WRITING
Processes and Intentions

WRITING
Processes and Intentions

Richard C. Gebhardt
Findlay College

Dawn Rodrigues
Colorado State University

D.C. HEATH AND COMPANY
Lexington, Massachusetts   Toronto

COVER PHOTO: Computer Graphic by Earl Glass/Stock, Boston
COVER DESIGN: Carmela M. Ciampa

Published simultaneously in Canada.

Printed in the United States of America.

International Standard Book Number: 0–669–09132–4

Library of Congress Catalog Card Number: 88–81108

10   9   8   7   6   5   4   3   2   1

To the Teacher

Writing is a dynamic process that does not fit easily into course plans and textbooks. Various lines of current research point to the complexity and individuality of the writing process. In the effort to help students understand and use the writing process some teachers and text authors oversimplify by attempting to impose a linear and restrictive set of instructions on writing. We believe that this pitfall can and should be avoided. It is challenging to write a textbook that does justice to the complexity of writing, to the teacher's need for flexiblity, and to the student's need for direct and practical instruction, but we feel that such a book is necessary and vital for the effective teaching of writing. *Writing: Processes and Intentions* is our answer to that challenge.

Overview

Writing: Processes and Intentions is built around two central concepts: the *processes* of writing and the *intentions* (or motives) that guide a writer at various points in the life of a writing project. The *processes* of writing are mental (memory, logic, intuition, emotion, conscious and subconscious reactions), and physical (movements of the hands, use of the eyes, awareness of sub-vocalized sound, etc.). These processes are dynamic, interconnected, recursive, and non-sequential. The *intentions* a person has while writing influence how that person writes, and these intentions vary at different points in the life of a writing project. For example, the initial motive to "just get started" shifts to the need to get a rough draft done, and later to the intention of tightening and sharpening the draft.

By stressing *processes,* this text helps students to understand the complexity of writing and to appreciate the freedom this complexity provides—the freedom to draft spontaneously *or* pre-plan *or* shift approaches, depending on what works in a given writing session. By emphasizing *intentions,* this text offers very practical instruction in applying writing strategies that correspond to the different stages in the life of a writing project. Indeed, the text contains dozens of suggestions about how to approach different writing assignments, how to draft productively, how to revise and edit drafts, how to use the computer as a writing tool, and how to work collaboratively with other writers.

Contents

Chapter 1, Processes and Intentions, suggests how the brain, hands, and eyes interact in writing, and how different intentions or motives influence a writer. Chapter 2, Generating Ideas, presents several ideas and activities designed to enhance coordination of the writing processes, developing the capacity for writing freely and spontaneously. Chapter 3, Drafting: Growth Through Change, offers specific suggestions for effective drafting. Chapter 4, Revising and Editing Finished Drafts, extends the principle of "growth through change" into strategies for reseeing and reshaping drafts. Chapter 5, The Writing Situation, highlights the roles that audience, subject, and attitude play in the writing process. The focus of the last few chapters is on writing projects based on personal experience, reading, and reasoning. The relevance of process and intention is further explored in the context of these specific types of writing assignments. Chapter 6, Writing Projects Based on Personal Experience, discusses the possibilities for integrating personal knowledge, experience, and opinion into a piece of writing. Chapter 7, Writing Projects Based on Reading, deals with reading-writing strategies, critical reading questions, summary-reaction writing, analysis and comparison of sources, and other issues related to the use of published sources. Chapter 8, Writing Projects Based on Reasoning, stresses the reciprocal relationship between thought and information in academic writing (such as critical reviews and problem-solution papers), and presents suggestions for evaluating the logic and evidence in source materials and in student drafts. At the end of the text we have included two appendixes that supplement features in this text. Appendix A, Computer Writing, contains additional tips and information for using computers to help develop writing ability. Appendix B, Teamwork Writing, provides an overview of teamwork writing, and explores how it might be used most effectively.

Instructional Features

Each chapter contains one or more *Idea Files,* which provide tips and information for computer writing. These Idea Files are a valuable resource for students who use a word processor. They help students to adapt strategies and suggestions from the text for use with the computer.

At the end of each chapter, we've included a *Teamwork Writing* section to help students work collaboratively on their writing.

The Idea Files and Teamwork Writing sections support and supplement the text. However, the text does not depend on these features, so that you can decide whether to emphasize them or make them optional.

Throughout, the book offers numerous practical hints and writing strategies, often illustrated with student examples, including journal entries, drafts, and finished papers. One suggestion we make is that students keep a writing log to encourage them to write freely and to provide themselves with a record of their experimentation and growth over the term.

Following each chapter are *Writing Exercises* designed to help students use ideas from the text and build them into their repertoire of writing skills. If you decide to ask your students to keep a writing log, you may wish to ask students to keep assigned exercises in the log.

Each chapter ends with several *Suggestions for Writing.* These suggestions relate to the emphasis or focus of the chapter. You may assign these projects, as they are presented, or modified for major course papers.

Flexibility

Writing: Processes and Intentions is a flexible and adaptable textbook, one that need not be covered in a linear and sequential way. Our approach in this text allows for a variety of student needs and teaching styles. Teachers can adapt the textbook to fit specific course requirements and instructional priorities. Students will find it to be a useful guidebook for writing.

The degree to which you utilize features in this textbook is ultimately up to you. The text can be applied on a number of levels. For example, the use of computers can be a major focus of your course, or you may touch on it briefly, or not at all. Whichever option you choose, you will discover that you can adapt the text to your needs. If you prefer to encourage collaborative writing in your course, you may choose to emphasize the Teamwork Writing sections. But if you dislike group writing, you might eliminate this requirement completely. For a course that focuses on writing processes, you might choose to emphasize the first half of the book, assigning a writer's log and requiring students to complete most of the Writing Exercises in the first four chapters.

We believe that *Writing: Processes and Intentions* has the dynamic qualitites necessary for teaching a dynamic subject. The multitude of options and possibilities for writers are presented in a clear and coherent manner. By actively exploring these options through writing, we hope that students will become more confident and skillful writers.

Acknowledgments

No good composition text gets written in a vacuum. Long before ideas and words see ink and paper, authors work with students—sharing their frustrations and successes, learning how well instructional approaches work with students or why they don't work. Over the past twenty years or so, several thousand students at Findlay College, Michigan State University, Colorado State University, and New Mexico State University were our collaborators as we developed the instructional approach of this book.

Authors also work with ideas—finding in articles and conference papers concepts that explain student difficulty and suggest directions for effective teaching. Behind *Writing: Processes and Intentions* are many debts of this kind—for instance, to Kenneth Bruffee, Peter Elbow, Janet Emig, Linda Flower and John Hayes, James Moffett, Barrett Mandell, Donald Murray, Sondra Perl, and Nancy Sommers.

Writing: Processes and Intentions also has been influenced by our colleagues, at our own institutions and elsewhere, whose conversations and arguments, have clarified our ideas of composition and its teaching. Many people have helped Rick in this way, among them, Paul Beauvais, Robert Ewald, Robert Rennert, Barbara Genelle Smith, and Kathleen Welsch—colleagues and former colleagues at Findlay College—as well as Lynn Z. Bloom, Robert Boynton, Audrey Roth, and Lynn Quitman Troyka. While working on this book, Dawn was fortunate to have the support of her new colleagues at Colorado State University: Jean Wyrick, Kate Kiefer, and Steve Reid. She thanks them for their indirect assistance with this project. Their continuing discussions about composition theory and practice make teaching and writing about composition a joy.

The reviewers helped shape the direction of the book, too. A special thanks to the following people: Bruce C. Appleby, Southern Illinois University-Carbondale; Stephen A. Bernhardt, New Mexico State University; Lynn Z. Bloom, University of Connecticut; William A. Covino, University of Illinois-Chicago; Jean Lutz, Miami University (Ohio); Ben W. McClelland, University of Mississippi; Kim Moreland, Auburn University (Alabama); Christine Neuwirth, Carnegie-Mellon University; Alvin Past, Bee County College; Linda Peterson, Yale University; Duane Roen, University of Arizona; Philip M. Rubens, Rensselaer Polytechnic Institute; Donald Stewart, Kansas State University; and William Wresch, University of Wisconsin Center-Marinette County.

Paul Smith, Senior Acquisitions Editor for English at D. C. Heath, is decisive in manuscript acquisition and creative, patient, and candid in manuscript development—qualities essential to the completion of this book. As Production Editors, Rosemary Rodensky and Linda Belamarich tried to keep us on schedule and succeeded in ironing out dozens of questions and problems as the book moved toward production.

Finally, Dawn sends a personal "thank you" to her husband, Ray, and son, Brad, for taking over household chores when she was too busy writing to help, for going to football games and other events without her when necessary, and for giving her first rights to their best computer as she worked on this book.

Contents

7 WRITING PROJECTS BASED ON READING 191

8 WRITING PROJECTS BASED ON REASONING   221

WRITING
Processes and Intentions

Introduction

Writing: Processes and Intentions is a textbook about writing and about how you can work at writing effectively. It is a textbook that will encourage you to develop an awareness of yourself as a writer. It will help you to understand the processes you use as you write and it will suggest strategies you can follow as you work on different college writing tasks—strategies that will carry over to the on-the-job writing tasks you are likely to face after graduation. This book will also offer a perspective on writing—a way of thinking about your intentions as a writer—that can help you with your writing.

The Importance and Difficulty of Writing

Writing is one of the most important things you do in college. Good writing skills are essential to your success, whether you are writing reports on readings or lab work, preparing research papers, or taking essay tests. Working on those writing assignments is, potentially, one of the most difficult things you do in college. The *importance* and *difficulty* of writing spring from the same source.

The *importance* of writing derives from the way that writing makes your brain and senses work together to help you learn. You can see words appearing at the same time that you are thinking about the ideas, feeling your fingers write the words or press the keys, and perhaps even hearing yourself muttering words and phrases as you work.

What this coordination of the physical, the visual, and the mental means is that writing can help you learn. It focuses your mental, physical, and emotional resources on the same facts and ideas at the same time—a good opportunity for you to discover insights, or at least to see connections between your classes, your reading, and your personal experiences. This interaction also helps you "dig into" a subject more deeply, as you learn about it, finding ideas you did not have before and looking for the words to express those ideas. And it gives your fragile, developing insights the permanence of ink on paper (or of storage on a computer disk), so that they do not slip away like so many "good ideas" you have but later forget.

The *difficulty* of writing grows from the same coordination of hands, brain, and eyes. Writing may help you discover and organize ideas, because it draws on your mental, physical, and emotional resources. But this means that your efforts to write can be sabotaged by thousands of different mental, physical, and emotional problems or distractions—everything from a headache or the noise of a roommate returning from a bar, to nagging worries about finances, to feelings of anxiety you may have about writing.

In general, the difficulty of writing is the reason that some publishers publish oversimplified textbooks and some colleges offer tightly controlled writing classes. Most students go to college with fairly little writing experience and with practical reasons for wanting to learn how to write. Writing texts and courses want to give students instruction to help them cope with the blocks and frustrations that often seem to accompany writing. Sometimes, this results in oversimplified information about the "right" way to write, or the "steps" to follow in order to write well.

We don't plan to oversimplify. There are no tricks, no easy steps. In fact, if you try to follow some of the tricks you've heard about, you may have more difficulty than if you didn't follow them at all. For example, if you believe, as some students do, that you *have* to develop ideas mentally before you can start to write, you may waste a lot of time and suffer a lot of frustration waiting for "inspiration" to strike. Or, if you believe that in order to write you need to follow a clear-cut series of stages or steps, you may start to believe that there is some single, "correct" way to write. If you believe that, and (like most people) you do *not* write that way, then you may start to doubt writing habits that are working for you. Like a good batter who slumps when trying to switch-hit, you may hurt your writing by trying to change your habits when you really don't need to.

The Approach of This Textbook

As a writer, whenever you write, and no matter how far along you are in a writing project, you are involved in the processes of writing: your eyes are observing what you've written, your mind is reflecting on the ideas, and your hand is actively producing more text. Your *writing processes* are at work throughout the entire project. When you are writing casually, intending nothing more than to get some thoughts on paper and generate ideas, you feel and act differently than you do when you have to produce a finished essay before tomorrow. The approaches or strategies you use as you write vary with your motive for writing, or what we will refer to as your *intention* for your writing session.

Experienced writers—both student writers and professional writers—feel and act differently at different times in the life of a writing project. At the beginning, when they have no pressure, they usually spend some time *generating ideas*. Later, often when a deadline is nearing, they move on to the task of *drafting*—developing a preliminary version (a *draft*) of their work. Different writers may begin drafting with different *intentions*, or motives, for their writing. They might consciously decide to produce at least a portion of a draft by the time they finish for the day. Then, during their next writing session, they might focus on *revising*; but if they discover that their draft is underdeveloped, in spite of their deadlines, they will shift gears and consciously attempt to generate more material before setting out once more to draft their way to a finished project before their deadline. A writer may write many drafts before producing the *final draft* or completed piece. Furthermore, effective writers allow themselves the flexibility to shift intentions for all or part of their writing sessions, when necessary and as time permits.

Writers rarely move from generating to drafting to revising in exactly that order. A more likely pattern is for writers to shift intentions frequently as they work, depending on how their writing project is taking shape. Moreover, each writer's overall writing processes will differ from one task to the next. And no two writers' processes will be alike. Having a variety of strategies to use as they shift intentions for their writing helps writers complete their writing tasks confidently and competently.

We believe that writers can develop their writing abilities by learning how to adjust to the demands of the task at hand. We feel that if writers consciously establish an intention *before* they begin a writing session, they can prepare their minds for the way they want to write—the strategies they want to use *as* they write. If they are honest with themselves in establishing their intent, then they will not be disappointed if, by the end of a writing session, they have produced nothing more than a loose collection of ideas—for they may have *intended* only to generate ideas that day. On another day, they might feel a need to get a draft completed. Establishing an intention for their drafting session can help them accomplish their goal.

But we know from our own experiences as writers (even from our experiences writing this text) that writing involves many complex processes with emotional, physical, and mental dimensions. Thus we will not suggest that *Writing: Processes and Intentions* offers a foolproof method for writing well. What we will do, however, is

1. help you use, as fully as you can, your intuitive sense of writing as a process of discovery.

2. present the concept of *intentions* in writing, helping you note how your writing processes change when your intention changes.

3. offer some fairly specific directions for things you might try as you write, but not because they are the "only" or "right" ways to work. As a student in a writing class, you are looking for strategies that might work for you.

Throughout this textbook, we will try to help you expand the number and range of strategies you have to draw on as you write. We will stress the twin sides of writing—exploration and communication—and we will offer instruction and writing exercises to help you move, as you work on a writing project, from early drafts written for yourself toward drafts that are increasingly intended to be clear and effective for other readers.

Organization and Contents

If you glance over the Table of Contents, you can get a good sense of how the text incorporates ideas from this introduction. Chapter 1, Processes and Intentions, asks you to take a fresh look at writing, observing what writers do as they compose their ideas. Also, this chapter introduces you more fully to the relationship between writers' *processes* and their *intentions*. We demonstrate how different intentions or motives influence what a writer tries to do at various times in a writing project. By asking you to complete a number of writing exercises, we give you an opportunity to develop a better sense of what you do as you write.

Chapter 2, Generating Ideas, helps you learn how to write freely so that you feel more confident when you sit down to write with the intention of generating ideas. Chapter 3, Drafting—Growth Through Change, builds on the ability to write spontaneously, that you developed through exercises in Chapter 2. It offers fairly detailed suggestions about what you can do while you are working and reworking your ideas in the drafting process.

Running through the first three chapters is the underlying assumption that writing is quite dynamic, and not a simple movement through separate stages. As exploration, writing is a way to locate ideas, and so either *generating ideas* or drafting are good first steps for beginning a writing project. But the special nature of academic assignments, and the tight deadlines within which college writers usually have to work, often make more systematic exploration strategies helpful. Thus we include systematic strategies in later chapters.

Much of what you do while drafting is revising: making changes in ideas, in word order, in word choice, in spelling and punctuation, and so forth. But producing an article or report that is clear, effective, and interesting to read usually requires revision of a completed draft. And so, Chapter 4, Revising and Editing Finished Drafts, suggests strategies that are useful for the completion of a writing project.

Chapter 5, The Writing Situation, explains how understanding such things as subject, audience, and purpose can improve the effectiveness of all your writing projects. The remaining chapters in the book focus on specific kinds of writing projects that you will be asked to work on in college: Chapter 6, Writing Projects Based on Personal Experiences, presents strategies writers can use when they are assigned such projects; Chapter 7, Writing Projects Based on Reading, helps writers understand important connections between reading and writing; and Chapter 8, Writing Projects Based on Reasoning, stresses the importance of logic, evidence, and critical thinking in academic writing.

■ Special Features: Computer Writing and Teamwork Writing

You will also find two special features scattered throughout the text— some ideas about writing with computers and some information about *teamwork writing,* what some texts refer to as collaborative writing. The Idea Files we include in each chapter will help you use this text if you happen to write with a word processor or if your class has access to a computer lab. And the teamwork-writing sections at the end of each chapter will give information about using collaborative-writing strategies so that you and your classmates can help each other write more effectively. We have deliberately separated these sections from the rest of the text so that you can skip over them if they are inappropriate to your needs.

An Introduction to Computer Writing

No matter what your intention and no matter what the nature of your assignment, if you have access to a personal computer, you can certainly use your word processor to practice any of the writing strategies we suggest in this text. A word processor offers writers a variety of possibilities, possibilities that may interest some of you in the future even if they do not seem useful right now.

With a word processor, writers can expand on an idea, or add supporting ideas or more precise words, by simply moving the cursor to the appropriate point and typing. Writers can see the changes they make—in ideas or structure or word choice—occur instantly as text is added or deleted. Writers can, with a few keystrokes, move a concluding paragraph to the beginning of a paper to see whether it might serve as the start of an introduction; similarly, they can try out different organizational arrangements by reshuffling the sections of a draft. They can leave a draft, thinking it is complete, and return to it later to add new supporting material. They can save the different drafts that result from such changes and decide later which draft to use towards a completed paper. And, as many students discover, the speed and sense of freedom they get from a word processor can increase the flow of ideas and encourage them to make the changes through which writing grows.

For all of these reasons, we have included Idea Files in this textbook. These Idea Files explore various aspects of computer writing, and occur at least once in each chapter. Those of you who are doing your writing assignments with a word processor will easily be able to locate computer ideas.

An Introduction to Teamwork Writing

Just what *teamwork writing* or collaborative writing is will become clearer as you work, especially if your teacher assigns the teamwork writing sections that will appear as the last section of each chapter. The teamwork suggestions demonstrate what collaboration can mean for writers. You will be using teamwork writing if you follow our suggestion, at the end of this introduction, and talk with your classmates about your observations concerning writing. When you and another student work together as observation partners, and record your observations, you will be working at teamwork writing. By working together, each of you will be able to give, and receive, the cooperation and information you both need to understand your writing behaviors.

When you are working together on formal assignments, teamwork writing will provide you with a way to exchange assistance and information with other writers. By working with your peers, you will be able to make connections with other writers so that you can overcome two kinds of isolation writers face during much of every writing project. The first sort of isolation—emotional feelings of separation and fear of failure—is clearly expressed in these words by the American playwright William Saroyan:

> A writer *chooses* to write. He chooses to put himself aside at fairly regular
> intervals in order to make a work of writing of some kind. While he

works he is alone. If the work is difficult, as it almost always is, he feels alone, and sometimes even abandoned. . . . But the word [loneliness] itself isn't especially accurate, in any case: that which is named loneliness is probably more nearly ineffectiveness, a form of failure, a form of fear. . . .

Source: William Saroyan, "Why Does a Writer Write?" Reprinted from Floyd Watkins and Karl Knight, *Writer to Writer* (Boston: Houghton Mifflin Company, 1966), p. 30. Originally published in *The Saturday Review,* 1961.

Saroyan makes it clear that feelings like loneliness, frustration, and futility are perfectly normal during the all-too-frequent difficult times with a writing project. But being normal does not make them any less troublesome. Collaborative approaches work partly because they let you break through the loneliness and talk with others who also need support while they are writing.

Beyond these matters of loneliness and mutual support is another dimension of the writer's isolation—intellectual isolation from the responses of others about how effective or ineffective the writing is. As William Saroyan puts it:

When the going is good a writer knows very little, if any, loneliness. When it is bad he believes he knows nothing else. The flaw is the same in either event: when the writer thought the going was good and therefore felt no loneliness, the writing was not necessarily good, and when he believed it was bad and therefore felt ineffective, the writing may actually have been good. He just happened to feel loneliness at the time. If it wasn't something he ate, it was surely something that was eating him.

Source: Saroyan, "Why Does a Writer Write?" in *Writer to Writer,* p. 30.

This second kind of isolation is not, in itself, a bothersome feeling. It involves the fact that a writer working alone gets so immersed in the subjective feelings of the moment that he or she cannot judge very well whether drafts are "good" or "bad." Teamwork writing breaks through this isolation by letting writers help each other dispel inaccurate, subjective impressions about their work.

A thread that runs through these remarks on teamwork writing is the concept of *mutual assistance.* In teamwork writing, students will help you because they also want you to help them. For much the same reason, students treat each other candidly but kindly during teamwork-writing activities. All of you, after all, are in the same situation—opening up in front of other people, offering your ideas and words for the comments of other writers. *You* don't want to be treated rudely, and neither does anyone else. And since, in teamwork writing, the participants all have similar insecurities and fears, you all have a common motive to work sensitively for your mutual benefit.

Even if your teacher doesn't require you to work collaboratively on the teamwork-writing exercises included in this book, you can benefit by reading and thinking about how teamwork writing can help you.

You might even be able to do some of these activities independently by teaming up with a roommate or a friend in class to work on your writing.

Processes and Intentions Log

One way to work with this textbook is to keep a special kind of writing notebook: a *Processes and Intentions Log* in which you complete writing exercises, reflect on your writing processes, and note changes in your development as a writer. You can also keep a record of the writing strategies that work best for you—both pencil and paper strategies and computer-writing strategies.

At the end of each chapter you will find several Writing Exercises, tasks to help you build ideas from the text into your repertoire of writing approaches. Also, you will find Suggestions for Writing, which your instructor may choose to assign or to modify for use as writing assignments in the course. Your teacher may have other directions, but you might want to keep these exercises and assignments in your Processes and Intentions Log.

One approach to keeping a writing log would be to store all the work from your writing course in a large looseleaf notebook. In one section of the notebook, you could keep the exercises you complete from this text, each item numbered and dated. Another section of your notebook could consist of periodic entries that you make about your writing processes, about your intentions as a writer, and about the strategies that you use as you complete writing assignments. This section will help you focus on your development as a writer. It will help you get in the habit of writing about your writing as you work on a writing project. In still another section of your log, you might want to keep your finished assignments, along with all of the notes, ideas, and drafts that you produced as you worked on a given project. Thus, not only will you be able to observe your development of each piece of writing, but you will also be able to find—even as you work on another assignment—ideas that occurred to you during your earlier work. If you are using a word processor for your writing, you can create an electronic version of this writing log.

During a writing project, you should try to make entries in your Processes and Intentions Log

1. when you first receive an assignment, or within a few hours after you receive it.

2. after any "good" stretch of writing. (What made it a good, productive session?)

3. after frustrating, unproductive writing sessions. (What made this time ineffective?)

4. if you feel that you need to change your topic.

5. whenever you clearly sense that your intentions in writing are changing—for instance, when you know that you have finished getting started on a paper and are ready to draft for an audience, or when you consider a draft "finished" and decide to work to make it clearer and more effective.

6. when you turn in a paper, or within a few hours after you turn it in.

7. when you see your teacher's comments on a paper, or within a few hours after you read the comments.

Finally, as you make your way through the text, we hope that you will enter into a dialogue with your classmates and that you will record some of your observations about what writing is and how it develops. You won't become a different kind of writer overnight, but if you begin to think of yourself as a writer, and if you become conscious of your writing processes and intentions, this text can offer some useful strategies for tackling the kinds of writing assignments you will encounter, in college and on the job.

Processes and Intentions

1

A Look at Writing

What is *writing?* Is it the finished product people read—words, sentences, clever turns of phrase, and the like? Or is writing the set of processes by which the finished product came into being—hand pushing pen or computer keys; trips to the library to fill note cards; ideas and phrases tried out, rejected, or saved?

Writing is both process and result. Writing is the means by which writing is produced.

As a college writer—a person who needs to use writing in classes, a person likely to enter a career in which you will use writing—you have a stake in both meanings of the word *writing.* You have good reason to be concerned about the clarity, persuasiveness, originality, and wit of the papers you submit to professors and employers. To a large extent, these people will judge your intellectual mettle—the soundness and clarity of your thinking—at the same time that they respond to your writing.

Your professors will be expecting "good" academic writing from you: writing that communicates the author's message to the reader; writing that is appropriate for the occasion; writing that is clear, direct, and honest; writing that is suited to its purpose. As they read your writing, teachers and employers will judge it on the basis of its effectiveness in fulfilling a particular assignment. Of course, since writing tasks differ from one discipline to the next, what constitutes good writing for one professor may be vastly different from what another professor considers to be good writing. A chemistry teacher would not accept a personal essay on "Why I Like Chemistry" as a substitute for a controlled, objective lab report. A personal essay would be inappropriate for the occasion. Nor would an English teacher accept a chemistry lab report as a substitute for a personal essay.

Your professors will be judging the *results* of your efforts, your papers. But *you* need to be concerned about the strategies you use to produce these papers. After all, it is only through these processes that you can explore the subjects you write about and develop the insights that you will share with others through your writing. And it is by learning to adapt these strategies to the demands of each writing task that you can become a more efficient and effective writer.

Since this is a writing book, you really should use writing to *feel* what happens as you write. So before you read further about writing, we'd like you to do some writing. Get out some paper and a pen or pencil, or sit down at your computer, and spend several minutes on each of the following writing experiments.

■ The Thinking Pencil or the Thinking Keyboard

Writing Experiment 1:
Thought-Comes-First Writing

To begin with, try to think before you write. Close your eyes and fold your hands. If you are writing with a pencil, think about the words, *the thinking pencil.* If you are writing with a word processor, think about the words, *the thinking keyboard.* What are four different things these words could mean?

Think of these words as the title of the short essay you are about to write. Mentally decide what the words mean. Then mentally work out details that you could use to explain these meanings to people who have never done this exercise.

Plan in your mind a six-paragraph essay: an introduction, a paragraph on each of the four meanings of the title, and a conclusion.

When you have finished planning your paper (four minutes maximum), begin writing. As quickly as possible, pick up your pencil or start typing and transcribe the paper you have planned mentally. Move the ideas from your mind onto the paper or computer screen.

After you have worked at this experiment for a few minutes, proceed to the next one.

Writing Experiment 2:
The Thinking-Pencil Approach

This time, try to let your *thinking pencil* (or *thinking keyboard*) do the work. Pick up your pencil or pen, or start typing. Write about this topic: "How I Felt About the Writing Activity I Just Completed."

Make the pencil move right away, and keep it moving for three minutes. You could start by writing the title, and then just keep going. If you can't think of anything to write, write out some questions (What does this mean? Why am I doing this stupid exercise?) and then answer them. If you start to stop, write more questions and answers, or else just write "I've run out of stuff, I've run out of stuff, I've run out of stuff," etc. But keep the pencil or the keys moving nonstop for three minutes.

These experiments may have seemed a little strange or artificial to you. But if you made a serious try at both writings, you should have been able to feel some differences between two broad theories about writing. (If you have skipped over the preceding paragraphs, we suggest that you go back to the beginning of this section and do the two writings before reading further. Remember, it only takes about ten minutes to complete them!)

The first writing experiment introduced you to a *mental* or *thought-comes-first* writing approach, an approach of long-standing in American schools. In this view, thinking precedes writing, *causes* writing, so that it is reasonable to expect writing to proceed smoothly once you have captured ideas in your mind. You may have been given writing suggestions based on this theory, such as: find the thesis for a paper and *then* develop that thesis, or work out an outline for your paper and *then* follow the outline as you write.

It's not that outlining *never* works. Sometimes it does. And it's not that the mental-writing approach *never* helps a writer move smoothly and quickly toward a finished writing project. Sometimes it does help, and when it does, thought-comes-first writing can be efficient and exciting.

But when thought-comes-first writing does *not* work, it wastes a lot of time and it causes the sort of frustration you felt when you were working at the first experimental writing. Think about that assignment a moment:

1. It asked you to define an unfamiliar term in four different ways.

2. It asked you to locate clarifying examples for the general definitions, a task that requires completing the first step, remembering those four definitions, analyzing what about each definition might confuse a reader, and mentally searching for details to remedy the confusion.

3. It asked you to consider the final form and organization of the writing project, even before you had worked out basic points you may have wanted to make. In other words, it assumed that your intent was to produce a finished product—an impossible task when you hadn't yet worked out your ideas.

Each step in the instructions for the first experiment competed with the others for your attention. This may have left you wondering about where to try to start. Or, as you thought about one point, you may have forgotten some good idea you already had about another. In short, the first experimental writing task probably was impossible, because of two related facts:

1. It asked you to do more things than your active, short-term memory could keep track of at one time.

2. It prevented you from using paper and pencil or computer keys to relieve any of this mental strain.

From these twin roots grows the essential problem of thought-comes-first writing: *It can make you too dependent on your mind as you write.* To put it another way, thought-comes-first writing can cut you off from the insights and discoveries that the thinking pencil or the thinking keyboard can reveal as you work to spread words over blank spaces.

The second writing experiment introduced you to the way that active, physical writing can help your mind discover what you want to write. In this thinking-pencil or thinking-keyboard approach, writers find ideas and grope their way toward what they want to write while they work to push pens or to press keys. The instructions implied that your intent was to think on paper—to figure out what you wanted to say.

You may not be the kind of writer who writes to discover what he or she wants to write. You may be the kind of writer who thinks through a writing assignment well before putting pen to paper. Each writer is different. Furthermore, the strategies any individual writer uses change according to the task at hand. But no matter how effectively you may be able to think through your topic before writing, you will no doubt discover more about your topic *as* you write. Writers rarely think of everything they want to say before they begin writing.

Writing Processes

Writing is a way to explore material, a way to discover insights into subjects. Many of the most important processes in writing take place, invisibly and very privately, inside the writer's mind. If you are like most students, you probably change your mind as you write. Maybe you begin to feel troubled, as if you are running out of ideas. Perhaps you occasionally glance back over a few sentences before moving on at a faster speed. Sometimes you may feel yourself making a sort of mid-course correction—a change in the direction your ideas are going as you work at writing.

Some of our students have written about their writing processes. You might be interested in finding out whether your processes are similar to theirs. Reading about their experiences might also help you learn what to look for as you begin thinking about your own writing processes.

> GREGORIA: When I write, I like to sit somewhere comfortably and have thoughts run through my mind. I see pictures in my mind. This helps me know what it is that I'm trying to write. I always take a few moments to pause and then go back to my writing. When I pause, sometimes my mind will drift far away but other times it dwells on what I'm writing about. I think many sentences through carefully, sifting words out to make the sentence "sound" just right to me as I put them down. After I have written words, often I will reread them out loud to myself. If it sounds OK, I will leave it but other times I will change words to make them sound better.

> BECKY: When I write with a computer in the Apple lab, my thoughts flow quickly. With pen and paper, it takes me longer to write down what I'm thinking and I sometimes lose an idea before it goes down in words, or because of a silly problem like running out of ink. With a word processor I never worry about this because I always save my work on a disk and I can always wait to print it later if the ribbon is bad. If I get stuck on an idea, I sort through my text and find what is causing my problem. Sometimes I move a paragraph to a different point in my text to see if that helps me get going again, and I especially like to be able to stick new ideas right into the middle of sentences when I get a new idea. When I find mistakes, I can correct them right away (with the delete key) but what I like to do is just keep going until later and then go back to work with spelling errors and typing mistakes.

> SHARON: When I begin to write in my room, or actually before I begin, I like to organize my work area. Papers and notes stacked in neat piles are the only way I can function when I am doing a research type paper, or after I have already written earlier drafts that I want to use. While I write, I have the habit of filling the margins with ideas for additions and corrections. During short breaks, I tend to quickly reorganize the area since it does get messy while I work, especially if I am constantly referring to notes.

Most people who think honestly about their own practices as writers realize that writing is not like a quick drive along a straight interstate highway, but more like a meander along a winding road. Words may flow smoothly *for a while* onto paper or computer monitor. Inevitably, though, the hand pauses while eyes glance at or study what has been written. During these pauses, a great deal of important mental activity is taking place:

1. The eyes and brain together review the meaning of recent phrases and sentences.

2. The brain decides whether the draft is headed in the right direction and, if it is, projects how the next words should connect with what has gone before.

3. The brain may decide that the writing is heading down a dead end. It may discover an accidental new idea that requires some adjustment in the direction of the draft. It may find that a phrase or piece of evidence just doesn't work in some way. In such cases—and they are very frequent—the brain projects a new approach for the draft. In other words, it makes a change.

Writing, then, is often a form of changing your mind. The changes may be small, rather than especially noticeable. They may occur spontaneously, as a result of responses that you hardly notice, responses that you make intuitively during brief pauses in your writing. On the other hand, the changes may occur consciously as you study a completed draft, looking for ways to improve it. But changes there are, almost always, during periods of effective writing.

■ Observing Writing: Class Activity

It is difficult to remember much of what happens in your mind as you write. Even *you* probably can't reconstruct your mental processes accurately. But some of the mental activity shows in ways others *can* observe. The observable parts of writing form the basis of a classroom writing activity we'd like you to try.

But before you try these activities, you need a topic to write about. Here are a few ideas for you to consider:

1. What makes writing "good"? What makes writing "bad"? Bring some samples of good and bad writing to class. Use your samples as the basis for your response.

2. Young people today are frequently accused of being apathetic. Do you agree with this assessment?

3. What goals do you have for your career? What obstacles do you need to overcome in order to achieve those goals?

4. What do you know a lot about—a subject in school, a hobby, a sport, another part of the country or the world? Write about something that you think others in class would enjoy reading.

If these topics don't intrigue you, you might want to write about something that you need to write about anyway. For instance, if you have a writing assignment due for another course, you can use this occasion to complete that assignment. If you don't have a formal writing project due for another course, you might write about something you just read about in one of your textbooks. Writing about what you have read will help you remember the ideas in the chapter. Of course, how you write will depend on what you write. Writers use different processes for different kinds of writing tasks.

In order to take a *look* at writing, you'll need to cooperate with another person—ideally, a person in your class with whom you can work during a class session. Briefly, what you will do is take turns, one of you writing while the other observes writing behaviors, and then reversing roles.

Writing Behaviors

- *Rituals:* Adjusting chair, shuffling papers, tapping pencil, crumpling paper in disgust, sharpening pencils, organizing the writing area. If you are observing someone write at a computer monitor, notice any rituals that may be peculiar to computer writing: placing a notebook beside the computer, writing the title of the paper at the top of the page, opening a file even though the writer is not ready to write, getting a printed copy of every draft.

- *Movements:* Facial and body-language clues that indicate attitude, degree of involvement or boredom, amount of success or frustration, level of confidence or nervousness, etc.

- *Verbal Clues:* Talking to self, forming words silently with lips, muttering, significant sighs during writing, etc.

- *Doodling:* Drawing pictures, making random marks, jotting down a few words then quickly erasing them or (in the case of computer writers) deleting words with the backspace key.

- *Listing:* Putting down isolated words and phrases, making a scratch outline, not writing complete sentence after complete sentence. If you are observing someone who is writing at the computer, note whether any listing or jotting down of ideas is done at the computer. Note when this listing is done: before, during, or at the end of the writing session.

- *Sustained Production:* Fairly continuous production of sentence after sentence. If you are observing someone who alternates between writing by hand and writing directly at the computer screen, try to note when the writer changes from one method of production to the other. In either case, the *flow* of writing will be interrupted occasionally by the next several kinds of behaviors.

- *Glancing:* Quick movement of the eyes to scan words or phrases. It might happen while the hand continues to draft, or during momentary pauses in sentence-after-sentence writing. With computer-writers, notice how often the writer uses the arrow keys to "scroll" through the text.

- *Studying:* Eyes seem to pay more careful attention to words and sentences during longer pauses in sustained writing.

- *Changing:* Modifying a draft by adding and changing words, crossing things out, drawing arrows to indicate a changed order, etc. The changes are made *on* a draft, not by starting over on clean paper or in a new file. They may seem to be part of the ongoing writing, and may occur in brief pauses within the sustained production of sentences. Computer writers will probably make some changes as they write, but at some point they will get a printed copy of their writing. Note whether they begin making major changes at the computer or whether they make only minimal changes on the computer screen and then get a printed copy of their writing.

- *Redrafting:* Modifying a draft by working with fresh paper to do over an earlier draft, or a section of a draft. With computer writers this might mean beginning a new file. But it could also mean moving systematically through the file, making change after change—*as if* they were rewriting the entire piece. (Remember, since the computer file can be modified without being retyped, computer writers don't need to retype their papers in order to make changes.)

- *Unknown Pause:* Neither hand nor eyes seem to be working. Is the writer thinking hard about what he or she has just written and what should come next? Or is the writer daydreaming, procrastinating, worrying about problems unrelated to the writing project? What other possibilities can you suggest?

Writing Experiment 3:
Observing Writing Processes and Behaviors

Work with a partner so that you can observe his or her writing processes and behaviors. Then switch places, so that you serve as the subject of your partner's observations.

Here are some suggestions for a writing observation session, possibly a class period in which your teacher serves as a timekeeper:

1. Sit facing your partner across a desk, or some other writing surface, so that you are directly in front of your partner, and a few feet away. Position yourself so that you can see the writer's facial behaviors and eye movements, and also the movements of hand across paper. If your partner is writing at a computer, you should probably sit on one side of him or her, so that you can observe your partner's hands on the keyboard at the same time as you are able to observe facial gestures and body movement.

2. Do not sit too close, and avoid making movements or noises that would draw the writer's attention to you any more than the odd, artificial situation itself is bound to do.

3. Keep the list of writing behaviors (pp. 17–18) open in front of you as you watch, and jot down notes so that you can talk with the writer later about what you saw during the observation session.

4. As you observe, pay special attention to the behaviors we called Sustained Production, Glancing, Studying, and Changing. Keep these questions in mind as you observe:

   a. What does the writer do to get started writing?

   b. How does Glancing seem to fit into the writer's behaviors? For instance, you might note that your partner writes sentence after sentence for several minutes, then seems to run out of steam, glances back to see how things are fitting together, and then picks up speed again.

   c. Is there a relationship between Glancing and Studying and the Changes the writer makes during writing? For instance, do the eyes seem to be active just before the hand makes changes?

   d. When the writer makes Changes, do they involve words, phrases, whole sentences, or punctuation? Are they changes of elimination, addition, or substitution? (In other words, does the writer delete words in some places, add words in other places, or does the writer delete a few words and substitute other words?)

5. Try to find one or two points in your partner's writing that you can talk about later. Look for combinations of behaviors: Glances just before Changes; eye movements that seem to trigger hand movements; periods of slow, labored writing giving way to more fluid writing. Do you see points in your partner's drafting that make you wonder whether something significant was going on in the writer's head? If so, remember the place on the paper; later, ask your partner to talk about what was going on at that point in the writing.

6. Summarize what you have observed—the writing behaviors you have noticed. While you are writing your summary, your partner should write down what he or she thinks went on. Are there any discrepancies? Have a *debriefing* session with your partner, a session in which you read one another's summaries and then talk about your observations. Encourage your partner to talk about the session. What did you learn about your partner's writing behaviors? What did your partner learn about his or her writing behaviors? What processes did your partner engage in that were not observable?

7. Reverse roles, and follow steps one through six with your partner observing while you write. When you have completed two observations, each followed by a debriefing session, take five or ten minutes to discuss similarities and differences in your two writing approaches. Are there areas in which both of you seem to be writing in much the same way? Are there other areas in which your approaches are clearly different?

Even if everything goes well as you do the preceding experiment, you will probably still feel a little strange—performing for an observer, spying on a classmate's writing session. Don't think you are unusual. That kind of response is normal for this activity. And it is not as bad as it could be. If you were taking a tennis or golf clinic instead of a writing course, you and the other amateurs in the group probably would have to perform, all too publicly, under the gaze of clubhouse loungers as well as the teaching pro. But as you work on Writing Experiment 3 in class, your only audience will be a very friendly one—a "teaching pro" who understands the awkwardness of the situation, and students who feel just as awkward as you do about it.

We have watched hundreds of students work with the sort of observation and writing and discussion activity of the preceding pages. If your experiences are similar to our students' experiences, you will probably find it fairly easy to observe the writing behavior of another person. There he or she sits, hands moving or pausing, eyes visible as they shift back to read an earlier section. As your partner writes, you can look for items on the list of writing behaviors, make notes, ask questions. When you are the one being observed, all you have to do is write, just as you always do when a teacher asks you to compose on the spot, and let the other person see what he or she can. You probably will also find it easy—if somewhat awkward—to have someone else tell you how your writing process looked.

What you may find harder to do is to understand the significance of what you will see your partner do, or of what your partner will report that you did. If you are like other students who have tried to look at writing using the exercise in Writing Experiment 3, you will probably *sense* several basic facts about writing:

1. Different people write differently.

2. Some people seem to leap at a single bound from assignment to sustained writing, while others fidget, doodle, and outline their way toward sentence to sentence writing.

3. Once started, some people have long stretches of sustained writing during which their eyes glance back, as if they are working mentally to connect where they are going to where they have been. Others work in shorter stretches of sustained production, with pauses in which they look around the room or reread long passages.

4. Some people clearly seem to be helped along by words on the page. Their sustained writing slows, as if they are getting confused or running out of ideas; their eyes glance back and seem to spot something on the page, and the pace of their drafting immediately picks up.

5. Some people get similar help from the notes or outlines they scribbled earlier. They seem to work along, referring periodically to notes on separate paper.

From observing other students—especially if you have an opportunity to observe several people and discuss written reports from several partners—you will probably realize that what *writing* is can vary a good deal from person to person, from situation to situation. Writers may shift their strategies, depending on how difficult the assignment is, how tired they are, whether they have intended to come up with ideas or to produce a draft, or whether there are distractions around them. So a person who sometimes takes a long time to get started may, at other times, begin writing almost immediately without much hesitation. Clearly, this is one of the lessons we have learned from observing our students who have written notes like these to their observation partners:

MARILYN: It was interesting to watch you write, Kelly. You obviously are a well-organized person and self-disciplined. You spent the first few seconds thinking about the assignment, then picked up the pen and began writing rapidly. The speed amazed me as did your infrequent pauses for reflection. It looked like you knew what you wanted to say and how to say it. I was surprised to hear you say that you really weren't sure where your thoughts were headed. Anyway, you were self-disciplined, and it showed in your tight posture, your attitude, the way you gripped the pen, and the few body movements I was able to observe.

KELLY: The first thing I noticed about the way you did the assignment, Marilyn, was that you had some "rituals" it looked like you had to go through before you could start writing. You folded your notebook over very businesslike and moved around in the chair like you had to get some feeling or beginning. Instead of writing right from the start, you moved down the page a couple of lines. A second thing I noticed was that you did a lot of glancing. I thought I saw you looking back a couple of words to keep your train of thought. And you had a look on your face as if you were deep in thought. I was amazed to hear you tell me that you were daydreaming!

COLETTE: I was fascinated by the way you wrote. You started writing immediately at the computer screen, but you didn't seem to be writing your paragraphs in any special order. Then, after you took a short break, you came back to the computer and started moving paragraphs around. I was interested in what you told me when we did our debriefing—that during your break you thought about what you would write when you came back to writing. When you came back, I watched you add some ideas in some places, and delete other parts completely. You kept reading and rereading your work before you made changes. You had a satisfied look on your face after you moved things around. You got a printed copy of your draft after you did all of this. At that point, you seemed to be reading just to check for errors.

DAVE: You didn't even seem to notice me, Colette. You just started writing—well, listing, jotting down some notes—on paper. Then you opened a computer file and started writing—without even glancing at your notes until you had written over a page without stopping. Then you started adding ideas and creating paragraphs. I noticed that you used the arrow keys to move through your paper and to guide you as you reread what you had written.

SHARON: Ronnie, when you started you seemed to have an almost constant flow of ideas. But as you approached the middle of your paper, you began to spend more time pausing and glancing at what you had just written. You seemed to be quickly looking at the previous thought pattern before continuing on. (Does that sound like what you do?) You only made a few small changes, like adding or deleting a word after some of your pauses. You looked like your total concentration was on the paper before you, and you didn't make many body movements.

What is the right way to go about writing? From our experiences observing students and talking with them about their observations about writing, we have learned that there may not be any such thing as the *right* way to write, but there do seem to be ways that are more effective or less effective for certain writers on certain kinds of writing tasks. For instance, some students resist putting words on paper. They stall, telling themselves that they are waiting to "get an idea" or that they need to do more research. What they are really doing is preventing themselves from engaging their minds—from using the coordination of hand, eyes, and brain that we talked about earlier—to help them with their project.

Idea File: Computer Writing

Word Processing Strategies for Writers

Use Lists

List all the ideas that you can think of at the top of the computer screen. Next, rearrange the items on your list into some kind of logical order. Then start writing. As you think of new ideas to add to your list, just move your cursor back to the beginning of your writing and add the new idea to your list wherever it seems to fit. Then return to wherever you were in your writing and keep on going.

Create "Great Idea" Collections

As you write, you will think of many ideas that may or may not be related to the section of the paper you are working on at the moment. If you want, you can type those ideas with your word processor and store them in an easily accessible location in your current file or in another file on your disk. Some writers like to use the "go to the end of the file" command of their word processor so that they can write their "great idea" there. Other writers like to create separate "idea files." These writers use the commands of their word processors to access the idea file and move the "great idea" of the moment to that file.

Even when they are sitting before their desks or computers, some students don't seem to try to engage their mind by looking at the words they have written and then writing in response to new ideas that are triggered by this kind of activity. They may look at the ceiling or close their eyes while they think about what to write next, and then put those words down before thinking some more. Sometimes writers need to close their eyes to get away from their text and clarify an idea. But they probably shouldn't use that strategy all of the time. A more effective approach would be to look at the idea they've just expressed and use it to propel them forward in their writing.

On the other hand, some writers pay so much attention to the words they've already written that they can hardly write more words. They reread and correct, putting so much effort into spelling and punctuation changes, and efforts to find "just the right word" that they have a hard time moving on toward a finished paper.

We firmly believe that the "right" writing approaches for you are those that work best for you. In this book, you will have an opportunity to practice different kinds of writing strategies and writing behaviors so that you can discover those that work most effectively. Of course, some of the processes you have already developed may work quite well. In writing, whatever *works* is probably a good approach. If a completed project is clear, detailed, interesting, and persuasive, then apparently your approach to the project was acceptable. There is a similar cliché in aviation: If you can walk away, it was a good landing. In both cases, though, there are more or less effective ways to reach the same goal. As a passenger, you would prefer to smile at the flight attendant as you walk out the door up the jetway into the terminal, than to slide down an emergency shoot from an airliner that had skidded off the runway. As a college writer, you probably should not just blunder ahead on a major project, waiting to see your grade before you decide if your approach has worked or not. And by looking at writing, you may already be forming some ideas about how you could make your writing more effective. Most of us can improve our writing strategies even if, in general, we are satisfied with the results of our writing.

■ Reexamining Your Writing Processes

Usually, when students think about writing processes and behaviors carefully enough to observe them in other people, they begin to reexamine their own writing processes. And the reports they get on their writing from observers further stimulate their interest. People may doubt what observers tell them or they may agree with the reports. But later, they begin to notice more things about their own writing processes, such as

1. times when they "know" what they want to write and seem to write it down almost by dictation.

2. places where some word or phrase triggers a change in what they are writing.

3. points where they "get stuck" or "run out of steam," and immediately reread the previous sentences until they sense, once again, how they should proceed.

4. times when the pauses in their writing are *not* focused on their writing—when they look around the room or daydream instead of glancing back to their developing text—so that their eyes can't help them sense where they are trying to go with their writing.

5. start-up procedures that seem to recur whenever they face a new writing task.

6. habitual tendencies, like the need to correct any spelling or punctuation error they see, whenever they see it—even if that breaks the flow of their thought and interrupts the production of words.

7. alibis like "I can't write unless the room is quiet," or "unless the stereo is on," or "unless I've got my feet on a pillow and hot cocoa in my green mug."

8. times when the writing is going so well that writers consciously shift gears. They may start out intending to produce a finished product; however, they may decide as they work that it would make more sense to slow down and generate ideas for awhile.

Once people begin to notice what they *do* while they are writing, we have found, they are more interested in working with writing, and better able to benefit from instruction. That's why we wanted to start this book with a series of class activities and writing assignments that can raise your consciousness about what it is *you* do when *you* write. Knowing what you do can help you decide what you would like to continue doing and what you would like to change.

Processes and Intentions

We'd like to extend your knowledge of writing by focusing not only on the *processes* writers use as they write, but also on how those processes interact with the varying motives or *intentions* writers have for different writing sessions. As you become more aware of your writing processes and intentions, you will be able to take charge of your writing, adjusting your processes and your intentions to the varying demands of writing assignments in different disciplines.

■ Understanding More About the Writing Processes

Writing makes use of complex, mysterious processes—mental, physical, and emotional activities that interact to allow ideas to grow. These activities are *not* things that happen in a controlled sequence, like following a recipe or the directions for setting up a stereo system. Instead, these processes work together naturally and simultaneously, as you already have seen if you observed another writer's eyes glance back while his or her hand continued to put words on paper.

Table 1.1 tries to outline our ideas about how writing processes work:

1. Table 1.1 suggests that as a writer writes, thinking does not always come before physical writing behavior (although it may). That is, observing what is going down on the page (represented by the arrow from "Observe" to "Think" in the table) can stimulate thoughts, just as thoughts (following the arrow from "Think" to "Move Hand") can prompt the production of words. To put it differently, the hand can work spontaneously as well as take "dictation" from the mind.

2. The table indicates that "thinking" is not all logical and conscious. A writer's subconscious, intuitive, and emotional activity is extremely important to what that person writes, even to whether the person can write at all.

3. The table suggests that conscious and subconscious responses to the written words—including the decision to revise them—can trigger further ideas and more words. That is why this book emphasizes rapid or spontaneous writing—what we called the *thinking pencil* or the *thinking keyboard*. What is essential is getting the words out to where the eyes and brain have a chance to respond to them,

TABLE 1.1   *Writing Processes*

Mental and Physical Behaviors That Take Place (Often Simultaneously) at Any Time While a Writer Is Generating, Drafting, or Revising.

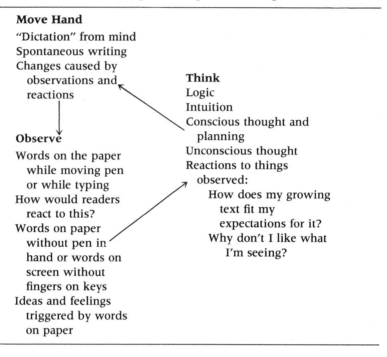

Move Hand
"Dictation" from mind
Spontaneous writing
Changes caused by
    observations and
    reactions

Think
Logic
Intuition
Conscious thought and
    planning
Unconscious thought
Reactions to things
    observed:

Observe
Words on the paper
    while moving pen
    or while typing
How would readers
    react to this?
Words on paper
    without pen in
    hand or words on
    screen without
    fingers on keys
Ideas and feelings
    triggered by words
    on paper

    How does my growing
        text fit my
        expectations for it?
    Why don't I like what
        I'm seeing?

giving words permanence on paper or computer screen rather than trusting your memory to hold ideas that develop as you write.

■ A Writer's Intentions

In addition to developing an awareness of the writing processes you are using as you write, it may be useful for you to focus on your *intentions* as a writer—the different motives you have when you sit down to write. Most of the suggestions we'll give you throughout this book won't deal with the *processes* of writing as much as with the *intentions* or *motives* you have at different times in a writing project. When your conscious intention for your writing session shifts, what you do as you write—your writing processes—changes, too.

Writing is not linear and orderly, but more like a rotating merry-go-round. And, in a sense, you can jump on the composition carousel at any point—by physically moving pen or computer keys, or by observing words you have written, or by thinking about your topic and what you hope to write or what you have written during your last writing session. With experience, you can learn how to shift intentions for your writing sessions and also how to recreate the mindset or intent you had during a previous writing session. You can learn how to jump back into a writing project after having been called away from it by the press of daily activities. Being conscious of your intent as a writer helps make that jump easier to negotiate.

As you read the next few paragraphs, keep in mind that a writing project is partly a matter of time. Assignments for college papers indicate the date they are due, and essay tests tell you how many minutes you have to write on each question. Similarly, journalists know the deadlines they have to meet for a story to make it into print in the next edition or on the air for the six o'clock news. In fact, author and writing teacher Donald M. Murray feels that one of the main pressures that helps a writer work is

> the approaching deadline, which moves closer day by day at a terrifying and accelerating rate. Few writers publish without deadlines, which are imposed by others or by themselves. The deadline is real, absolute, stern, and commanding.
>
> *Source:* Donald M. Murray, "Write Before Writing," College Composition and Communication, 29 (December 1978), p. 376.

A deadline may cause you stress—especially at its "real, absolute, stern" worst just before an important paper is due. But if you are honest, you probably know that you need deadlines in order to finish your papers. Five weeks before a research project is due in your economics class, you can wander from one interesting idea to another in the library, taking breaks whenever you like and not really putting your brain, hands, and eyes into the sort of coordinated activity through which writing can discover meaning. But if, on the night before you must submit a proposed thesis statement for the paper, you discover that all you have is a pile of unconnected note cards, the very pressure of the deadline helps you create the thesis you must have. The deadline is part of your motivation as a writer affecting how your writing processes work.

Each time you sit down to write, you have a chance to make a conscious decision about what you intend to do that day. Do you intend to play around with ideas? Do you intend to produce a draft because you'd like to get your project moving along rapidly, or because your assignment is due tomorrow? Or do you want to rework a previous draft? The way you write will be affected by your intent or motive for writing.

Your intentions or motivations for each writing session will change as your project takes shape. *Intentions are psychological phenomena in a writer who is facing a writing task.* Intentions are characterized by different mindsets, different inner states. They are functions of what you know (about your subject, your readers, and the writing approaches that you can use). They also are functions of how much time you have until you need to turn a finished piece of writing over to the readers. The main intentions most writers report are generating, drafting, and revising.

Generating.   Generating reflects the need you have to explore, to find information, to clarify, and generally to make a start on a writing project—or to restart when you stall. It is a time for you to write for yourself in order to understand your topic and for you to do whatever focusing you need to do. You may find a need to generate ideas at any point in your writing.

With extremely familiar sorts of writing (like a note to a friend) or very tight deadlines (like an essay examination), your *intention* to discover material may govern your writing processes for only a very brief period of time. It may not even seem separate from drafting; you may "just start" to write, as suggested in Table 1.1. But in many college and professional writing projects, there is a period when deadline pressure is low enough that you do not have to worry too much about how other people may react.

Drafting.   Drafting (and redrafting) becomes an intention or motive as you sense the direction you think you should take in your writing project, and as deadline pressure begins to figure in your priorities. As a writer drafts, the text is constantly adjusted or revised.

Extremely tight deadlines will force you to begin drafting immediately. But in many college writing projects, you will have the luxury of writing for yourself until you sense some fuzzy plan, some kernel of meaning you want to communicate to your audience. Then you can "draft your way" forward toward that plan.

Of course, even if you think you sense the direction your project should take, you still may end up changing your mind. Any time you are writing, your eye may observe something that triggers a revision in your plans, or your mind may uncover problems or new promising points that demand a change in what you are writing.

As you draft, you proceed differently than you do when your intention is to generate. You probably *feel* different about your writing, too. But your intention to draft never completely replaces the need to generate material and to find a focus for your writing. The exploration of your subject continues as you draft and revise, even though the need to build a complete draft has become your overriding intention.

Revising.   Revising (along with editing—making surface changes) becomes an intention later when, with deadline pressure building, you turn to a draft you have "completed" in order to improve its organization, examples, sentence structure, and word choice, as you try to make your writing more effective.

Here, too, generating and focusing may continue to take place, though to a lesser extent because you don't have the time to completely redo your writing. You may think, as you study a draft, that you are only trying to locate surface errors such as confusing sentence structure, spelling errors, lapses in diction, and so on. But once your eye and mind begin to respond to your text, you may see things that alter the focus you have on your subject or that trigger the need to revise by adding new material. When that happens, you might decide to shift intentions; you might decide to generate some ideas or you might decide to draft a new section. But if making the best you can out of the draft in front of you remains your primary motivation, then your *intention* is to revise.

Once again, these general intentions or motives—generating, drafting, and revising—are not the processes of writing. Your writing *processes* are working—your hands are busy, your eyes are moving, your mind is judging—regardless of whether you are trying to generate material, to create a draft for others to see, or to improve a completed draft. The intentions you have at different times in a writing project *influence* the way those processes of writing work for you.

Idea File: Computer Writing

Adapting Your Writing to the Computer

Different writers adapt to word processing in different ways. You need to experiment until you find some ways that seem suited to your own writing processes and intentions. Here are some possibilities:

1. Generating
   a. Use paper and pencil to gather ideas and then move to the word processor when you are ready to draft.
   b. Try to generate ideas directly at the monitor and then get a printed copy of your ideas before you begin drafting at the computer screen.
   c. Create an outline with either a computerized "outline generator" or with a word processor. Then get a printed copy of your outline. Revise your outline before you begin drafting.

2. Drafting
   a. Try to compose directly at the monitor. Some writers maintain that they think more efficiently when they compose at the keyboard than when they use pencil and paper. After you have drafted for awhile, get a printout of your writing and use a pencil to cross out what you don't want to use.

Then return to the word processor and delete the excess material.

b. Draft on paper and then enter your draft at the computer. But don't just type! Redraft as you proceed.

3. Revising

a. Try reorganizing your writing directly at the monitor. Some writers maintain that revising this way helps them to focus their attention on their ideas.

b. Get a printed copy of your draft and make changes in it with a pencil. Then return to the word processor to revise text according to the changes you made in pencil.

c. Proofread and edit both at the computer screen *and* on paper. The different media affect the way you see your text. Some errors will be easier to locate on paper than on the computer screen. Other errors will be easier to spot on the screen.

■ Processes and Intentions at Work

We have discussed how writers' intentions affect their writing processes. You will need to observe your own shifting intentions as you work on your next writing assignment. Try not to feel self-conscious *as* you write. Let the processes involved in writing happen naturally, and try to let your intentions for your writing sessions shift as your project takes shape. But after each writing session, try to re-create in writing what you accomplished and how you felt as you wrote. If you record your processes and intentions on several writing projects, you will be able to trace patterns in the life of your writing. Only after getting a clear idea of *what you do* can you determine *what you might do better.*

Table 1.2 gives you an overview of writers' intentions and how they vary as deadlines approach.

■ Different Intentions, Different Strategies

If you learn to establish intentions for your writing, you'll discover some practical consequences, for each intention calls up concrete strategies for writing that you can use—sometimes consciously and deliberately—to move your writing project along from inception to completion. And these strategies will be a central concern in much of this book.

In Chapter 3, we will present some strategies you can use when you are generating ideas and moving to a focus. In Chapter 4, we will give you some insights into strategies that work well when you are

TABLE 1.2   *The Life of a Writing Project: Intentions That Affect Your Writing Processes*

Intention 1: Generating Material and Finding a Focus

Main Intention:	To discover and to clarify.
Deadline:	Usually fairly remote.
Main Audience:	Yourself.
Methods:	Uncensored "rapid writing" to explore.
	Systematic exploration strategies.
	Just starting to write.

Intention 2: Drafting and Revising for Purpose and Audience

Main Intention:	To communicate ideas at least partly discovered and clarified already and to continue drafting and redrafting until you feel that you've said what you want to say.
Deadline:	Closer—and getting closer with each day, and each new piece of your draft.
Main Audience:	You *and* your anticipated reader.
Methods:	Generating and focusing continue.
	Revising continues.
	Text constantly adjusted in line with your developing plan for the project and your sense of your audience.

Intention 3: Final Revising and Editing

Main Intention:	To alter a "completed" draft in line with your plan for the project, your sense of your audience, and any new information you have discovered.
Deadline:	Closing in on you.
Main Audience:	Your readers.
Methods:	Vary considerably from writer to writer. Some writers allow generating and focusing to continue, redraft large sections and whole sentences, and alter the order of sections. Other writers do most of their revising while drafting and only edit sentences and words at this time.
	Altering the order of sections.
	Editing sentences and words.

drafting. And in Chapter 5, we will give you some practical advice for honing your final revising and editing strategies. Throughout, we will remind you that your processes and intentions will vary from one assignment to the next. But as you develop an awareness of your needs as a writer, you will be able to determine how to proceed on each new project, establishing appropriate intentions before you begin each writing session and incorporating efficient strategies as you write.

Summary

As we have suggested in this chapter, successful writers don't try to do everything at once. Each time they sit down to write, they determine their intention for their writing session. They consciously decide whether they intend to generate ideas, to draft, or to revise and edit.

The amount of time writers have for their writing project helps determine how they will proceed. When they have a writing assignment with a remote deadline, they allow themselves plenty of time to collect information and to *generate* ideas before they decide they are ready to push toward a draft. As they push toward a *draft,* however, they allow themselves the freedom to shift intentions should the need to shift become apparent. They keep in touch with their needs as writers and monitor their progress. As the deadline for their writing project approaches, effective writers set aside a separate writing session in which they consciously intend to do nothing but *revise.* Again, should the need to redraft become apparent, they allow their intentions to shift. But the need to finish the project compels them to return to revising whenever they can.

Finally, after they have finished revising, successful writers allow time in which they focus their intention for their writing session on proofreading for errors. They shift intentions briefly, and only if necessary, to make minor revisions or to redraft a section.

Throughout this chapter, we have asked you to consider the processes you use as you write and to reflect on your writing behaviors. In Chapter 2, Generating Ideas, you will have an opportunity to begin refining your writing processes as you practice several strategies for collecting material and discovering ideas to write about.

TEAMWORK WRITING

Teamwork Agenda A

You can start using teamwork writing even before you begin a writing project. Here's a *teamwork-writing* activity for you to try that will help break the ice:

1. Take a moment to think about writing experiences you have had in school, on the job, or in your private life. Then spend five minutes writing in response to these questions: When is writing easy? When is writing hard?

2. Get together in groups of four. Select someone to lead your discussion and another person to take notes. If you haven't met one another,

take a few minutes to introduce yourselves to one another. Then select someone to act as recorder and gather a list of your responses to the preceding questions.

3. Select someone to act as reporter. This person should summarize for the whole class what your group has talked about. After each reporter presents the key ideas of his or her group's discussion, other group members should have time to ask questions or to comment on what was talked about.

Teamwork activities help in different ways at different times. In the earliest stage of a writing project's life (when you are trying to understand an assignment) teamwork writing can help you discover various subtopics within a broad topic, decide what approach to an assignment or topic might be most efficient, and locate sources of information in your experience and the library. These are some of the benefits of teamwork activities. You can do all these things alone. But you can also use teamwork writing strategies so that you do not feel lonely, and so that you can benefit from several points of view while you generate material and find a focus.

While you are drafting, your brain, hands, and eyes are engaged in a complex and private process. You undoubtedly want to be alone at this time. Information others gave you earlier may prove helpful while you draft, and you can use the support of others after a lonely drafting session. During a drafting session, any sort of distraction can be an irritant. But immediately after a drafting session, you may enjoy talking with your peers about how your projects are going. Sharing successes and frustrations can help reassure you that writing is filled with ups and downs, backward and forward movements.

Late in the life of a writing project, you begin to look closely at a "completed" draft with the intention of revising: improving the draft's clarity, its impact on readers, its flair and interest, and its accuracy. You can do this revising—this reviewing—alone. But you can also use teamwork writing so that several sets of eyes and several different brains help tighten and improve your draft.

Teamwork Agenda B

Learn what you can about one another's writing processes by answering the following questions and then discussing your similarities and differences as writers:

PART 1

Answer the following questions on a separate sheet of paper, then take turns telling one another about your responses.

1. Think back to your last writing project. How did you get started? How did you feel about the assignment?

2. How do you usually get started? How do you usually feel at the beginning of a writing task?

3. Do you have any special rituals that you follow when you write? Do you use any special writing tools? (For example, some writers always use yellow pads to draft, other writers always use the computer.)

4. Do you have any secrets, any special techniques or strategies that you have adopted over the years?

5. What are your main problems as a writer?

PART 2

After you have shared your responses to the questions in Part 1, organize your findings by creating a chart based on the following outline:

Our Group's Writing Processes and Strategies

• Similarities

• Differences

• Special tips or techniques

Each group should report its findings to the entire class. Perhaps someone in the class will volunteer to produce a master list of your class's writing processes. You can save that list, and later, at the end of the term, see if your processes and strategies have changed in any way.

Writing Exercises

1. Keep a Processes and Intentions Log for the duration of this course. (See additional explanation in the Introduction on pp. 8–9.) Set aside a section of your notebook for your log or use a separate notebook. As you work on exercises and writing suggestions in this text, you will be growing and changing as a writer. Let your Processes and Intentions Log be a record of the changes in your writing processes and behaviors, including your changing attitudes about writing. As soon as you finish a writing assignment, make an entry in your log. Note which strategies and suggestions in the text seem useful to you and why they seem to help. Also indicate which strategies seem inappropriate, at least for the task you are completing at the time. Remember to date your entries.

2. What makes writing good? What constitutes bad writing? Collect samples from the newspaper, from your textbooks, from novels and short stories. Attach each sample to a page in your notebook. Write a brief comment about why you feel that each sample is an example of either good or bad writing.

3. Look over the list of items people often notice about themselves while they are drafting (p. 24). With your notebook in front of you and a pen in your hand, "think" about these questions: Have there been times when such things showed up in your writing practices? When? What was happening? Use a separate piece of paper for each of the eight items in the list. Number each page and write a sentence that identifies the item you are thinking about. For instance: "There are times when putting down one word seems to trigger other words" (no. 2), or "Lots of the pauses in my writing fill up with daydreams instead of thoughts about my writing" (no. 4).

    Write a series of these *assertions* about your practices as a writer. Then, as quickly as possible, use your *thinking pencil* or your *thinking keyboard* to put down examples and clarifying statements that support the accuracy of each assertion.

4. Processes are influenced by intentions in other areas besides writing. To see the parallels, try to think of a situation in which you've had to consciously change your behavior or your actions in order to accomplish what you needed to accomplish. Or maybe you can think of some occasion when you "caught yourself" in one mode of behavior when you knew you needed to switch to another. Here are a few examples of how people's actions are affected by their intentions:

    Jim is a long distance runner from Pennsylvania. He claims that he has his own way of running—sets of running processes—that he uses when he is in training. Long before the day of the competition, he trains differently from the way he trains a week or several days before the competition. His *intent* for the earlier training sessions is different from his intent in later sessions. In early sessions, he intends to build his stamina gradually. When it is close to the day of the race, he intends to push himself to the limit.

    Patti is a watercolor artist from Las Cruces, New Mexico. She accepts commissions to do paintings of birds, desert scenes, and local people. When Patti begins to work on a painting, she draws several sketches of what the finished piece might look like and shows it to her client. When she draws these sketches, she feels free to do anything she wants without penalty. She *intends* to try out a few possibilities and to imagine how they might work. But when she and her client settle on an idea for a painting, Patti goes about her work differently. Early in the process, she takes her time, waits for insights, talks about possibilities. Once her project gets rolling, her *intent* shifts; she needs to make her finished product look something like the sketch. Her painting *process* becomes more intense, more controlled. Sometimes, however, she goes back to the drawing board and starts sketching again. When she sketches, she is most comfortable, she feels less constrained. Somehow, in the sketching mindset, she can work out problems that seem impossible with watercolor.

In your log write about how *your* processes and *your* intentions are linked as you complete some kind of activity other than writing.

5. As you work on each writing assignment in this course, keep a record of when and why you shift intentions. Compare your responses with other students in your class. Discuss the relative ease or difficulty with which you shift from one intention to another.

6. Interview someone in your major or field of interest. Ask the person you interview to tell you about the kinds of writing he or she does in a given week. Learn what you can about his or her writing processes. See if you can also find out whether your interviewee has deadlines for most writing tasks. In class, share what you have learned with your classmates. Try to discover whether the writers who have deadline pressures use different writing processes than the writers who have considerable time for their projects.

7. Examine several college textbooks. Look at the organization. How easy are they to read? If you find one textbook easier to read than another, try to determine what causes that difference. Unless you can interview the authors, you can only speculate about the writers' processes and intentions. But venture some guesses about the authors: What writing behaviors do you think the textbook authors exhibited as they wrote these books? Record your reactions in your writing log.

Suggestions for Writing

1. Choose a writing assignment that you can begin now and keep working on as you do other assignments this semester. Working on a topic over time will give you a chance to write over time—a different kind of writing experience from the routine assignments you get in college, yet an assignment that will help you learn how to tackle extensive research papers that you may have to do in upper-level courses. By writing over a long period of time, you learn how to dip into and out of a writing project. Think of some topic that you'd really like to explore in depth, something that you need to know more about or that you'd like to know more about. Choose a topic that has some immediate interest for you. If a relative has a serious disease, learn what you can about that disease. If you are upset about a local issue—such as a plan to dam a river and thus destroy the natural habitat—take the time to learn more about the topic. If you are curious about sexual trends on your campus, do some research. See if you can identify sources in the library or through a computer data base that will help extend your knowledge of the topic. Start writing this paper now, but keep exploring the

topic all semester. Take notes, interview people, write spontaneously on the topic at least once a week. Whenever you feel ready, start drafting a section of the paper. Then explore the issue more—delve deeper into the topic, read more about it, talk to experts—and write another section of the draft or a completely new draft. Keep a record of how you proceed and be prepared to discuss your writing processes and shifting intentions with your classmates.

2. Write a fictional report on yourself as a writer. You can use some of the ideas you developed in the writing exercises in this chapter. Since you have already generated plenty of material for this assignment, you can start drafting immediately. Remember, the report should be fictional, so, if you want, you can write about the kind of writer you want to be rather than the kind of writer you are. Refer to yourself by name, or as she or he. Have some fun trying to fool your reader by giving your report the feeling that someone else is writing about you.

3. Write an essay about your writing processes and intentions for a class collection entitled *Portraits of Students as Writers*. Your individual topic might be something like "What I Do When I Write—and Why." Use some of the ideas you came up with as you completed the exercises in this chapter to help you get started. Be sure that you include specific, personal details.

4. Interview several professors at your campus who frequently publish their writing in the form of journal articles, scientific reports, textbooks, novels, non-fiction essays, or poetry. Write an essay in which you focus on the similarities and differences amongst the writers you have interviewed. Or, if you would prefer, write about one of your professors' writing processes. Consider submitting your piece to the campus newspaper, but be sure to let your sources know before the interview if you plan to publish your writing. For now, use whatever generating, drafting, and revising strategies that you are comfortable with. Return to this essay toward the end of the semester and revise and reshape it, using strategies presented in later chapters of this text.

Generating Ideas

2

What You Know and What You Need to Find Out

To generate is to spark ideas, to trigger insights, to activate thought processes—to somehow muster the information and insights you need for a writing project. The need to generate ideas can surface at any time while you are writing, drafting, revising, or editing. But, when you have the time, you should pay particular attention to generating as much material as you can at the beginning of a writing project. By gathering the information you need before drafting, you give yourself an opportunity to get a head start on your writing project. With the content of your paper under control, you can focus on other matters while you draft.

Generating ideas can be an enjoyable process. After all, when writers are generating ideas, they are free to say what they want to say, to think what they want to think, and to break as many rules of grammar and punctuation as they happen to break. They know that worrying about their writing can make them censor their words and ideas. They know that attention to small matters of mechanics can distract their attention. And so they free themselves from these concerns during generating sessions. They fill the page or the computer monitor rapidly, with no other intent than to think about ideas and capture them in words. They let their *intention* (to generate ideas) affect their writing processes and they are often surprised at how many good ideas can show up.

In this chapter we will help you develop strategies for discovering what you know about a topic and determining what you need to know. Although we want to stress the generative power of rapid writing as a way of discovering ideas, we will also suggest other strategies that you can try when you begin writing projects, or any time that you feel a need to gather more material or to generate additional insights about your topic.

Developing Confidence

Confidence that you can write and freedom from self-censorship when you start to write are two requirements for writing sessions in which you generate ideas. But how can you develop this confidence and freedom if you don't already have it?

First, you need to write. And next, you need to write under conditions that help you become more spontaneous and free. You need to write successfully, seeing ideas appear on your paper or monitor, so that you develop a positive "I can do it" attitude about writing.

Locating Promising Topics

Before you can write, though, you need a topic to write about. But you do not need just any topic, you need a topic with the potential for success. A promising topic is a topic that

- is appropriate for the course in which you are writing and for the general assignment given by the instructor.
- you care enough about to work hard on.
- you understand well or are interested in learning about.
- is interesting enough or important enough that other people will care about it, or can be made to care about it.
- can be adequately developed through knowledge gained from your own experiences and from research.
- is limited enough for you to develop it thoroughly, yet broad enough that you do not get bogged down in extreme specialization, jargon, and trivia.

Suppose you've been asked to write on a topic that is related to your major or to the profession you plan to enter. There is so much you could write about. You might consider writing a career profile—a kind of character sketch of someone in a profession that interests you. Or, you could write an essay in which you explore some problems in your chosen field.

How do you know which topic will work for you? Try to determine which of the topics below would be promising topics for a student who is interested in careers in television or radio:

1. A Typical Day in the Life of a Television Newscaster

2. A Profile of Ann Jackson, Local News Commentator

3. Problems Facing Communications Majors

4. *Broadcast News:* The Movie vs. the Reality

If you are like most people, you probably think that topics 1 and 3 are too broad. The first topic could be revised to read "A Typical Day in Tom Brokaw's Life." However, it's not always possible for someone other than the writer to determine whether a topic is promising. Only the writer himself or herself can determine the full potential of a given topic. For instance, the topic "Problems Facing Communications Majors" appears much too broad. But what if the writer knows three or four issues that indeed do cross all communications fields (for example, low pay, fierce competition, and inequitable promotions), and what if, further, the writer has many examples to support each of several points? Then, a seemingly broad topic might be the basis for a compelling essay. In general, though, writers tend to avoid broad topics; they search instead for narrower versions of their topics. For instance, in her book *And So It Goes,* Linda Ellerbee focuses on her own experiences in television news as a way of suggesting overall problems in the broadcast media field as a whole.

Once you have a topic—whether it has been assigned or is a topic you have developed yourself—you have the kernel of a paper. But how successful your paper will be depends on what else you do. Too many students try to move directly from a kernel of an idea about their topic to a finished paper by using a few ideas they already have and a few more that they locate on a brief trip to the library. Since they really have little to work with other than a general topic, such as "The Communications Business Today," these students usually end up with generalized, unconvincing essays that lack any sense of their personal involvement in the topic and any substantial support for their generalized statements. To avoid such ineffective writing, you should try to generate as many ideas, supporting points, facts, examples, and interesting sidelights as possible about your topic before you begin drafting. However, don't be surprised if, even though you've spent considerable time trying to focus your topic, you find yourself needing to focus it still further as you begin writing.

By generating ideas about your topic you not only discover how much you know about it, you also find out how much additional time you'll need to spend collecting material from other sources (such as books, field trips, and interviews with experts).

Just Writing

Many times, one of the best ways to generate ideas about a topic is to plunge in and write. Since your mind and your hands coordinate naturally, and often spontaneously, during composition, you may find that you can write well by just sitting down at your desk or computer and going at it. You don't need to have any particular strategy in mind in order to generate ideas. All you need to do is write.

So pick up a pen and put a sheet of paper on your desk. (Or, if you prefer, turn on your computer and load its word processing software.) Now, write. Never let your fingers stop as you write for three minutes on this topic:

Writing Assignment: Part 1

What are you putting your energy into these days? Why? What keeps you motivated? Who helps you stay motivated? How long do you think you'll stay interested in this same thing?

As soon as you read the assignment, get your fingers busy forming words—any words. You might begin by copying the assignment. Then you might write out something like this:

So that's the assignment? I wonder what I'm going to write? Maybe I should write about . . . .

In other words, just let your writing processes get started; let your hand, your brain, and your eyes work naturally. Try to write something related to the topic. Later, if you feel yourself running out of things to write about, you might write something like this:

I seem to be running out of things to say. I wonder why? Is this topic boring to me? Is there something I've missed here?

Work for several minutes to experience what writing this way feels like and to discover ideas as you go. In a sense, try for rapid writing that fills the paper or computer screen. Don't worry about mechanical errors, silly ideas, problems in grammar, or spelling.

Could you write on demand, keeping hands always in motion? Reflect on what you've just written and on the way you went about writing it. Now, try to write rapidly, nonstop, and margin-to-margin on this topic:

Writing Assignment: Part 2

When I think back on the writing assignment I described a few minutes ago, what is it that seemed most difficult or frustrating about the topic and the situation?

If you are anything like the students we have watched do Part 1 of this writing assignment, you were able to do it fairly well. Oh, you may have felt silly, or irritated at the arbitrary orders about nonstop writing; or worried when you sensed an error and wanted to go back to correct it. But probably, you were able to do as well, writing on demand, as this student did on a different topic:

> The first in-class writing in English 101. I'll never forget it. The teacher told us to write for fifteen minutes of "personal narrative." He said he needed a short example of our writing style and ability. Everyone else started filling sheets of notebook paper with sprawling lines of prose. But I sat there wondering what to write, what would be interesting. What if I write something stupid? What if I say it wrong? Don't writers need "inspiration," and I certainly didn't have any that cold winter morning.
>
> Oh, no! My fifteen precious minutes was almost half gone already. I just had to start. So I began to write, jotting down words as they came to my mind. The first rough sentence appeared on my paper, and I sensed that there was something there I could write. In the few remaining minutes I tried to add ideas and some examples to make a passable one page piece. I wasn't all that proud when I handed it in, but I was relieved that I had gotten anything done to hand in at all.

Some people like to write spontaneously and use this strategy a lot; others prefer to spend their time listing ideas, jotting down notes, or just thinking for awhile about their topic. You may not want to generate ideas in the same way all the time, but there are many times when spontaneous writing will work for you. Try spontaneous writing when

- you can't seem to come up with any ideas.
- starting to write feels like the only way to begin.
- seeing a few words you didn't expect to write helps ideas start to flow.
- you want to explore a topic to discover whether you know enough to write about it.
- you feel (at any point in your writing) that you need to just let words roll freely on the page or computer screen: if you began a particular writing session intending to draft, you may feel a need to shift gears, relax, and write spontaneously for awhile; if you intended to revise, you may, nonetheless, discover that you need to sit back, reflect, and work out some problem by writing freely about it.

Ideas may have come easily as you wrote about yourself in the preceding writing assignment. You may have had some general idea in mind before you started to write. But almost certainly you saw new things appearing, and your brain responded to these discoveries by making some adjustments in the idea you might have had originally. This is the phenomenon we called the thinking pencil or the thinking keyboard earlier. It is also an example of another phenomenon in writing—growth through change. Words on the page affect the growth and shape of words not yet on the page. Because of the spontaneous coordination of brain, hand, and eyes, writing can be a source of ideas and a means to change your point of view about a topic while you are trying to write down your present point of view.

Rapid Writing

When you write quickly in order to discover or generate ideas, you are using one of the most common tricks writers and writing teachers use to build spontaneity in writing. The technique is known by various names—free writing, wet-ink writing, rapid writing—all of which stress the ease with which words flow. Here is how freelance writer and novelist Gene Olson describes this sort of writing:

> The trick is to keep the words flowing, rolling, sliding upon the paper. You're creating at this stage, not being picky-picky. Go with the flow, then push it a little, just sort of nudge it along. Before your eyes, a few words turn into a sentence, a sentence into a paragraph, and a paragraph into a composition . . . in the rough.
>
> *Source:* Gene Olson, *Sweet Agony: A Writing Manual Of Sorts* (Medford, Oreg.: Windyridge Press, 1972), pp. 34–35.

Gene Olson's words convey a good deal about free writing. First, when you are writing freely, your words are "flowing, rolling, sliding upon the paper." Since they are so flexible and changeable, the words you write during rapid-writing sessions need not be objects of "finicky" worries or "picky-picky" self-censorship. The student who described her difficulty writing a short, personal narrative (see page 43) was frustrated precisely because she was not free of such inhibitions. Instead of starting to write, she worried that she had nothing to write, that she could not start writing, that everyone else in the room was a much better writer. And magnifying all those worries was another inhibition: the student wanted so much to give her teacher a good example of her style and skill that she started treating a minor, first-day writing assignment as if it were really important—as if what she wrote would be "engraved in stone."

If you don't think you can get your golf ball over the water hazards, you probably will lose a lot of balls every time you play golf. If, when you sit down to write, you doubt that words will flow and roll onto the paper, then you will have a hard time following Olson's advice to "go with the flow" as you watch "a few words turn into a sentence, a sentence into a paragraph." Such lack of confidence is evident in the student sample on page 43. The student wasn't too confident to begin with, and as she looked around the room and saw everyone else writing, she realized she was not writing and that made it even harder to get started.

IDEA FILE: COMPUTER WRITING

Rapid Writing

Whenever you need to generate ideas, just start writing. Rather than sitting at a blank computer screen, open a file and start typing in ideas. Remember, your words on the screen are not permanent. They are merely electronic dots until you save and print your file. Try the following strategy:

1. Start writing at the top of your file. If you feel like listing ideas or writing in fragments, that's okay. You are writing only with the intention of capturing *ideas,* not with the intent of creating sentences and paragraphs as you would if you were drafting.

2. When you have gotten some ideas on the screen, move your cursor to a clean spot and start over. Push your list of ideas or your sentences off the screen so that you don't see them. Don't look back at what you wrote. Then start writing. Focus on your topic. Write for at least five minutes. Save your file when you finish.

3. Now read through your writing and delete everything but the ideas you want to build on later when you draft. Then save your file with a *different name* so that you have both a record of your original rapid writing and a collection of "worthwhile ideas" in your new file.

We recommend that you try rapid writing whenever your intention is to generate ideas or to write toward a focus. Remember, you can shift intentions at any time while you are writing. You may begin drafting only to discover, in the midst of a drafting session, that you need to return to generating for while. As you get to know your needs as a writer, you will learn how to change your writing strategies as you change your writing intentions.

In writing, as in many activities, success tends to bring more success. Successfully getting words down during low-pressure sessions of free writing promotes a positive attitude that can help you write effectively at other times.

Using Structured Rapid Writing to Explore Your Topic

Rather than just sitting down and writing about your subject, you might prefer a more structured approach to generating and clarifying ideas. To help you get used to rapid writing, we would like to suggest some ways that you can use it to help you learn more about your topic. Focusing upon different aspects of your topic and approaching your topic in a number of ways adds to your understanding of it.

Learning About Your Topic

Here are some ways you can explore your topic:

1. *Write what you know about your subject.* Following the "nonstop" technique of rapid writing, try to get down on paper as much information as you can about the subject you think you will write about. Try to be factual, and to use writing as a way of creating a helpful record of factual information that you might be able to use later.

2. *Write what you feel about your subject.* Use rapid writing to explore your responses to the subject you plan to write on. Are you interested or bored? Why? Are there things in your biography, your religious convictions, or your political ideas that color how you feel about the topic? Would any of these things make good material in a paper about the subject?

3. *Dissect your assignment.* If you have a specific writing assignment to work with (whether a teacher made it or you have developed an assignment for yourself), use writing as a way to make sure you understand it. Concentrate not on the subject (such as "Planning My Financial Future") but on the specific details the assignment requires you to deal with as you write about the subject: how much research is required, should there be formal documentation, how does the assigned length affect the amount of detail needed, who will the readers be, is "financial future" a term I need to be more precise about before I can do a good job on the assignment?

4. *Write about what you should do next with your writing project.* Following the nonstop technique of rapid writing, consider where you are in your efforts to complete the writing project. What are your intentions at this point in the project: to generate material and find a focus, to draft for an audience, to refine a completed draft? Given the amount of time left before the project is due, should you be farther along or are you moving so fast that you are not letting good ideas develop? Given the specific information you have "dissected" out of the assignment, what should you plan to do the next time you get out your project and start working with it?

5. *Write for different readers.* You can discover still more about your topic

by varying your approach to it. As you focus on your topic by applying the preceding suggestions, try writing for different readers:

a. *Write a letter to a friend.* Before you start, think of a real friend or a family member. Jot down a casual and personal letter to this person. As in any friendly letter, report on what you are doing and ask questions that return correspondence may answer.

b. *Write a letter to your teacher.* Take the same approach as in the preceding suggestion, but use the letter as a way to communicate with your instructor. If your teacher replies, you may get some very helpful responses in a completely non-threatening way.

c. *Discuss your topic with your "clone."* Pretend that you are two people. You are exactly alike except that your clone is more analytical and skeptical than you are. Your clone is a person who really likes to ask tough questions and find the "loopholes" in people's arguments. As you write, try to get a dialogue going with this person.

   Another approach for using this technique is for you to write about the topic, then have your clone turn his or her skeptical eyes to your words and write a comment or question he or she would ask. Use some distinctive mark to identify the clone's comments. Next, respond to the comment or answer the question in "your" voice, and so on. Try to let the comments and questions trigger more writing about the topic, so that "you" and your "clone" act as cooperative collaborators. As you begin to develop a draft of an assigned project, you could start one of your rapid writing sessions by having your clone examine and pose some tough questions about the draft. Then you could respond, have the clone comment on how you have responded, etc.

d. *Write an entry in a diary.* Pretend that you are writing for no eyes but your own within the total privacy of a diary. (If your teacher plans to check your daily writings, make sure "DIARY" stands out prominently at the top of the page so he or she can skip over the entry.)

You can experiment with different combinations of topic focus and approach during your daily writing sessions. Table 2.1 shows how you can come up with sixteen different combinations of *focus* and *approach* for your writing. By working through the sixteen combinations from top to bottom—doing all four approaches to no. 1 before starting on no. 2, and so on—you can turn your daily writing into a three-week exploration of one subject. In fact, if you have a paper due at the end of three weeks, your sixteen writings would allow you to

• clarify for yourself what you know about the topic, and to do this at different points in your developing understanding of your subject and your plans for the paper.

TABLE 2.1 *Rapid-Writing Grid*

		Approach		
Focus	A—Letter to a Friend	B—Letter to a Teacher	C—Talk with My Clone	D—Diary Entry
1. What I Know	1A	1B	1C	1D
2. What I Feel	2A	2B	2C	2D
3. Dissect the Assignment	3A	3B	3C	3D
4. What Next?	4A	4B	4C	4D

- explore your feelings about the subject several times, even as your feelings are changing because of your ongoing work on the paper.

- receive from your teacher up to four different responses on your ideas about your focus, and on the progress you are making in your work.

- probe for logical gaps and "thin" spots in your writing during four conversations with a friendly clone, to close loopholes that some outside readers might discover in far less friendly ways.

Here are some examples from one student's practice writing sessions on the subject of "Stress Management." Notice how the combinations of *focus* and *approach* from Table 2.1 helped her to explore her topic in a variety of ways.

Topic: Job Stress

Focus: 1—What I know about "Job Stress"

Approach: D—Diary entry

```
Stress is common among today's Americans. It seems like
wherever I go pamphlets, signs, TV shows and news re-
ports all warn of stress. Heck, I didn't even realize
it was something to worry about until I opened my eyes
to the media. Thanks guys--you've helped create stress
in me just warning about the blasted stuff. But stress
on the job is a narrower topic. Let's see, I know that
almost all executives have a rough time with this. All
the pressure and responsibility they have is bound to
result in something bad. Heart attacks are big time
problems with executives who just don't know how to
```

release their stress. But I don't know enough about
the kinds of stress lawyers face. . . .

Topic: Job Stress

Focus: 4—What next on "Job Stress?"

Approach: A—Letter to a friend

I told you you would be hearing from me again soon,
Doug—here I am. Thought I'd just give you one more
report on how well the paper is going for Gebhardt's
class. Last night I really took a close look at one
of my sources. It looks like it will be helpful. I took
notes on about 15 cards. I wish I could find some information on how lawyers are affected by job stress.

Topic: Job Stress

Focus: 3—Dissect the assignment

Approach: B—Letter to a teacher

It seems as though my ideas for my "job stress" paper
are finally coming together. I must admit I was somewhat worried that I wouldn't find any material for my
paper. But I've interviewed a lawyer, and I'm beginning to get a lot of information. I've learned that
everyday work is often routine for some lawyers. It's
only when special cases come in that the stress mounts.
There are a few more questions I need to ask Attorney
Heberling, though. And I need to read a few more articles about stress in general. As you look at my draft
you will see the listings of sources I have found. Most
of these, I feel, are worthwhile sources. Do you feel I
have enough research here to get an overview of my topic or is more necessary? I am unclear as to the amount
of documentation required. The paper doesn't really
require much documentation, does it? I know there is
a section where I put bibliography entries of my sources.

Topic: Job Stress

Focus: 2—What I feel about "Job Stress"

Approach: C—Talk with my clone

 Job stress should be interesting to most anyone.
[That's an assumption you shouldn't make. If you go in-

to a paper with that attitude, you're liable to avoid creative flair and just rely on reader's interest.]

I believe in a holistic approach to health care. By taking such an approach, one must look at all components of health. Stress is one of these components. It has physical debilitation, emotional influences, and for some spiritual debilitation.
[That might be an area you'll want to touch on in your paper. It helps the reader recognize the significance of stress and how it affects the whole person.]

It affects practically everyone in the working world to some extent. If it doesn't face them now, it most likely will later. I think it was at the root of my father's heart condition. When he first began having heart attacks he was working a very tense and pressure-filled job. He was unhappy with his job but stayed there regardless. Now he has already had one double bypass and is about ready to have surgery again.
[This helps emphasize the fact that coronary disease is a major result of stress, and it also lets you show a "personal" connection to or expertise about your topic.]

IDEA FILE: COMPUTER WRITING

An Electronic Writing Log

If you want, you can use a word processor to do some or all of your log entries for this course. Here are ways you might proceed:

1. *Create a table of contents file.* Dedicate an entire disk to your *electronic log*. If your computer has a hard disk, you can create a "subdirectory" called "log" (or whatever your word processor will allow, such as "log.doc."). On that disk, create a separate "Table of Contents" file. Type the following (or an equivalent):

> **Table of Contents**
> **Topic/Assignment:**
> **Focus:**
> **Approach:**
> **Date:**
> **File name:**

Copy this framework (or template) for your file several times, then save your file under a name you will be sure to remember. For example, you might name it the "Contents" file.

2. *Update the "Contents" file regularly.* Whenever you are ready to write a log entry, open your "Contents" file and fill in the appropriate spaces:

> **Table of Contents**
> **Topic/Assignment:** Editorial on political campaign for political science class
> **Focus:** What I know
> **Approach:** Letter to a friend
> **Date:** 9/12/88
> **File name:** politics

3. *Use a separate file for each log entry.* Open a new file for each new topic or assignment. Be sure to use the file name listed in your "Contents" file.

4. *Recycle parts of your entries.* Use segments of your rapid writing as you draft your paper. As you are drafting, remain alert for places where you could use a "chunk" of text from your log file. Learn how to "merge" the sentences from your log file into the file you are using to draft your paper. (Note: Not all word processors allow you to move material from one file to another or from one disk to another. You may need to retype your ideas from a printed copy of your rapid-writing entry.)

Other Generating Strategies

Many students like to generate ideas through writing. But other students prefer more structured activities such as the Rapid-Writing Grid (see Table 2.1). Here are a few other strategies that you might experiment with as you move through different assignments for this course:

1. *Question your topic.* You've probably heard of the journalist's five W's: Who, What, When, Where, and Why. Most news stories answer these questions since they tell *who* was involved in a story, *what* happened, *when* it happened, *where* it took place, and *why* it happened. These same questions can be altered to fit almost any topic. For instance, if you are doing a profile of someone in your chosen profession, you might ask: Why did you decide to become a journalist? What experiences did you have in school that helped you in your career? Where did you work? When did you decide that journalism was the field you'd enter?

Practice developing *who, what, when, where,* and *why* questions for your own and your classmates' topics. By learning how to ask questions, you learn how to find information and ideas to answer those questions in your writing.

2. *List and classify ideas.* Before you have done any rapid writing or after you have written for awhile about your topic, make a long list of ideas, insights, and other fragments of information about your topic. Do not worry about whether items fit together. Just aim for as comprehensive a list as you can possibly gather. Next, place the same number or special symbol (an asterisk, for example) by each item on the list that "fits" with other items on the list. After you've sorted your list into different categories, recopy your list so that you can see what you've got.

IDEA FILE: COMPUTER WRITING

Listing and Classifying

Listing and classifying ideas works especially well at the computer screen. Suppose you are writing an essay defending television programming. In order to gather ideas, you might jot down the following items, and then add symbols identifying items that match. You can also add "notes to yourself" in brackets. Finally, you can use the "move" command of your word processor to reorganize your list.

$$ television shows bring family members together

$$ shows such as "Family Ties" and "Cosby" stress the importance of close family bonds

& even police shows emphasize the difference between good and evil [INDICATES SOME VALUE IN TV]

& shows that include a lot of sexual material help introduce youngsters to these ideas at home before they hear about them at school [INDICATES SOME VALUE IN TV]

my dad and brother like sports [SHOWS HOW THERE'S SOMETHING FOR EVERYONE]

my sister and mom like game shows [SHOWS HOW THERE'S SOMETHING FOR EVERYONE]

$$ we all like cartoons

I like some educational shows like National Geographic Specials [SHOWS HOW THERE'S SOMETHING FOR EVERYONE]

You don't even have to retype your notes to yourself. Just write out the common link between several of your items and then "copy" your text to the appropriate spots. (If your word processor has "glossary" capabilities—a feature that allows you to insert prefabricated words and phrases with certain keystroke commands—then you can avoid retyping by using that feature.)

3. *Look at your topic from different disciplinary perspectives.*

TOPIC: Politicians

Literature: How do politicians influence the kind of literature produced in a given decade?

Sociology: How do politicians influence social trends and patterns?

Science: How can politicians help scientists get additional funding for their experiments?

Recreation: What is the best way to get politicians to understand the recreational needs of a state?

4. *Probe your topic using standard thinking patterns.*

TOPIC: Politicians

Compare your topic with something similar: How is the way politicians are "sold" similar to the way that products are advertised?

Define your topic: What are politicians? What is an honest politician?

Look at *causes and effects:* What kinds of things are caused by politicians? What is the effect of political maneuvering?

Classify your topic: What different kinds of politicians are there?

Analyze your topic by dividing it into various components: What is politics made up of? How do individual politicians fit into the picture?

Different Writers, Different Assignments, Different Strategies

The strategy you choose will vary depending on the nature of the assignment, your deadline, and your personal preferences. If you are taking an essay test, you may have only a few minutes to collect ideas and let your mind roam. If you are working on a casual assignment, you may know enough about your topic to begin by writing freely until you generate sufficient information to move to drafting. If your assignment is more complex, however, you may need to do some initial reading, note taking, and thinking before you try to generate ideas in writing. And you may find a need for a structured generating strategy to help you get started.

Your knowledge of the topic will also affect your choices. For one thing, if you don't know much about your topic, you'll have to do a lot of reading or searching for information. And you'll need to take notes. Then, before you actually start writing sentences, you might want to jot down a list of all the ideas you'd like to cover in your writing. But we want to make sure you understand that you don't need to use any particular strategy for generating ideas: You can generate ideas by writing. You don't need to go through any excessive preparation. You can just sit down and write whatever comes to mind—whether you know a lot about your topic or not.

Not everyone likes to start writing projects in the same way. Some writers think best by using complete sentences and just letting go with ideas. Other writers like to jot down ideas in lists or answer questions about their topics. Still other writers like to use special idea-generating strategies that we will cover later in this textbook. As you experiment with new strategies, reflect on their usefulness to you as a writer. Note which strategies help you in specific circumstances. In this way, over time, you will learn how to adjust your writing processes to your varying needs as a writer.

What to Expect from Generating Activities

This chapter has explored how rapid writing and other generating strategies can be spontaneous and filled with discoveries; it has provided suggestions and ideas on how you can make your generating sessions become more fluid and free. If you have tried some of the ways to use rapid writing, you have probably discovered how—by writing freely about your topic or by using such strategies as writing about your topic in a diary, dissecting the assignment, or writing a letter to your clone—you can gradually develop a clear notion of what you want to say in your paper or how you can write your way out of a tricky point in a drafting session.

Do realize that generating activities do not always lead to immediate results. You shouldn't be disappointed if your spontaneous writing doesn't result in more than a rough collection of ideas. You shouldn't feel that you've done something wrong if your responses to questions are getting you nowhere. Just be honest with yourself. If, for instance, you discover that you have said nothing useful or that you have written in circles, admit it and determine what to do next. Think about your options. You can start over if you want. Or, you can read through your writing and your lists of ideas, and collect the useful nuggets of information. Then you can use those ideas as the basis for additional generating activities.

From Generating to Focusing: Writing Thesis Statements

After you have generated sufficient ideas and details about your topic, try to sharpen the focus of your topic into a main idea—a thesis statement—that will control and unify the whole paper. Perhaps in an early writing session you discovered that "The Florist Business" was too broad a topic to offer you much hope of success. You might have decided that "Attractive and Unattractive Aspects of Being a Florist" could work as a topic. But what specific focus will the paper have? Being a florist is attractive and unattractive for whom? Attractive and unattractive according to what criteria? Do attractive and unattractive features exist in equal parts?

What you would need before you could move much further with this paper would be a more sharply focused *thesis* statement that unifies your writing—one that indicates not only the topic, but the specific direction that you plan to take as you discuss the topic. For example, notice how this thesis statement establishes a clear focus on the general topic:

General Topic: "A Vocational Area of Interest to Me."

Focused Thesis Statement: "Even though I realize that owning my own florist business will involve long hours, volatile prices, seasonal sales fluctuations, and the risk of failure, the personal satisfactions of the florist business still attract me."

For Whom? The writer.

What Criteria? Amount of work, security, chance of success, personal satisfaction.

What Reasons? Competition, erratic prices, the seasonal nature of the business.

Equal Parts? No. Attractive personal factors outweigh unattractive economic factors.

Read over your responses to generating activities to see if you've already written your way to a focus or to see if you've already written a sentence that states your main idea. Then, in a separate sentence or in a few sentences, write out your main idea. You can state your idea using whatever words come to mind, knowing full well that (1) this idea might change as you draft and (2) the sentence or sentences that you write at an early stage in your writing will not necessarily bear any resemblance to those that appear in your finished theme or essay. By writing down a thesis statement or main-idea sentence, you will be forcing yourself to focus your thoughts.

It's usually wise to establish a focus before you start a drafting session. Then, as you draft, you have a sense of where you're going with your ideas as you shape them into sentences and paragraphs. Here are some examples of how our students used rapid writing to help them develop their thesis statements.

Student: Marilyn

Topic : The Oprah Winfrey Show

Excerpt from Rapid Writing :
I really like Oprah Winfrey's shows. They are educational, in a way, but you don't notice that as you're
watching. What happens is that you get caught up in
the ideas. l started to watch them closely, trying to
figure out how Oprah does it. How she manages to keep
everyone's attention, that is. It seems that Oprah
presents all sides of an issue using a personal approach. She's not afraid of controversial issues either.
One show presented parents of children who had committed suicide. . . .

Proposed thesis statement :
The Oprah Winfrey Show presents all sides of a given
issue in an exciting talk show.

Thesis statement from finished essay :
Oprah Winfrey enraptures her audience with provocative
issues that most people haven't heard about or thought
about. Unlike other talk shows, which primarily present
one side of an issue, The Oprah Winfrey Show presents
all sides, demonstrating a clear understanding of the
day's topic so that viewers and audience participants
can come to their own conclusions.

Student: Dean

Topic : Movie ratings

Excerpt from Rapid Writing :
I really detest violence, but I know that in some
cases, moviemakers have to show violent scenes explicitly. I've started noticing, though, that not all
R—rated movies are equally violent. Some are handled
in such a way that a viewer like me can tolerate what's
happening. But others are more than I can handle. Last
week I walked out of one movie and into another one.
Both movies had R—ratings, but one was much more well
done, and the other was more than my stomach could
handle. I decided to do my next paper on the problem.
After reading about the movie ratings codes and how
they came about, I think I finally learned why the ratings are so ambiguous. . . .

Proposed thesis statement:

Not every R-rated movie is disturbing to watch. Some
are even well done. This makes me wonder why the
rating system provides such an ambiguous guide for
filmgoers to make viewing choices by.

Thesis statement from finished essay:

It's movie night, and you and a friend decide to see
what's playing at the local triplex. As you stand in
the lobby looking over your choices, you notice that
all the movies showing are rated "R." You choose
Scarface over Ruthless People, but being of weak stomach, you leave early and catch the rest of Ruthless
People. In this movie the comic portrayal of violence
is nowhere nearly as graphic and unsettling as that
shown in Scarface. This makes me wonder why the rating
system provides such an ambiguous guide for filmgoers.
The answer lies in the Motion Picture Production
Code of 1968, which is in use today.

Student: Susie

Topic: Surrogate parenting

Excerpt from Rapid Writing:

It might be okay for a woman who can't get pregnant to
hire a surrogate. But what about a rich woman who just
plain doesn't feel like having a baby? That's different and could get out of hand.

Proposed thesis statement:

It seems very possible in our society that surrogate
parenting could get out of hand and we need to do
something about the problems.

Thesis statement from finished essay:

To control the problems involved in surrogate parenting,
agencies should apply stringent screening procedures to
all parties involved.

After you've settled on a main idea for your writing, you still may
want to do some additional planning and organizing before you begin
drafting. Or you may want to move directly from spontaneous writing
to drafting. Chapter 3 offers some specific suggestions on how you
might try to build up words on paper as you draft and how you can
control your writing processes as you "write" your way to a finished
draft.

Summary

In this chapter, we have suggested some strategies for gathering ideas and information for your writing projects. Consider using them whenever your writing schedule allows you the time to ponder and reflect. You should remember, of course, that much of the information you come up with by using these strategies may not fit into your rough draft. Think of generating sessions as times to think on paper, not times to produce actual sentences and paragraphs for your finished assignments.

We have also covered focusing at the end of this chapter—for an important reason. If you end a generating session with time left to look over your work and write down a thesis statement, you'll know where you are and where you need to go when you sit down to write a rough draft—the subject of the next chapter.

TEAMWORK WRITING

After all members of your writing group have experimented with some of the generating suggestions in this chapter, it's time to use these strategies for a purpose—to help you generate ideas for an actual writing task. Get together on several different occasions to help one another move from choice of topic to generating to drafting.

Help One Another Select and Narrow a Topic

1. If you don't know what to write about, let your group members help you decide. Tell them what your interests are. Ask them which of your interests they'd like to know more about.

2. Even if your teacher has assigned a topic, you still need to personalize the topic. You might do some rapid writing to help you come up with your own angle on the topic. You may need to focus on a few different angles to help you develop an overall focus on your topic. You can also talk about your topic in order to get a clearer grasp of what you want to focus on. Take turns telling one another what you think you'll write about and why you've chosen your topic or why you plan to write about a particular aspect of your topic.

Help One Another After Generating Sessions

1. Get together in your writing groups to talk about your experiences with trying to come up with ideas. Share your successes and failures.

2. Get together to help one another plan writing strategies:

a. Group members can take turns talking about how far they are in their writing projects. If someone is ready to shift intentions and start drafting, that person should explain why he or she feels ready to move on. If others feel that they've still not clarified their focus, they can talk about what they might do next.

b. Group members can talk about why they feel a certain strategy will help more than another one. One person might plan to use some of the diary strategies suggested in this chapter. Another person might want to use focused rapid writing exclusively. Group members can help one another make decisions about their writing processes.

c. Group members can talk about their previous successes as writers. What strategies worked for them in the past? What strategies did not work? Why? By listening to others talk about writing processes, each group member may begin to realize how individualized writing is—how differently one person writes from the way another person writes. What works for one person may or may not work for another person. Group members should consider trying other peoples' strategies, realizing that ultimately, each writer must use the strategies that work best for him or her.

Review One Another's Responses to Generating Activities

You can help others in your group move from rapid writing (or other generating activities) to drafting, by reviewing one another's early efforts. Reviewing doesn't necessarily mean reading. You have many choices:

1. Tell one another about what you've got so far and what your focus is. Then ask for responses. Your partners might tell you what they'd like to know more about, what they are most interested in, where they feel you might be digressing.

2. Read over one another's writing in response to directions from the writer. For instance, one person might say: "When you read this, I'd like you to tell me which ideas you think I should omit when I draft." Or, you might say, "See what you think my focus is in this piece."

3. Write down thesis statements and share them with group members. After one person reads a main-idea sentence, the others can tell that person what they'd expect to hear about in a draft on the topic. Having heard others' expectations can help a writer remember to remain "on topic" as he or she drafts.

Writing Exercises

1. Plan to do some "Daily Rapid Writing." Each day for the next several weeks, write rapidly and margin-to-margin, as you did earlier

in this chapter. (Yes, you can take some days off.) Start with a five-minute free-writing session; each day stretch the session by two minutes so that after the ninth day you are writing spontaneously for at least twenty minutes.

a. Keep this writing organized in your Processes and Intentions Log or in any notebook, so that you can see the gradual lengthening of your entries over an extended period. Try to write at about the same time each day, so that you start building writing into your subconscious "schedule" of the day. Jot down the starting and ending times of each writing session—just to help keep you honest about how much time you are spending on your writing.

b. Apply your writing practice to some of the work assigned in your writing class. If your teacher assigns a paper as you begin this series of daily writings, you will get some special benefits out of your work. Since writing is a good way to discover what you are going to write about, your daily rapid writing can become a tool to help you do well on the paper.

c. Write about one subject or one aspect of your subject in each rapid-writing session. You've got to write about something, and this *something* is the *subject* of a session. Your subject may be a large question mark: "What will I write about today?" It may be a general impression: "Since I need to write something, maybe it would be interesting to write about that weird piece of sculpture they just put in the art gallery." It may be something focused on your class: "Let's see, that next paper has to be related to my financial plans for the future." But, unless some other subject just burns itself into your attention, use your daily writing to help you explore the writing assignments your teacher is making.

d. In your daily rapid-writing sessions, work with the different combinations suggested in Table 2.1.

2. Look over your "Daily Rapid Writing" entries to learn what you can about your writing processes. Which strategies seemed to fit you the best? Check to see where your writing seems most fresh and vivid. Which strategies seem to fail? Look for places where you seem to have written in circles. Write a journal entry summarizing what you have learned about yourself as a writer as a result of doing this exercise.

3. Collect thesis statements from feature stories in newspapers, books, or magazines. Write them in your log. Then examine each thesis statement to determine how well it is focused. Does each sentence contribute to the meaning of the essay? Where is each sentence

placed? Record your answers so that you can share them with your classmates.

Suggestions for Writing

1. If you have some idea of what career you might enter after college, write a paper about it. You might do a profile of a person who is successful in your field. What kinds of writing does that person do? What does the person like about his or her job? What is a typical day like? What is his or her lifestyle like? What issues concern him today? What are his or her concerns for the future? What advice does this person have for aspiring professionals? Remember to keep all of your drafts and your notes for this paper in your Processes and Intentions Log so that you will be able to remember the procedures you followed as you worked on this paper.

2. Start working on an assignment you have to complete for another course. Write spontaneously in your journal to prepare for your first drafting session. Dissect the assignment using one or more of the approaches described in this chapter. Write a "letter to your teacher" to help clarify your understanding of the topic. Do some spontaneous writing and develop a main-idea sentence to help you prepare for drafting. Then draft your paper using whatever techniques have worked well for you in the past. Keep a record of the techniques you use so that you can continue to reflect on your writing processes throughout this course.

Drafting: Growth Through Change

3

Productive and Efficient Drafting

In Chapter 1, you took a brief look at the writing process and saw how your mind, your eyes, and your hands work together dynamically *whenever* you try to get words down with pen or word processor. Inevitably, the words you got down helped you to think about your subject. In Chapter 2, you worked on some activities that helped you to generate ideas. We hope you learned how to be less critical of your writing so that you can loosen up and continue to think on paper at any point in the life of your writing projects.

As you completed the various Writing Experiments and Writing Exercises in Chapters 1 and 2, your *intention* was to generate ideas. You didn't think about what a finished draft of your writing would look like because your intent was not to produce a finished version. Your intent was to produce ideas in those exercises; you wanted to let your writing help you discover what you had to say about a topic.

These activities were a necessary prelude to Chapter 3, Drafting: Growth Through Change. This chapter aims to extend the spontaneity of your writing. But in addition to generating ideas as you write, you will be *drafting*, pushing toward a rough approximation of what your writing might look like. To be productive as you draft, you need to know what you are drafting toward—what shape you want your writing to take, how you want to sound to your readers, what effect you want to have on them. As you write, you need to keep "tuned in" to your evolving text.

Efficient drafting implies a conscious control on the writer's part—an attempt to be productive. During drafting, writers develop a kind of "productive thoughtfulness." They maintain some of the spontaneity of earlier writing sessions, but they add another dimension to their writing. They begin to make intuitive decisions *within* the flow of words—decisions about sentence structure, paragraph form, word choice, etc. They pause *while* they write—"hardly-noticed intuitive responses during brief pauses in your hand's journey," as we put it earlier. They do not allow logical or critical thinking to operate consciously, the way they do when they read a completed draft to find its weak spots and revise them; instead, they develop a spontaneous way of monitoring their writing processes. In this chapter, we will show you how to move from rapid writing to productive drafting.

Generating, Drafting, and Revising

As we have mentioned earlier in this text, the processes of writing are at work whenever you are writing. But they work differently, depending on whether you are generating ideas, drafting, or revising. When you are motivated to generate new ideas and discover material for a paper, you write differently from the way you write when your primary intention is to produce a draft as quickly as possible. Similarly, when you revise a finished draft, you work differently from the way you worked composing that draft.

When you are deliberately *generating* material, spontaneity is very high because you have comparatively ample time and because you have not yet developed any content or shape for your project. During rapid writing, you may constantly find new ideas, and frequently change your mind about your subject and how to approach it. You may feel these changes to be somewhat aimless. While you are deliberately working to generate material, every idea or example or witty phrase you discover could be the key to what your writing project will become. But each one also competes with all the others, so that you may feel a disturbing lack of direction as you write.

Drafting allows you to continue some of the spontaneous observations and changes of rapid writing. But now your *intention* for your writing session should change. You should feel ready to draft. You should have at least a kernel of meaning you want to communicate to your audience to give direction to your writing. As you write, you will probably find that new ideas or concrete examples or clever phrases appear; when they do, you should respond to them in terms of your general plans. Maybe the new idea fits your emerging plan and, by the very fact that it appeared while you drafted, carries you closer to completing your plans. That's a kind of growth in your draft. Maybe a new idea or example does not fit your plans, and you realize that your intended kernel of meaning needs to be changed so that it can fit. That also is growth through change. Maybe the new material seems so irrelevant to your plan that you realize how definite your overall idea is becoming. And that is growth, too.

Writing can *grow through change* at any time in the development of a piece of writing: while the writer is generating material, drafting, or revising. After all, you can change your mind and reword a sentence or recast a paragraph whether your primary *intention* is to generate material on a new topic, create a draft, or revise a completed draft. But the most productive growth through change takes place when you are drafting—when you are working to fill paper or computer screen, margin-to-margin, with words.

When your primary motivation or intent is to *revise* a completed draft, your writing processes work differently than they do when you are drafting. When your intention is to revise, you see new ideas and discover alternate points of view in your work, but you feel at least some commitment to the content and shape that the project has assumed through days or weeks of drafting. And you may have comparatively little time to make changes before your deadline. Together, these factors, attitude and time, usually limit your spontaneity as they focus your attention on the task of improvement. When you are consciously revising, you usually ask yourself *not* "Have I found an interesting idea yet or should I be on the lookout for something better?" but instead, "Am I getting my ideas across to readers clearly and effectively?"

■ From Rapid Writing to Drafting

Everyone's drafting behavior will differ, but looking at how others proceed can help you determine how to proceed yourself. Having a sense of what drafting is for others can help you evaluate and assess what drafting should be like for you. Looking at samples of other students' writing—from generating sessions and from drafting sessions—can help you understand the difference between the two.

To get a feel for how rapid writing differs from drafting, read the following sample of a student's rapid writing. Notice the loosely structured sentences and the rambling flow of thoughts and ideas. Then read the student's draft on the same topic, observing the different features in the writing:

```
Tobogganing can be a very hazardous sport if you
don't pay attention to what's going on around you. I
had my back turned to the top of the hill and when I
turned around it was too late to get out of the way of
```

a toboggan with two people on it flying down on the
ice. It hit me and flipped me over onto my head. The
next morning I woke up with a terrible headache, felt
sick to my stomach, and very dizzy and drowsy. The
symptoms remained the same for two days before I went
to the hospital with a very bad bloody nose. I had
skull x-rays and they were negative. I had a mild concussion. I rested for a week which is the only remedy
for a concussion. I'll know to watch out for other people next time.

Source: Jeff Porter. Printed with permission.

In this rapid-writing exercise, the writer tries to get down all of
what happened—the accident, the next day, the hospital, the meaning
of the event—in one burst of thought. His writing can't be judged for
anything but intent. If he got down what he wanted to get down, he
has succeeded.

When asked to move from rapid writing to drafting, Jeff's writing
behavior changes. He wants the result of his drafting session to constitute a *draft*—an unfinished piece of writing that bears some resem-
blance to what the finished writing will look like. Note the
"thoughtfulness" of the writer emerging in this draft:

If you don't watch the action that's going on around
you, tobogganing can be a hazardous situation. It was
a cold, stormy night and my visibility was limited. I
had my back toward the top of the hill as I sped down
the first slope on my toboggan. Hearing voices from
another toboggan all too close, I turned around to
see just how close they were. It was too late. The
oncoming vehicle, flying down the ice with two people
aboard, made hard contact and flipped me over onto my
head.
    Somehow, I got home. The next morning I awakened
with a terrible headache and an upset stomach. I
thought I'd feel better if I got up. Not so. I was too
dizzy and drowsy to move. After two days of these continuous symptoms, complicated by a bad bloody nose, I
finally went to the hospital.
    In the hospital I had a skull x-ray taken, which
turned out negative. I felt lucky to get away with
just a mild concussion. I rested for a week after the
accident, which was the only thing I could do. I'll
know better next time and watch the action around me
when I go tobogganing.

Source: Adapted from Jeff Porter essay.

In the second example, the writer has obviously begun to draft. As he has moved from the first to the second sentence, he has almost intuitively sensed a need to give the reader some background information: "It was a cold, stormy night. . . . " He explains why he had his back turned (he had already started down the slope) so that the reader will understand why he didn't have enough time to avoid the other toboggan. He becomes conscious of paragraph structure and starts new paragraphs for different episodes—the next day, the hospital—seeming to want to sort out the stages of his experience in separate chunks of information.

The writer has allowed a thoughtfulness into his writing behavior, a productive way of thinking that becomes a spontaneous, natural way of responding as he writes his way toward a completed project. Jeff explains his writing behavior in this way:

> I knew that I wanted to use the tobogganing accident for my essay because when I first wrote about it, I kept thinking back to that night and wishing it would have been different. In other words, I knew that I wanted to write about that topic, that's why I knew I was ready to draft.
>
> When I wrote the draft, I felt like I needed to explain everything. But I knew that I was supposed to get the draft done before class, so I kept writing. I thought about how the ideas fit together whenever I paused. I read over my sentences before I added the next one. I read over my rapid writing—even used one of the sentences exactly as it was—until I read it. Then I changed it, too. Then I kept on writing. I wrote about the next day. But I realized that I needed a new paragraph, so I started one. I knew that I wanted to say more about that day, but I wanted to get the draft done, so I let that go and I moved on to the hospital part. I know that the last sentence still isn't what I mean—I'm going to have to make the whole thing look less like I learned so much (I didn't) but at least I've kind of framed my story and I feel that it's now a draft.

Barrett Mandel, a professional writer, talks about making the same kinds of instant judgments and decisions in his writing:

> Consciousness instantly accepts or rejects . . . what it sees spill onto the page. Sometimes, I wind up scratching out what I have written because it does not conform to what I thought I'd write. Sometimes, I reshape it to fit the "logic" I now feel it requires. Sometimes, I save what I've written because it transcends what I thought I'd write.

Source: Barrett Mandel, "Losing One's Mind: Learning to Write and Edit," *College Composition and Communication,* 29 (December 1978), pp. 364–365.

Thoughtfulness (or what Mandel calls *consciousness*) is crucial to effective writing. It allows both Jeff, the student writer, and Barrett Mandel, the professional, to see ideas they did not have when they started to write. It lets them discover new connections between ideas, and develop new perspectives on material they are writing about. It lets them change emphasis or direction during the act of composition so that, by the end of a productive writing session, they have written beyond where they could have hoped to write when they started. In short, their thoughtfulness lets writing grow—in concept, organization, clarity, and tone—so that the finished piece is far different from what they planned to write. This is what we mean when we speak of writing as *growth through change.*

Of course, just how much change will occur as a writer writes will differ from one assignment to the next. Sometimes the sentences of a draft fall into place more readily than at other times. Sometimes more changes take place as the writing grows than at other times. As a writer, you need to let the requirements of each writing task guide you. Remember, as your tasks differ, so your processes and strategies will differ from one writing task to the next.

The past few paragraphs reflect our own writing experience, as well as experiences that professionals we know have had and that many student-writers in our classes have encountered. You may not have had the same experiences, but we think you will understand and feel what we mean by *growth-through-change* when you write your next draft.

Writing, like painting or golf or any other complex act of coordination, can only be learned by *doing*. Learning to draft effectively demands that you start drafting. As you draft, you need to remember that only you will be able to determine what writing strategies are best for your assignment. Thus, the rest of this chapter is going to give guidelines you can follow (and later adapt to your own writing style) as you learn how to allow drafting to be a time of productive growth through change.

What to Do Before Drafting

How can you prepare for a drafting session? How do you know if you are ready to draft? Writers prepare for drafting sessions in different ways, but they start by making sure that they have selected a subject they are comfortable with. Some writers prepare for a drafting session by writing down a main idea or thesis statement to help them clarify their attitude toward their subject. Some writers use questioning or listing strategies. Some writers work from a rough outline or map of what they think they'll write. Other writers do a lot of rapid writing before they even think of drafting. Writer Susan Horton has a unique way of knowing she's ready to draft:

> I know it is time for me to start writing first drafts when I start sleeping restlessly and keep jumping out of bed to take more note slips, and when the rubber bands around them can no longer hold the stacks together, and when I am afraid that if I do not capture some of the ideas and sentences that are running through my head, I will lose them forever and be sorry to have lost them.
>
> *Source:* **Susan R. Horton,** *Thinking Through Writing,* (Baltimore, Md.: Johns Hopkins University Press, 1982), p. 191.

Every writer is different and has different ways of knowing what to do before beginning to draft, and different ways of knowing that it is time to draft. You need to decide what's best for you and for the assignment you are working on. If you choose to do an outline before drafting, be sure that you don't consider it as anything but a guide. Writers need to feel open to new ideas as they write. So begin any way you want, but work at keeping in touch with your evolving meaning as you write.

◼ Planning a Draft: Some Guidelines for Writers

Before beginning a drafting session, you need to take stock of your assignment and of your readiness to begin writing:

1. *Review the assignment.*
   a. What is the assignment? Dissect the assignment if you haven't yet done so; write about the specific details and requirements you need to work with.
   b. What will your purpose be as you complete the assignment? Determine whether you want to tell a story, to persuade your readers to change their beliefs, to explain your topic, etc.
   c. What should the assignment look like when it's completed?
   d. Who is your audience? In other words, who should you assume will read your finished work?

2. *Assess your writing needs.*
   a. What kinds of information do you need for the assignment?
   b. Do you need to generate more material?
   c. Even if you do need more material, do you have enough to allow you to begin drafting?
   d. Have you established a main idea for your writing?

3. *Clarify your intent for your drafting session.*
   a. What are your goals for the draft? (In other words, you know

you intend to draft, but how complete a draft do you want to produce?)

b. What do you need to keep in mind about your topic and your audience to help you draft productively?

4. *Select appropriate drafting strategies.*

   a. What strategies seem suited to this assignment?

   b. How will you proceed?

   c. What is your plan?

5. *Do some start-up activities to get ready to write.*

   a. Collect, on paper, as much information as you can about your subject.

   b. Explore how you feel about your subject; decide whether you are angry, happy, confused, accepting, etc.

   c. Write about how you plan to organize or give shape to your writing project.

What to Do While Drafting

You have some choices. If you know your material well, your draft may begin to take shape naturally. As you write, you can strive for structure and organization. But if you are not yet in control of your material, you can use rapid writing, while drafting, to help you establish a focus and an overall plan. Or, if you have a general sense of your material but are unsure of how to proceed, you can draft to find out where you are in your writing project. As your sentences and paragraphs emerge, you may or may not rework them. Some writers push themselves more rapidly through a draft than others. Whatever you do, we hope that you will discover strategies that are efficient. No one feels good about wasting time or getting nowhere in a writing project.

IDEA FILE: COMPUTER WRITING

Drafting Strategies

1. If possible, draft directly at the computer. Drafting at the computer is, to a large extent, the heart of "computer writing."

2. Don't worry about making silly mistakes or about writing down "dumb" ideas. The computer makes it easy for you to change your mind as you write.

3. Take advantage of the power of your word processor. Computer drafting lets you really experience growth through

change almost instantly. You can add whole sentences and juggle the order of paragraphs almost as easily as you can delete words or phrases.

4. Try skipping over rough spots and thin spots—places where you have a point in mind but can't seem to think of good phrasing or examples for it. You can leave a reminder for yourself with a few touches of the return key and a note set off with a distinctive marker or with some distinctive character style:

   [Check *Newsweek* for that AIDS story]

5. What if you want to reshuffle your paragraphs? The computer makes it easy: you can save your original version, reshuffle it into a new configuration and write in that direction, then save the new version. Later, you can compare the two approaches and decide which approach to take. You can even delay deciding and work alternately with both versions until, through drafting, you discover which approach makes the most sense.

By observing experienced writers as they write, researchers have learned what strategies those writers use naturally. They have found that experienced writers use their eyes and the words building up on their paper (or monitor) to help them draft more efficiently. In brief glances, experienced writers let their eyes drift back to previous sentences so that words already on the page help them create the words that are just forming. In other pauses, they check their emerging words to see how they fit their general plans. When they lose their forward momentum (as writers often do) they review what they have written, look back at general notes they made earlier, or think about their writing and about what may have gotten them off the track.

Many less-experienced writers do not take the time to pause and think about what they are writing. Instead, they may charge ahead, nonstop, until they run out of ideas. Then they may sit, fidget, and glance around the room, wait for ideas to come from somewhere, and grow more frustrated when they don't.

Less-experienced writers often have a limited sense of what they should react to during the pauses in their drafting sessions. They may worry so much about mechanics, for instance, that they don't think about ideas. They may be so concerned with specific words that they pay little attention to the concepts expressed by the words, or to the logic connecting words, sentences, and paragraphs. They may spend so much time trying to cut out or replace small details that they miss the chance for wide-scale reshuffling of their drafts.

Even though what you do is up to you, we can give you some guidance. Scanning your writing-in-progress and pausing to reflect on your developing draft seem to be characteristics of effective writers. So one thing you can do to make your drafting sessions more successful is to develop the habit of taking productive pauses while you draft. Trying to broaden the range of what you respond to intuitively during your pauses can help you to become a more effective drafter. Don't get too "conscious" about your responses. But as you draft, remember that the feelings and intuitions you have as you pause and scan can deal with any of the following aspects of your writing:

1. main ideas and key sentences in which you state your central ideas most directly

2. broad organizational patterns—the shape created by the sequence of key sentences and ideas

3. sentences and ideas that support and connect with the main idea of your paper

4. the quality of supporting statements and examples

5. the readers of your finished paper—your audience

Redrafting

Sometimes you need to write several *rough* drafts before you feel satisfied with your writing. One version of your draft is finished when you have pushed yourself to move from the beginning of your writing project toward an almost completed piece of writing. But though one *draft* is finished, your *drafting* may not be finished. Most writers find that they need several rough drafts before they are ready to shift their intention from drafting to revising their draft.

A review of the *processes and intentions* concept may help you understand why redrafting is necessary before revising and editing take place. Throughout a writing project, the writing *processes* are at work. Your hands are moving, your mind is working, your eyes are scanning your text. But as your project moves from beginning to mid-stage to completion, your needs change. In the beginning, you needed to get ideas as you generated material with rapid writing or other strategies; thus your intention in your early writing sessions was different from your intention in later (drafting) sessions. Writers' intentions differ depending on where they are in their current project and what they need to do to proceed.

After you complete a draft of your writing project, set it aside for a while. Plan to redraft when you return to it later. Proceed in whatever way seems best for you. Writers proceed differently as they scan a completed rough draft and begin redrafting. Some start all over; some shift intentions and generate more ideas for awhile; others just rework parts of the draft that need to be reshaped. (Many people would call this revising. You can call it that, but if you are still working on getting an acceptable draft, and not paying too much attention to sentence structure and grammar, then your main *intention* is probably still to shape a draft.) We are using the term *redrafting* to refer to the strategies writers use as they actively reshape or reconstruct an existing draft.

IDEA FILE: COMPUTER WRITING

Redrafting Strategies

1. *Play "what if."* As you redraft, you may want to clarify or focus some areas. Try playing *what if. What if* you moved one sentence to another position? Would the paragraph be clearer? *What if* you began with another introduction? Would your readers get a better sense of your topic at the outset?

   Use the "block move" commands of your word processor to experiment with possibilities—to play *what if.* Before you move text around too much, though, make a copy of your paragraph (or of your entire draft). Then you'll always have a record of the way your text looked before you began to change it.

2. *Experiment.* As you redraft, you may need to work out the best way of expressing an idea. If you are not satisfied with a sentence or a paragraph, you can experiment with rewording it or developing alternate ways of expressing your point. As a rule of thumb, don't ever delete your original work until you are sure you want to replace it with an alternate version. Write first—delete later.

3. *Reuse material.* You can save work from each drafting session. Rather than recopying earlier work, in just a few minutes at the start of a later session you can combine material from different sessions by loading (or "merging") parts of files onto the screen in any order you like. And then, without tedious copying, you are ready to let this "new" draft continue to grow.

Drafting Behavior

Your drafting behavior will vary from one assignment to the next. If, for instance, you have only a short time in which to produce a finished paper, you'll have to deal with many more aspects of your paper while drafting than you would if you had several weeks to work on your draft. Most often, though, you'll consider your draft finished when you feel satisfied that you have managed to convey the content and basic organization of the finished assignment.

■ One Student's Drafting Behavior

Take a moment to read a portion of a student writer's draft-in-progress along with our annotations. Jerry drafts directly at the computer monitor, so we can watch his writing unfold. Notice how Jerry's attention shifts from one sentence back to the beginning of the previous sentence as he allows his eyes to glance over what he has just written. Almost instantly, he makes additions and deletions, but he doesn't stop trying to build an idea:

```
Why don't we treat older people
with more respect? How can young
people begin to develop a respect
for their elders?
```
Jerry quickly types these two questions.

```
Why don't we treat older people
with more respect? How can young
people begin to develop a respect
for their elders? One way younger
people might have an opportunity
to develop some understanding of
the older generation is
```
After reading the first two sentences, he pauses and begins to add a new sentence. But he doesn't complete the sentence.

```
Why don't we treat older people
with more respect? How can young
people begin to develop a respect
for their elders? I'd like to sug-
gest one way younger people might
be able to get a better under-
standing of the older generation.
```
Instead, Jerry pauses briefly and then deletes the word "is." He then re-reads the entire passage and recasts the last sentence (adding the words "I'd like to suggest" before "one way . . . ," he removes the capital "O" from "One" and changes it to an "o," and finally he adds a period to the end of his now-complete sentence.

```
How can young people begin to de-
velop a respect for their elders?
I'd like to suggest one way youn-
ger people might have an opportu-
nity to develop some understanding
of the older generation. We could
```
Jerry moves his cursor to the beginning of his paragraph and deletes his first sentence ("Why don't we treat older people with more respect?"). What was

invite a wide variety of retired
people to talk not just about
their careers, but about themselves, their views about current
events, about historical events,
about aging.

How can young people begin to develop a respect for their elders?
I'd like to suggest one way younger people might have an opportunity to develop some understanding
of the older generation. Students
in an English class could invite a
wide variety of retired people to
come to class and talk with us.
not just about their careers, but
about themselves, their views
about current events, about historical events, about aging.

How can young people begin to develop a respect for their elders?
I'd like to suggest one way younger people might have an opportunity to develop some understanding
of the older generation. Students
in an English class could invite
representatives of the "older generation" to come to class and talk
with us. We could invite a wide
variety of retired people to talk
not just about their careers, but
about themselves, their views
about current events, about historical events, about aging. We
could ask these people what life
was like when they were our age.
We could ask what our guests' attitudes are toward different topics that we care about: financial
matters, family life, dating, sex.
Then we could share our views on
these topics with our guests.

previously his second sentence is now his first sentence. He then revises the
sentence that follows,
changing "be able to get a
better understanding of
the older generation" to
"have an opportunity to
develop some understand-
ing of the older genera-
tion." Next, he adds a
third sentence.

Jerry revises the third sentence. He deletes "We"
and replaces it with
"Students in an English
class." Then he concludes
that sentence with the
words "to come to class
and talk with us." He is
left with a sentence fragment.

Rescanning his text, Jerry
continues to rework this
third sentence, changing
"a wide variety of retired
people" to "representatives
of the 'older generation.'"
Then he fixes the sentence
fragment that his revision
has created: He revises the
fourth sentence to the way
it had been earlier, beginning it with "We could invite a wide variety of retired people to talk . . . . "
Then he completes this
passage by adding three
more sentences at the end.

Since Jerry drafted at a computer screen, he could change his sentences instantly to conform to his shifting notion of what he wanted to say. As his attitude toward his topic developed, his paragraphs took shape, and within his paragraphs, sentences and words appeared, disappeared, and shifted positions. If Jerry's *intention* for his writing session had been different—that is, if he were generating ideas instead of drafting—he would never take the trouble to change sentences and delete parts of what he had just produced. But having first done some rapid writing, Jerry's *intention* for the writing session that followed was to write a draft of his essay.

Here is Jerry's own account of his drafting session:

> This is what happened. I had done some rapid writing, but I still didn't know how to begin. So I decided not to begin at the beginning. I wanted to write about one way of getting to know older people—an idea I could use somewhere in my paper—probably as a paragraph toward the end. I asked a question and then I answered it. I kept writing sentence after sentence, almost as I had in rapid writing, but because this might become a finished paper, I seemed to care more about how I started my sentences. And I tried to make what I was writing look like a paragraph. That meant that I didn't let myself ramble much. I tried to answer the question I asked myself. Not the one about why do younger people act the way they do—the one about how the situation can change. I guess that meant I was writing a question-answer type of paragraph, the kind I remember my high school teachers talking about, but I didn't think about doing this, I just did it. As I wrote each of my sentences, I was trying to match the way I had written the previous one. For example, after writing "We could . . . " I started the next sentence in the same way (with the words "we could") because I wanted it to match the last one. Then I guess I thought of another idea as I wrote the next sentence. I honestly didn't know I had another idea, but it came out. Since I had at that point said basically what I wanted to say in the conclusion, I moved on to other parts of my essay on the elderly. Maybe it's strange that I didn't start at the beginning, but having drafted a part I liked helped me get going on the rest of the paper.

Drafting: Shaping Paragraphs

In the act of producing drafts, writers build paragraphs. Writers don't usually ask themselves, "What paragraph pattern shall I use?" or

"Where shall I start a new paragraph?" Typically, writers let paragraph patterns and shapes emerge naturally. As Erika Lindemann puts it, "We begin with content, and in the act of drafting, discover form" [*A Rhetoric for Teachers*, (New York: Oxford University Press, 1982), p. 153].

In the preceding example, Jerry's main idea is that the old and the young don't seem to understand each other. To develop one facet of that idea, Jerry writes down a few questions at the beginning of the paragraph. Then, he narrows his focus to answering one of these questions and deleting the other. As he answers this question, he inadvertently produces a paragraph pattern that is sometimes called *question-answer* paragraphs.

■ Using Topic Sentences As a Drafting Aid

The sentence that announces the main idea or topic of the paragraph is sometimes called the *topic sentence*. In Jerry's case, the question that forms his essay's opening sentence could be called the *topic question* of that paragraph. It announces to the reader what the paragraph will be about and helps the writer know what to say in the rest of his paragraph. As Jerry puts it: "I asked a question and then I answered it. I kept writing sentence after sentence, almost as I had in rapid writing, but because this might become a finished paper, I seemed to care more about how I started my sentences. And I tried to make what I was writing look like a paragraph. That meant that I didn't let myself ramble much. I tried to answer the question I asked myself."

Writing topic sentences, then, can help writers move their ideas along as they draft. If they begin with a general statement of their main point, they can complete their paragraph by writing several sentences that support that idea. Basically, paragraphs take shape as writers explain their general statements with supporting material.

■ Letting Paragraph Patterns Guide Your Drafting

Some patterns that often emerge as writers draft include: comparison-contrast, cause-effect, classification, and definition. As you draft paragraphs, you do not usually intend to produce the patterns that emerge. What probably happens is that the topic sentence somehow naturally pushes the paragraph toward an identifiable pattern. You will realize quickly, however, that most paragraphs do not have distinct patterns. They have, instead, a lead sentence announcing a topic and subsequent sentences developing it. Occasionally, when writers become consciously aware that their paragraphs lend themselves to specific shapes or patterns, they will try to follow through on those patterns, knowing that a well-structured paragraph will be easier to follow for a reader, and realizing that by completing the structure, they will be responding to the topic sentence in an orderly way.

Although writers may create tentative paragraphs while drafting, before they finish drafting (or during revision), they reexamine their text, and reconsider their paragraph breaks. Paragraphs are conventional ways of letting readers know which ideas go together as units. Knowing that readers expect to find paragraph breaks in a piece of writing, writers can influence their readers by taking advantage of their reader's expectations: they can group together sentences so that they are thought about as a unit; they can consider the value of having the reader process a complex idea at once or in smaller units.

Try an experiment. See if you can tell where Jerry began new paragraphs in the following rough draft of his essay on the elderly. Don't look ahead to see how Jerry divided his ideas. Decide for yourself:

```
 1  A lot of young adults go to extremes to avoid taking
 2  their parents and other older adults seriously. I
 3  decided to major in business not because I'm sure I
 4  want to be a business executive, but because I don't
 5  want to even consider being a doctor--what my father
 6  thinks I should be. We want to think for ourselves,
 7  we say. Then why can't we at least listen to our
 8  elders? I've got an uncle who was a doctor. He's
 9  in a nursing home now, so I don't even think of
10  asking him about his profession. I'm a typical
11  college student. I'm prejudiced against my elders.
12  Yet I want to change, and I think my friends who act
13  this way would be willing to change, too. Perhaps
14  understanding why we act as we do would encourage us
15  to change--to do something about the gap between
16  young and old. It may be that there's no one to
17  blame but ourselves, but other influences just
18  might have contributed to our attitudes, too. For
19  one thing, maybe some of the tension between young
20  and old is caused by social trends and patterns.
21  The nuclear family no longer exists. Most of my
22  friends' parents are divorced. My friends don't
23  talk to both of their parents on a regular basis.
24  Also, children move much further away from home
25  these days than they used to. I never got to know
26  my grandparents. We moved to Colorado when I was
27  five. Then there's the media to blame. How many
28  television shows and movie heroes are old? Cosby's
29  just middle-aged, so he doesn't count. Rocky and
30  Rambo--not the Golden Girls--are the heroes of the
31  younger generation. Commercials and advertisements
32  don't help much either. The models in ads look more
```

33 like us than like our elders. I read in yesterday's
34 paper that models are older today than they
35 were several years ago, but I haven't noticed those
36 changes yet on the shows I watch. I guess the
37 "national character" is another culprit. The
38 American ideal is the self-made man. Even Emerson
39 said to "trust thyself." Carried to an extreme,
40 that kind of fierce independence can build
41 barriers between generations. Americans don't
42 learn much from the past either, or so it seems. I
43 was too young to follow Watergate closely when it
44 happened. But older Americans who did follow those
45 events didn't seem to learn much. A lot of
46 deception has continued, as the Iranian arms-for-
47 hostages scandal has demonstrated. In all honesty,
48 though some of the above reasons may be valid, I
49 feel that a person must be responsible for his or
50 her own actions. Blaming won't do much good. So
51 I'll accept the blame. Now toward changing the
52 situation. How can young people begin to develop a
53 respect for their elders? I'd like to suggest one
54 way younger people might have an opportunity to
55 develop some understanding of the older generation.
56 Students in an English class could invite
57 representatives of the "older generation" to come
58 to class and talk with us. We could invite a wide
59 variety of retired people to talk not just about
60 their careers, but about themselves, their views
61 about current events, about historical events,
62 about aging. We could ask these people what life
63 was like when they were our age. We could ask what
64 our guests' attitudes are toward different topics
65 that we care about: financial matters, family life,
66 dating, sex. Then we could share our views on these
67 topics with our guests. We might find out that we're
68 not as different as we thought we were. And even if
69 we are different, we'll find out why. If we can
70 begin to pay attention to older people we don't
71 know, then we can surely start paying more
72 attention to our own "elderly," our parents,
73 grandparents, and relatives. Next week, I'll visit
74 my uncle in the nursing home. Maybe I do want to be
75 a doctor after all. And maybe not. But at
76 least I'll consider it.

If you felt that a new paragraph should begin in each of the following places, you made the same choices Jerry made:

We want to think—(line 6)

```
Perhaps understanding why we act as we do—(line 13)
It may be that—(line 16)
Then there's the media—(line 27)
I guess—(line 36)
Americans don't—(line 41)
In all honesty—(line 47)
How can young people—(line 52)
If we can begin to pay attention—(line 69)
```

But there are other places where paragraph divisions might occur. Here's another way that occurred to us:

```
I've got an uncle—(line 8)
For one thing—(lines 18–19)
Now toward changing—(line 51)
If we can—(line 69)
```

The latter division of ideas produces a larger middle paragraph, which might work just as well as, or better than, the former. Did you come up with any other ways of paragraphing Jerry's draft? Trying to determine why you paragraphed as you did should help you develop paragraph sense. If you use a word processor for your drafting, you can easily experiment with different paragraph breaks in your own writing.

IDEA FILE: COMPUTER WRITING

Paragraphing Strategies

1. If you're not sure where to start a new paragraph, don't worry about it as you are entering text. Just get your ideas down. When you feel ready to pause in your drafting, read over what you've written. Whenever you shift to a new idea in the middle of a chunk of text, move your cursor to that location and press return (or whatever command creates a blank line on your word processor).

2. If you think that your paragraph looks underdeveloped, just move your cursor to a point where an idea, an illustration, or an example would help develop your point and start typing. Your word processor will make room for your added thoughts (assuming that the INSERT function of your word processor is on).

3. If you think you need to cut some ideas from a paragraph (and the changes you intend to make are small), first print out a copy of your existing paragraph, then experiment with

deleting words, phrases, or sentences. If you cut out something that you later decide you want to include, you can just move the text of your choice from your copy of the paragraph to the correct location in the "new" paragraph.

4. If you plan to make major changes as you redraft, be sure to save your original draft. File it under a different name from the name you use for the revised draft.

Basically, paragraphs take shape as writers use supporting material to explain their general statements. Think of a paragraph as a topic-comment unit. After writers state a topic in the first sentence or two, they comment on it—they explain what they mean—in the succeeding sentences. Writers don't usually stop and say to themselves: "Now I need an opening sentence. Let's see. Shall I begin with a question or shall I begin with a generalization?" Rather, writers think in ideas and the ideas produce sentences. Just thinking "paragraph" often helps writers come up with enough ideas to develop the paragraphs.

After Jerry said "other influences just might have contributed to our attitudes, too" he almost had to tell what those influences might be. What if he couldn't think of them all at once? He could have put a note in the margin of his paper (or between brackets on his computer screen) saying: [ADD SEVERAL IDEAS HERE]. Jerry didn't say to himself: "I wonder what paragraph pattern I should use." He didn't go to a textbook and look at such paragraph patterns as generalization, classification, cause-effect, and question-answer. He merely let his ideas carry him along as he wrote.

Achieving Coherence in Paragraphs

Of course, writers try to produce paragraphs that are coherent, that is, paragraphs in which the sentences and words "stick together," enabling a reader to follow the writer's intended meaning. In a coherent paragraph, each sentence should be related to the preceding sentence and to the following sentence. Now some of that coherence can be worked out later, when a writer is consciously revising. But some of the words and phrases that produce coherent writing occur to writers naturally—either immediately, as they set words to page (or screen), or shortly afterward, as they pause and reread what they've written, shifting material, cutting out unnecessary copy, and connecting passages more smoothly. We wouldn't want you to concern yourself too much with paragraph structure and coherence while drafting. As long as you get the essence of your idea down clearly, you'll be able to return later to reconsider word choice, sentence structure, and connections between sentences.

■ Observing Coherence Markers

By looking closely at some sample paragraphs you can observe how writers create coherence—usually while drafting, sometimes while revising. Notice how coherence can be created or enhanced through the use of

1. repetition (of key words, ideas, phrases).

2. synonyms.

3. pronoun references.

4. transitional markers.

Students tell us that they never noticed all the connections writers use to make their paragraphs and essays clear and readable until we ask them to pause and take a look. You, too, may be surprised when you stop and observe how rich and varied are the inter-sentence and inter-paragraph links in most well-written writing.

As readers read, they focus on meaning, not on stylistic features of text. On occasion, however, it can be useful to pay close attention to *coherence markers*. Read through the following writing selections, noting how the writers build coherence in their texts. Then read through several passages that you and your peers have written. Discuss ways you might strengthen your own writing.

Example 1.   In the following passage, William Bennett presents his views on student academic performance. Notice how he uses pronoun references and synonyms to emphasize his focus on "students," "testing," and "writing." We have indicated these areas of emphasis as follows:

Double underlining: indicates references to "students."

Bold print: indicates references to "tests."

Underlining: indicates references to "writing."

> Among the generally high-performing students who take the **College Board achievement tests**—graded on the same 800-point scale as the **S.A.T.s**—English composition scores have risen ten points since 1979. But the general picture for all students is still no better than it was in 1974. And N.E.E.P.'s evaluation of its **most recent (1984) assessment** is that "**performance** in writing in our schools is, quite simply, bad."
>
> Fewer than one-fourth of all 17-year-olds **tested** in 1984 were able **to perform** at an "adequate" level on writing tasks considered essential to academic study, business, and professional work. Only about 20 percent of them, when **asked to write a letter to their** principal requesting permission to take a particular schedule of classes, handled this **relatively simple assignment** satisfactorily. A similarly small

<u>percentage</u> **performed** "adequately" when **asked** <u>to write an imaginative passage</u> describing a hypothetical situation and <u>their reactions to it.</u> Only 2 percent of 17-year-olds gained highest marks on this task by <u>writing a clear, detailed, and coherent narrative.</u>

Source: William Bennett, "American Education: Making It Work," reprinted in *The Chronicle of Higher Education,* May 2, 1988, p. A31. (Emphasis ours.)

Example 2. In the following feature article, columnist Ellen Goodman tells about a recent interview she had with Maggie Kuhn, leader of the Gray Panthers. In her article, Goodman wants to do more than tell about the interview. She wants to develop an analogy between war and the actions Kuhn and others are taking to make Americans aware of their point of view. We have underlined words and phrases that refer to war so that you can see how repetition of key words can help a writer emphasize her point. As you read the passage, noting the references to war, also try to find other coherence markers:

OLD, YOUNG MUST UNITE TO HELP BOTH

These days it isn't always easy to find the peacemakers, the bridge builders between the old and young. There is a generational <u>struggle</u>. Not a <u>hand-to-hand battle</u>, but a prolonged <u>tug of war</u> over money from the federal pockets.

In this <u>tug</u>, the elderly often have the more impressive <u>troops</u>. I saw them recently, a single <u>regiment</u> of notch babies crawling over the Capitol. These seniors born between 1917 and 1921 fell into a mathematical dip in their Social Security payments. They were in Washington claiming, simply, more.

But there has been no such enormous, persistent, grassroots constituency for the real babies of our society, for child-care or infant-mortality programs.

In such a national atmosphere, it was a pleasure to sit down for a few minutes last week with Maggie Kuhn, founder of the Gray Panthers. At 82, and not without the signs of her age, she talks less of <u>age wars</u> than of partnerships.

She has another model in mind. "It's the model of the tribal elder. That means a concern for children as well. It seems to me that older Americans are most free to transcend special interests and seek public interests."

Kuhn, who has no children of her own, lives in shared housing with young people in Philadelphia. She was in Boston, as she is in many cities, lecturing for the Gray Panthers—an anachronistic name for such a peacemaking group—that publishes a newsletter with the motto, "Age and Youth in action."

"Do you want to hear what the old and young have in common?" she asks over tea. "First of all, we are both marginalized out of mainstream America. We are both told, 'What do you know about it, you are too old, you are too young.'

"Second of all, we are both relatively poor. The young have a terrible time getting a job. The old have a terrible time keeping a job.

"Third of all, we are both into the drug scene, though we have different pushers. The old get addicted to Valium and Thorazine.

"Fourth of all, we are both going through body changes." And, she concludes looking at her middle-aged interviewer, "we are both in conflict with the middle generation."

Is that enough? The notch babies are the most glaring example of me-firstism. The organized clout of the senior Americans is enormous. Their political weight is measured in mailbags. They vote.

Even Kuhn admits that it will be very hard "to break down the special-interest perspective. The membership of her own modest group is 70,000, compared to the 24 million in the more aggressive American Association of Retired Persons. And there are indeed unmet needs among the elderly.

But there is greater recognition of the cost when there is a <u>struggle</u> between the generations, and the <u>risk of casualties</u>. A child in this country is already six times as likely to be poor as an elder.

As the population ages, the <u>tug</u> may increase. But for a few minutes, while one member of the older generation, Maggie Kuhn, talked as a tribal elder, the rumble of the <u>generational wars</u> seemed a bit more distant.

Source: Ellen Goodman, "Old, Young Must Unite to Help Both," *The Coloradoan*, May 20, 1988, p. A10. (Emphasis ours.)

Example 3. The primary way that Jerry, our student writer, achieves coherence in his sentences is by repeating *key ideas* and *key words* and by using *synonyms* to substitute for ideas in previous sentences. Reread one of Jerry's paragraphs, noting the connections that serve to clarify and focus the piece. We have indicated critical connections as follows:

<u><u>double underlining</u></u> indicates ideas related to social trends and patterns (divorce, moving away from home).

CAPITALIZED WORDS indicate references to family members (children, parents, grandparents).

<u>underlining</u> indicates differences between young and old.

Perhaps understanding why we act as we do would encourage us to change—to do something about <u>the gap between young and old</u>. It may be that there's no one to blame but ourselves, but other influences just might have contributed to our attitudes, too. For one thing, maybe some of the <u>tension between young and old</u> is caused by social trends and patterns. The <u><u>nuclear FAMILY no longer exists</u></u>. Most of my friends' <u><u>parents are divorced</u></u>. They don't get to talk to both of their parents on a regular basis. Also, <u><u>CHILDREN move much further away from home these days</u></u> than they used to.

```
I never got to know my GRANDPARENTS. We moved to Colo-
rado when I was five.
```

Another way that Jerry achieves coherence is through *pronoun refer-ences*. After he talks about "acting as *we* do" in one sentence, he uses the pronoun "ourselves" in the next sentence to form a connection. Af-ter talking about the "gap between young and old," he begins the next sentence with "it." And finally, Jerry achieves coherence by using *transitional words:* words such as *perhaps, for one thing,* and *also.* (Table 3.1 lists some transitional words and phrases.) Let's look at the same paragraph, this time looking only at the transitional words and the pronoun references. We have indicated these elements as follows:

CAPITALIZED WORDS indicate pronoun references.

underlining indicates transitional words.

```
    Perhaps understanding why WE act as WE do would encour-
age us to change--to do something about the gap be-
tween young and old. IT may be that there's no one to
blame but OURSELVES, but other influences just might
have contributed to OUR attitudes, too. For one thing,
maybe some of the tension between young and old is
caused by social trends and patterns. The nuclear fam-
ily no longer exists. Most of MY friends' parents are
divorced. THEY don't get to talk to both of THEIR par-
ents on a regular basis. Also, children move much fur-
ther away from home these days than THEY used to. I
never got to know MY grandparents. WE moved to Colo-
rado when I was five.
```

Since Jerry's own record of his drafting behavior reveals that he produces one sentence directly after the next rather spontaneously, it is not surprising that his writing automatically includes coherence ties. He doesn't consciously attempt to produce them.

TABLE 3.1 *Some Commonly Used Transitional Words and Phrases*

also	for example	rather than
although	for instance	since
and	furthermore	so
because	however	still
but	in fact	that is
consequently	in other words	therefore
even though	instead	thus
finally	nevertheless	too
first, second, etc.	on the other hand	while
		yet

Productive Drafting: A Few Suggestions

There is no *one, right way* to fill pages margin-to-margin with words. We want to stress the importance of every writer developing his or her own processes and strategies for generating, drafting, and revising. As far as drafting is concerned, if your pages fill up, you are probably drafting well. Still, it is possible to offer some suggestions so that your drafting sessions will reflect and extend the spontaneity you have started to develop in rapid-writing sessions.

Read through the next several pages, but don't try to follow all of the suggestions in this chapter at once. Instead, work gradually on these suggestions *while* you are working on your next few writing projects. Try the writing strategies that make sense to you and that seem to "work" for you.

Build up the basic *discipline* of drafting—sitting still and doing it— by working with the first suggestion during one drafting session, and then following the second suggestion during subsequent drafting sessions. Later, work at the third suggestion, pausing and scanning; and then try some of the ideas in the fourth suggestion. Finally, try to implement the practices explained in suggestions five and six: adding road-map making to your drafting habits and thinking about when you might want to consider your reader.

1. Extend Rapid Writing into Productive Drafting.   Clear off your desk and lay out paper and pen, or if you prefer, load word processing software into your computer. Then do some rapid writing about the topic you have selected for your current writing project. After you have filled a page or two, put your writing aside for awhile. When you come back to it, read over it quickly, and then shift your intention from generating material to thinking about what the finished product might look like. Then start drafting.

Try to keep yourself completely engaged in writing. Keep your hands and eyes busy. Keep the gradually-developing draft in front of you. As you draft, work as *constantly* as you can. Don't try for speed as much as for extended stretches of work with hand, eyes, and brain. At first, try for at least thirty minutes of uninterrupted concentration on drafting. In other words:

a. Do not get up from your seat.

b. Do not take your mind or your eyes off your writing. When your hand stops moving, resist the urge to glance around the room or to think of other things. Try to stay fully engaged with your writing— really work at it.

c. Gradually, extend the length of drafting sessions from a half-hour, to forty minutes, to an hour and more.

d. Gradually, begin to expand your *thoughtfulness:* As you feel yourself leaving one idea and moving to another, look back at a longer group of words—a paragraph or section—to let your subconscious orient itself to the way your paper is going and to generate new ideas.

2. Pay Attention to "Start" and "Stop" Points. Getting started is often the worst thing about drafting. Once a draft is moving well, new ideas come up that tend to "pull" the writer along. That's one of the reasons we have been urging you to keep your attention focused on your words and to try to extend the length of writing sessions. It usually makes drafting more effective if you work for reasonably long stretches of time.

We're not advocating marathon periods of drafting, just sessions long enough to be productive. After all, each time you start to draft, you may take five minutes to find pen and notebook, or to start your computer and load the right file from a disk. Then you may spend another five or ten minutes fidgeting, finding where you left off at an earlier session, and trying to decide how to move on from that point to fill more blank paper. If your "start-up" practices are anything like that, you may waste from 40 to 60 minutes—up to one-fourth of your time—in four *one-hour* drafting sessions, but only 20–30 minutes in two *two-hour* sessions.

There are a few other simple things you can do to help with the start-up frustrations of drafting sessions:

a. Don't stop a drafting session when you are "cold"—out of ideas, frustrated, tired. The unpleasant associations of these feelings will make it harder to force yourself back to your desk later, and harder to start again when you do return to drafting. So if you feel all "written out," try to make some sort of a "breakthrough" in your work before you end your sessions.

b. End a drafting session when you know where you are going next and feel confident about it. Write your way up to a point that feels complete but that connects to another point you plan to make. Make a few notes to yourself about what the next point will be and how you plan to connect it to the draft-in-progress. Then leave your desk feeling good about the drafting session—and about the one that will start tomorrow.

c. When you begin a new drafting session, check your notes from the end of the previous session. Then reread the whole draft-in-progress to see where you are in the project and how you should continue drafting. If you then see a different *connection* than what is jotted down in your notes, fine: go with what your intuition tells you is the way you should go. If not, reread your notes one more time. Then start drafting again.

3. Don't Be Afraid to Stop and Think While Drafting. Scanning the writing-in-progress and pausing to reflect on the developing draft seem to be characteristic of effective writers. So one thing you can do to make your drafting sessions more successful is to develop the habit of taking productive pauses while you draft. Here are some tips for making your pauses productive:

a. Keep your eyes, and your thoughts, focused on your draft-in-progress.

b. As you feel yourself leaving one idea and moving to another, look back at preceding words, paragraphs, or sections to let your subconscious orient itself to the way your paper is going and to generate new ideas.

c. As you succeed in building more productive pauses into your drafting sessions, begin to work with the next suggestion.

4. Expand the Range of What You React to During Pauses. Working gradually to broaden the range of what you respond to intuitively during your pauses can help you develop your draft more efficiently. Don't become too self-conscious about your responses. But as you draft, remember that the feelings and intuitions you have when you pause and scan can deal with many different elements of your writing: ideas and key sentences, broad organizational patterns, supporting material, paragraphing, sentences, words and spelling, and punctuation. Any of these elements can be changed in different ways to create various effects. You can make changes of different kinds. You can

a. shift the position of written copy—move sections of text, paragraphs, sentences, phrases, or words.

b. add material—paragraphs, sentences, phrases, words, new research, or punctuation.

c. substitute material.

d. cut material.

e. clarify connections within your writing.

5. Develop a "Road-Map" for Drafting. While you are drafting (or after you have done some rapid writing and before you begin drafting), you may feel an intuitive sense of what the overall shape of your writing project should be. When this happens, try to pin the intuition down on paper in rough outline form. Keep an extra pad of paper handy at your desk while you write, and use it for this purpose. After all, any idea about the overall structure of a writing project can be a very valuable thing—too valuable to trust to memory. Such an intuition can give you direction as you draft. It can help you sense how the sections of your project should relate to each other. Also, an intuition about the overall structure of a piece can help you know where to end one drafting session and how to begin the next. If you can capture some sense of this intuitive structure on paper, you can use it as a sort of "road-map" during later drafting sessions.

What we are suggesting here is *not* formal outlining, but quick sketching (following rapid-writing rules), such as Jerry's account of his drafting behavior, which he jotted down after his first drafting session. Jerry had drafted toward a sense of how the whole paper might look. As a result, he was able to produce the following rough outline or "road-map" for future drafting.

Begin with a general situation.
Explain what might have caused the situation.

- changing societal patterns

- the media and ads

- adult behavior—failure to learn from the past

End with a section suggesting how things could change.

When you begin to write down such an outline, you should expect to change it many times. In most really productive drafting sessions, you see new connections and ideas that cause you to redefine your writing project. In fact, you might like to leave lots of space between items in the outline, so that you can add details and modifications as they occur to you during drafting. (At the computer, you don't need to leave space in your outline. Just move your cursor to the spot where you'd like to add ideas, press the "insert" command, and start typing. Your word processor will automatically adjust and give you the space you need.)

As you follow the road-map of a rough outline, keep in mind that side-excursions (and even complete departures from an original itinerary) are possible for any traveller. You may discover, during any productive drafting session, that you feel a *new* intuitive structure for your project. If so, jot that down, too. After all, this change of direction may be just what you need for your writing to grow toward a completed project.

IDEA FILE: COMPUTER WRITING

Computer Outlining

Even if you don't usually like to outline, you might try *computer outlining*. You can outline quickly, without worry, because you can also revise and recast the outline at will; you can draft for awhile, then return to the outline and develop it; you can draft first and outline later. Here are some possibilities:

1. Whenever you feel that you have a general sense of what you want to say, you can start outlining. Type your main points into the computer.

Title: Computers in Society
I. Introduce by talking about the kinds of changes computers
   have made.
II. Talk about the positive effects of those changes.
III. Talk about the negative effects of those changes.
IV. Come to some conclusion.

2. Having entered a tentative outline, you have your choices. You
   can move your cursor to any point in the outline and start
   drafting. For instance, if you want to write your conclusion
   first, you can. Then, if you are ready to write your introduction—how computers have changed things—you can. But if
   instead you would prefer to develop your outline, you can do
   that. Just move your cursor to any point in your outline and
   start adding subpoints—details and examples to prove your
   point.

Title: Computers in Society
I. Introduce by talking about the kinds of changes computers
   have made.
   a. Telephone information is often computerized.
   b. Grocery store pricing is computerized.
   c. Banking is computerized.
   d. Shopping is becoming computerized.
   e. Libraries are computerizing their holdings.
II. Talk about the positive effects of those changes.
III. Talk about the negative effects of those changes.
IV. Come to some conclusion.

6. Don't Forget Your Reader—Unless You Want to. If you
want your writing to be clear and interesting to the people who read
it, you need to consider your readers at some point during your pause-
and-scan time. But that does *not* mean that you should worry about
readers *all* the time you are drafting.

The first time you sit down to work on a writing project, you may
find it productive to use some of the rapid-writing strategies discussed in Chapter 2. (Write for your diary, or write a letter to a friend,
or talk with your clone.)

You might find, even in the first drafting session on a project, that
writing for your intended audience brings out ideas about your subject that would not otherwise occur to you. Clearly, you will need to
take your reader into consideration during some of your drafting sessions, even if you do not want to during the earliest ones.

When you *do* want to remember your reader in a drafting session,
here are a few suggestions to keep in mind:

a. "Remember" your reader or "think of" your reader, but do not
   "worry about" your reader. Your reader probably will not read what
   you've written during a drafting session.

b. Let your sense of a reader guide some of the intuitive responses you
   have as you pause and scan. As your eyes flit back to a previous
   sentence or as you reread a paragraph, respond to what you see in
   terms like these:
   - How would this strike my reader?
   - Would this be clear? Interesting? Boring? Offensive?
   - Would this reveal things about me that I don't want to share
     with my reader?
   - What kinds of change would help?

When Is a Draft Finished?

Through the act of *drafting,* you will ultimately produce a complete
version of your paper, a finished *draft.* When is a draft completed?
That is a decision that the writer must make. Some writers are
satisfied with very rough drafts, perhaps because they are good revis-
ers. Other writers like to feel that they have their papers in almost
final form before they say that they've completed a rough draft. They
know they'll need to reconsider and revise their work, but they want
to feel somewhat finished when they say that their draft is done, so
they may even attend to such matters as paragraph structure, sentence
structure, and word choice as they draft or redraft.

Summary

In this chapter we have tried to give you a sense of what *drafting*
means—what it looks like, what it feels like, and its results. If you
have done some drafting recently, you may have been able to remember what a *drafting mind-set* (your state of mind during a draft) feels
like. But if you haven't pushed from generating activities toward
drafting recently, you may want to reread this chapter at another time,
checking to see if your experience compares with the kinds of drafting
behaviors we have described.

Some of the things we've talked about in this chapter may not be
new to you, but the idea of focusing on what you are doing as you
draft may be something you haven't tried before. By noting what happens as you write, you have an opportunity to strengthen your writing
processes by developing more efficient ways of drafting.

In the next chapter, we'll focus explicitly on revising. We think
you'll find that the motivation to discover ideas and connections while
drafting results in something different than what happens when the
motivation is to proofread or revise a completed draft.

TEAMWORK WRITING

Often, writers don't want to share their writing-in-progress; but they do want to talk about the problems that they are having as they write. If possible, get together in a group and talk about some of the following issues:

1. How are you feeling about your draft?

2. In what way is your draft going well?

3. In what way is your draft going poorly?

4. Do you want to test out an idea on someone?

5. Do individual group members want to request help with some problem they are having?

6. Do individual group members want reactions to a part of their draft?

7. Talk about what strategies you are using. What kind of writing processes are at work as you write?

8. What plans do you have for your next drafting session?

Sharing ideas and feelings about writing behaviors and writing problems helps writers develop their consciousness of writing processes and strategies. It also helps them develop confidence in those strategies, and in their own abilities to solve problems as they draft.

Writing Exercises

1. In order to strengthen your powers of spontaneous drafting, make periodic entries during the rest of the course in your Processes and Intentions Log (see p. 8). Write about the writing you are doing in your writing class and in other writing situations. You know that writing can be a way to find ideas, as the spontaneous coordination of brain, hand, and eyes brings them to your attention. So it stands to reason that you might get good ideas for a project if you were to write spontaneously for ten to twenty minutes about how things are going with the project.

2. Look at paragraph structure in several magazine articles, essays, or textbooks. Select two paragraphs that are particularly effective. An-

alyze them by recording the following information: coherence, transitions, development. For practice, write a paragraph of your own using one of these paragraphs as a model.

3. Examine several paragraphs in a *Newsweek* story to see if they follow any of these patterns: comparison-contrast, cause-effect, classification, definition. Try to describe the characteristics of any paragraph patterns you can identify. Write a sample paragraph of your own using one of these paragraphs as a model. Check to see if you have used any of these paragraph-types in drafts you have written so far in this course. How did this happen? Did you consciously attempt to write a comparison-contrast or a cause-effect paragraph? Most writers pick up these patterns from a lifetime of reading. If you need to become more conscious of the way writers develop paragraphs, devote some time to this exercise. Being aware of how other writers use paragraph patterns to develop ideas can help you develop your consciousness of writing and of yourself as a writer.

4. Check through the writing you have done so far this semester. See if some of your paragraphs follow a well-organized pattern even though you didn't consciously intend to produce a specific pattern. Use a journal entry or rapid writing to explain how you wrote those paragraphs.

5. You'll draft more effectively if you are writing about a topic that concerns you. For a more systematic exploration of material you could write about, spend an hour writing rapid but fairly detailed answers to the questions in any four sections of the following *interest inventory*. Keep your responses to these questions in your writing notebook and consult them whenever you need help in locating a topic.

Personal Interest Inventory

The Community

1. Where do I live?

2. What kind of community is my town or neighborhood?

3. What places or events in my community do I enjoy? Why?

4. What disturbs me about my community? Why?

5. What would I like to see changed about my community? Why?

Family, Friends, and Acquaintances

6. What is unique about my family?

7. Which of my relatives are especially interesting to me? Why?

8. What special customs or get-togethers does my family have?

9. What pets have I had, or would I like to have?

10. Which of my friends are especially interesting to me? Why?

11. Which of my neighbors are especially interesting to me? Why?

12. Do I know any really unusual people? What makes them unusual?

Education

13. What kind of educational background do I have? (Kindergarten? Elementary school? High school? Size of school? What did I learn? Which teachers impressed me? etc.)

14. What kinds of courses do I like the most? The least? Why?

15. What educational experiences have I had outside of formal schools and classes?

16. What would I like to see changed about the schools I have attended? About the overall education I have received?

Jobs and Career Interests

17. What kinds of jobs have I had? What was involved in doing these jobs?

18. What has most interested me about the jobs I have had? Why?

19. What has most disturbed me about the jobs I have had? Why?

20. What career am I interested in? Why am I interested in this field?

Hobbies and Leisure Activities

21. What hobbies do I enjoy? What makes each one enjoyable?

22. What kinds of movies, music, and books do I like? Why?

23. What is the most interesting place I have ever visited on a vacation? Why was it interesting?

24. Where would I especially like to travel? Why?

25. What kinds of extracurricular activities do I engage in at college? What do I "get out of" each one?

Personal Attitudes and Opinions

26. What event in the past year most captured my interest and enthusiasm? What was it that sparked my interest?

27. What event in the past year disturbed me the most? Why?

28. Do I think the technological changes going on every day are generally good or beneficial? Why or why not?

29. Do I think the social changes I have observed over the past few years are generally good? Why or why not?

30. What kinds of technological or social changes would I like to see take place? Why?

31. Have I experienced a change in my attitude toward any of these things: politics, religion, school, family, friends? If so, what was the change and what caused it?

Source: Adapted from Charles W. Bridges, "An Interest Inventory for Topic Discovery," *Freshman English News,* 7 (Winter 1979). pp. 12–13.

Suggestions for Writing

1. Follow the first four suggestions for productive drafting (see pp. 86–88) as you draft an essay on a topic that would be of interest to college students—of either traditional or nontraditional ages. To select a topic, look back over your answers to the Personal Interest Inventory to see if you'd like to use one of the items in the inventory as the basis for a paper. Or, consider the experiences—good or bad, serious or humorous—that you have had with one of these (or similar) topics:

   > Money, Money Management, and Financial Planning
   > Fitness
   > Fashion
   > Relationships
   > Personal Health and Health Care
   > Computers

   a. Draft for an hour on the topic of your choice, using the first two drafting suggestions—"Extend Rapid Writing into Productive Drafting" and "Pay Attention to 'Start' and 'Stop' Points." After an hour, take a break for at least several hours.

   b. Begin drafting again, for one hour, this time working at the third and fourth suggestions—"Don't Be Afraid to Stop and Think While Drafting" and "Expand the Range of What You React to During Pauses." Then, take a break for at least several hours.

   c. *Without looking at the work from the previous two drafting sessions,* spend at least an hour drafting your article from beginning to end.

   d. Put that new version into a readable form for your teacher and students in your class.

2. Use writing techniques from this chapter and from Chapter 2 to "draft" your way *toward* the "first draft" of an article that you might submit for publication in a magazine for college readers. Before you

start generating ideas and drafting, look through several campus-oriented magazines: *The Black Collegian, Campus Voice, College Entertainment Guide* are a few. Work with a topic that might be accepted by the editors of one of these magazines. You may decide to write about the same topic you chose for the preceding activity, or you may choose a new topic. You don't have to write on a different topic for this exercise if you don't want to. You'll be writing for a different purpose this time—since you will be adapting your topic to a specific magazine—so you'll have a chance to view your topic differently. For example, some of the general topic ideas suggested earlier might be revised as follows:

> Starting Today to Plan Your Financial Future
> Being Intelligent About Your Health
> The Impact Computers Will Have on Future Family Life

Whichever specific topic you work with, keep in mind that the primary goal of this project is to apply principles of drafting from this chapter. Follow these directions as you draft:

a. Do some spontaneous writing. Write a detailed *diary-type* pre-draft about *what you know* about the topic. (Review pp. 46–48 for additional information about this approach.)

For sixty (uninterrupted) minutes, do not move from your desk or computer; keep your hands in nearly constant motion, your eyes in nearly continuous contact with the words that develop. Remember: this is not a draft you are writing, but pre-draft material. So don't worry about appearance, form, or anything else except getting down as much information as you can about the topic and as many questions as you have about it.

Use the last five minutes of the drafting session to look over your pre-draft and make some notes about how you might start a new drafting session. Then put your work away and take a break for at least several hours.

b. For sixty (uninterrupted) minutes, write a *letter* to a specific, real person. Write about *what you know* about the topic, and about your *personal reactions to and feelings about* the topic. (Review pp. 46–48.)

In the last five minutes of the drafting session, read through the pre-draft and make some notes to help you start a new drafting session. Take a break for at least several hours.

c. Do some background reading on your topic in the library. Read some articles from the magazine that you plan to write your article for; read for information and to help you sense the sort of article you are trying to write. Jot down some brief notes and personal reactions to the articles as you read.

    d. For sixty minutes, write a *report to your teacher* about *what you plan to do* in your first draft (include what you learned in the library). Be specific; use paragraphs, not just sketchy listings of ideas. (See p. 47 for more information.)

       In the last five minutes of your drafting session, read through this pre-draft and make some notes to help you start a drafting session following the directions in part e (which follows this part). Take a break for at least several hours. Do some more background work in the library. *Take some more notes. React to what you've read in your writing log.*

    e. Draft for *at least* seventy-five minutes, or, preferably, for two hours. Work to produce a first draft by the end of this time. Look over earlier drafts and responses to the preceding exercises, but don't be bound by them. Turn in, for your teacher's comments, a folder containing all of the work from all four of the preceding drafting sessions. Arrange the work chronologically so that the first draft sits on top of your various pre-drafts.

3. Draft a second version of your article—one that is clearer and more effective because it reflects your continued attention, and your efforts to respond to comments from your teacher and from students in a writer's group.

    a. "Clean up" your first draft into readable, typed form—a "draft one and a half"—that you can share with several other students in a writer's group.

    b. Meet with your writer's group. Work together to improve each others' drafts.

    c. Reread your "draft one and a half" with the skeptical, questioning attitude of the clone you invented as part of the spontaneous writing activities in Chapter 2. Take into consideration comments by other students, suggestions from your teacher, and reactions *you* now have to the draft you prepared earlier.

    Finally, make some notes that would help you get started efficiently with a drafting session. Then take a break.

Revising and Editing Finished Drafts

4

The Need for Revision

Almost all writers revise not only as they write, but after they write. Why do they work this way? Why should you plan to dedicate some of the time you spend on a writing assignment to *revision*?

For one thing, it makes composing easier. Knowing that you plan to return to your work can free you to focus on ideas as you draft. The mind can only juggle so much at once. Setting aside some time after you finish a draft to do nothing but contemplate possible changes in your text can also make revision easier. Revising after drafting allows writers to objectively evaluate their entire text—not just the portion of their text that they have just drafted.

Seeing revision as something that you simply plan to do at some point in your writing—that is, seeing revision as "standard operating procedure"—gives you time to sit back, read what you've written, and take stock of what you need to do in order to improve it. When you take time to revise thoughtfully, you give yourself an opportunity to read your own writing as a reader would. And so you notice the gaps in thinking, the awkwardly phrased sentences, the disjointed paragraphs that you might not have noticed as you drafted. That's why, even though we encourage you to revise as you draft, we also encourage you to set aside some time for conscious revision after you have finished a draft.

By now you probably have some feel for your shifting intentions as a writer. You've gotten a sense of how, by adopting one mind-set or another—one intention or another—you can modify the way your writing processes work for you. In other words, you have learned that a *reflective, meditative mind-set* helps you generate ideas without criticism. You have learned, too, that when you draft, you can't be quite as easy-going about writing. You need a more *production-oriented* mind-set. You want to let your mind continue to reflect and respond to sentences as you write them, but you also want to encourage your mind to be productive—to work toward a finished product and to think of how that product should look *as* you write sentences that lead toward the product. Having learned how *generating* and *drafting* feel, you are in a position to focus your attention on *revising*.

This chapter will help you develop an awareness of how you can proceed when your intention is to revise. We'll encourage you to get a sense of how, in order to revise, you need an objective and critical *revision mind-set*. And we'll suggest strategies you can use as you let your revision processes work for you.

Revising and Editing

In order to develop a revision mind-set, you've got to understand what revision means. Revision means literally "to see again" or "to see anew." In order to truly re-see, you need to look at your writing in a more objective, critical way. And as you look again at your writing, you need to be prepared to reshape your text: move paragraphs and sentences to new locations, add sections, delete unnecessary parts.

The term *revising* is used differently by different writers. Sometimes a writer talks of *editing* and means the same thing as another writer who talks about *revising*. The terms *revising* and *editing* are used in many different ways to refer to a variety of strategies used by writers as they rework early drafts. Donald Murray likes to distinguish between "internal" revising, the kinds of changes that affect meaning, and "external" revising, the kinds of changes that affect the surface of the text—such as mechanical errors. [See Murray's essay in Charles R. Cooper and Lee Odell (eds.), *Research on Composing: Points of Departure* (Urbana, Ill.: National Council of Teachers of English, 1978).] We are using the term *revising* to encompass all kinds of textual changes that writers make when they specifically intend to rework their writing in order to prepare it for readers.

Proofreading is another matter. Most writers are in agreement about what proofreading is: something we've pretty much got to force ourselves to do! Proofreading refers to the very late-stage editing attention writers need to give to most texts in order to spot the kinds of errors that they are capable of spotting. (After all, why let a reader think that you made the error out of ignorance when, in fact, you erred out of neglect. *Don't neglect to catch what you can.*)

Revision Decisions

How do you know when you're ready to revise? There comes a time when most writers finally say: "That's it. I've said what I wanted to say. I'm done drafting." Just when that moment occurs will vary from one writer to the next. Some writers don't begin revising in earnest until their draft is completely organized, paragraphs in place, and development complete. But other writers are satisfied with a draft when they have finished writing about each of their main points. You have to be alert to your own tempo. Shift to revising when you feel ready to shift. Realize, of course, that you may in fact decide to return to drafting if you need to.

How much revising is necessary? It all depends. A lot depends on the nature of the writing task. A lot depends on the quality of the draft and on your response to the following kinds of questions:

1. Do you say what you want to say?

2. If you haven't said want you wanted to say, how important is it that you clarify your message?

3. If it is important that you clarify your message, then how much revising will accomplish the task?

■ How to Prepare for a Revising Session

How do you prepare for a revising session? Most of all you need some distance from your draft. Read something else about your topic. Break long enough to forget your words, and return to your draft with a fresh outlook. You've got to read your writing as if you hadn't written it yourself.

One way you can gain distance from your writing is by looking at the structure of your piece—how you've put your ideas together—instead of at the content. When you reread your own material for content, you can sometimes imagine that there are more connections than there are. To "see" the structure, try drawing it or diagramming it.

How you proceed from that point on is up to you. You need to make your own plans. You need to be able to adapt your revising sessions to your own needs and to the dictates of the assignment. Thus, before you begin to revise, you may want to take a few minutes to review the nature of your writing assignment and to assess your progress in completing it. The following suggestions can help you plan for a revising session.

Revision-Planning Guide

Review the Assignment

1. What was the assignment?

2. What should the assignment look like when it's finished?

3. Who will read the assignment?

4. What impact do you want to have on your readers?

Review Your Progress

5. What is the state of your draft? Are the paragraphs fully developed? Are you satisfied with the overall flow of ideas? If you haven't worked on paragraph coherence, as you drafted, do you need to revise your paragraphs for coherence? If you haven't yet worked on sentence structure, do you need to rework some sentences? What about word choice? Grammar? Punctuation? Other?

6. What are your goals for your finished draft? Do you hope to produce a powerful piece of writing? An acceptable piece of writing?

7. How much revising do you feel your draft needs? Only minor touchups? Total reshaping? Other?

Prepare for Your Revising Session

8. How will you proceed; that is, what should you work on first?

9. What strategies can you use to transform your draft into what you want it to be?

Extensive Revising

How extensively should you revise? When you have decided that a thorough revision is in order, you should sit down in front of your writing and assume that your revised draft will not look like a retyping or reprinting of your original draft. If you recognize that your draft needs substantial work, you will have considerably more to do than correcting punctuation and spelling. A draft that has been revised extensively usually demonstrates that you have made a number of the following changes:

REORGANIZED:	Ideas	Paragraphs	Sentences	Phrases	Words
ADDED:	Ideas	Paragraphs	Sentences	Phrases	Words
SUBSTITUTED:	Ideas	Paragraphs	Sentences	Phrases	Words
DELETED:	Ideas	Paragraphs	Sentences	Phrases	Words

The reorganizations, additions, substitutions, and deletions in the revised draft should reflect your thoughts about

- how well the different parts of the paper connect and "flow" together.

- the organizational signals your reader needs to follow the flow of the paper.

- how individual sentences and paragraphs help or hinder the development and flow of ideas in the paper.

- the examples and other "evidence" it may take to help your reader understand the paper and feel convinced by your arguments.

IDEA FILE: COMPUTER WRITING

Revising

1. When your intention for your writing session is to revise, save your original file. Give your original file a name that is different from the name you use to file your revision. For example, file the original as "Theme 1" and the revision as "Theme 2." Then you'll have a record of the original version of your draft, in case you need to refer to it. Frequently, writers return to their original drafts and use sections that work well.

2. If your word processor has "split-screen" or "windowing" capability, consider opening a new file in one of the windows. Keep the draft of your writing in the first window and use the new window as a "tryout area"—a place where you can write alternate versions of your sentences or paragraphs. That way, you'll be able to experiment with possibilities before moving your words and sentences to the window that contains your draft.

3. Another way to use the split-screen capability of your word processor as you revise is to load your file in both windows— renaming the file in one of the windows so that you can change it without changing the original. Then you can rework your sentences or paragraphs in context in one window and compare the results with the original version in the other window. Or, you can rework each file in different ways and compare the results.

Readability and Clarity

When you revise, what you are really doing is trying to make your draft more readable. When you decide that you are ready to revise, you adopt a new stance toward your material. While drafting, you can be inside your work, producing sentences quickly as you put your thoughts into words. As long as you've said what you want to say, you can feel satisfied with your rough draft. But when you revise, you need to be sure that your words and sentences are clearly expressed for your readers. You need to move outside your words and react to them as readers are likely to react.

In a way, drafting is like talking to yourself or like chatting with a friend. In contrast, revising a draft involves preparing your words for people you don't know, readers who need clear signals in order to follow your meaning. If possible, ask someone in your class to help you prepare for revising by reading your work for you and commenting on it; if you can't find anyone to help, then you need to read it yourself—putting yourself in someone else's shoes.

How can you make your writing more readable? We can offer you a few pointers:

1. Provide clear statements of your key points.

2. Organize key points so that writing flows *logically* toward the conclusions you want your readers to reach. By using smooth transitions, you can emphasize points and clarify the flow of your thinking. Connecting sentences to each other with transitional markers can increase coherence and help readers follow your intended meanings.

3. Be sure that your paragraphs emphasize points and support the logical flow of your ideas. Sometimes you can keep ideas moving along more smoothly if you combine shorter sentences by using effective connecting words.

4. Use examples and evidence from your research to effectively clarify and explain important points.

5. Provide introductions that prepare readers for what is to follow.

6. Use precise, unambiguous words.

7. Rewrite sentences that are too long to be followed easily.

8. Check to see if your sentences have enough variety in length and structure to keep your paper from being monotonous and boring.

Remember, when you revise for readability, as well as when you revise for other reasons, you must continually reread what precedes and what follows your change. *Every change affects the whole.* Don't revise one section for readability without looking at what precedes and what follows a given passage. Don't revise one or two sentences without rereading the entire paragraph in which the sentences appear. Always revise in the context of the entire draft.

■ Some Guidelines for a Revising Session

The following guidelines provide suggestions for what you might think about as you revise your paper and include questions that you may ask yourself about your writing. Answering these questions honestly should help you move toward a thorough revision of a rough draft. You should plan to take a good bit of time in answering the questions and in revising your draft.

At first, following the guidelines and responding to them may seem mechanical. But if you push yourself to answer the revision-guideline questions (especially after applying these guidelines to several papers), you'll begin to know what to look for without having to look at the list. Think of these guidelines as training wheels. When you become a more proficient reviser, you won't need the training wheels. Gradually, you'll begin to look automatically and intuitively at your draft and you'll consider the kinds of alterations suggested in these guidelines without being prompted to do so.

You should keep a grammar or English usage handbook near you as you revise, so that you can check any questionable areas you find as you work. Ask your teacher to recommend one if you don't already own one.

Revision Guidelines

Consider What a Reader's Response to Your Paper Might Be

1. First read your paper as if you hadn't written it. How do you feel as you read it? After you've read it?

2. What do you like about the draft overall? What disappoints you about it?

3. Do you notice gaps in your thought processes? Do you notice parts that seem confusing?

4. If you want, ask someone else to read your paper responsively. Ask for overall, general reactions before moving on to the more tangible concerns that follow.

Review the Overall Organization of Your Writing

5. Check to see if you have an interesting opening.

6. See if you can identify a clear, unifying idea that is limited, significant, and appropriate to the assignment.

7. Note whether you have discussed any subpoints (from your introduction and thesis statement) in the same order in which you introduced them.

8. Check to see whether you have a satisfying conclusion.

9. Determine whether you have maintained a smooth flow of ideas throughout the paper. Note where you need to improve the flow.

Consider the Tone of Your Paper

10. Read your paper objectively. Do you seem to have a genuine interest in the subject and a good grasp of the subject?

11. Pretend you just came across your paper and that you do not have any idea who wrote it. Does it sound as if the paper is written for a real audience? What particular kinds of readers would be interested in the paper?

Analyze Your Paragraph Organization

12. Does each paragraph "in the middle" of the paper relate to the main idea and to a specific subpoint?

13. Is there adequate support for generalizations and assertions in each paragraph?

14. Are transitions and sentence openers used within paragraphs to achieve a smooth narrative flow? Do your sentences flow smoothly?

15. Is supporting evidence handled clearly and smoothly (with effective lead-ins and lead-outs), and with accurate documentation?

Check Mechanics and Grammatical Construction

16. Does the paper show adherence to the rules of English grammar and mechanics of usage, or what is often called "edited American English"?

17. Does the paper avoid trite, clumsy, and wordy expressions?

18. Is there a variety of active, colorful verbs?

19. Is the sentence structure varied so that sentences are short, long, simple, or complex? You probably should have a few sentences of each type in your paper.

■ A Sample Student Draft: Before Revision

To give you an idea of how these guidelines can help you revise, we'd like you to read a sample student paper—a rough draft of a paper on AIDS (acquired immunodeficiency syndrome). The student chose the topic for this paper herself. She decided that she would write her essay in the form of a newspaper feature story, one that she might actually submit to the student newspaper. Read through the paper carefully, concentrating on the writer's ideas. Then reread the paper with the preceding list of revision guidelines in mind. Better yet, pretend that you wrote the paper, and respond (in your writing notebook) to the revision-guideline questions.

THE AIDS SCARE

Aids has been the hottest news topic around because it has affected more facets of American society than just those afflicted with it. Short of nuclear holocaust, AIDS is perceived as being the greatest threat to the health and well-being of millions of people. It has made herpes, the only other incurable sexually-transmitted disease, seem trite in comparison. (After all, herpes is an occasional bout with blisters; AIDS is an almost certain bout with death.) Furthermore, the disease has added a whole new dimension to the term "homophobia." It has also repopularized the old standby contraceptive, the condom, and has given the idea of cautious sexual behavior a positive connotation rather than a negative one. Virgins aren't prudish, they're proud!

The most obvious effect of the controversial AIDS threat is a slowing down of the rapidly growing sexual revolution. The "Love the One You're With" attitude of the sixties and the "Dating Game" mentality of the seventies have given way to the AIDS-plagued eighties, wherein the price tag for promiscuity may be much higher than an unwanted pregnancy or a shot of penicillin for an episode of gonorrhea.

Never before have staunch homosexual haters been given a better excuse to publicly express their views than now, when homosexuals, along with Haitians and drug abusers, have been distinguished as the primary carriers of the AIDS disease. Although its infiltration into the heterosexual population is growing, AIDS is still perceived as a homosexual disease, and has given rise to extreme prejudice against gays. For example, declarations by religious leaders attesting to this "divine revelation" of the evil of homosexuality have not been uncommon in recent months. Condom manufacturers have benefited immensely from the onslaught of AIDS. Teenage boys no longer exclusively support the condom industry. Women are a new and promising target for condom sales, as evidenced by the growing number of condom advertisements in women's magazines. Touted as

being the only form of birth control that can reduce
the risk of AIDS, condoms may well become the preferred
contraceptive. "National Condom Week" in February of
1987 kicked off a drive by government officials and
health practitioners to promote condom use. Condoms
aren't kid stuff anymore.

The effects of AIDS on society has now given rise to
speculation as to its effects on society in the future.
As U.S. News & World Report (February, 1987) predicts, the number of individuals expected to succumb
to AIDS should rise to a yearly toll of 54,000, nearly
equivalent to the number of casualties in the Vietnam
War. If a cure is not forthcoming, we may see blood
tests that screen for AIDS become mandatory. Dating
services may lure customers by promising disease-free
dating partners, and wallet-sized certificates declaring a clean bill of health may become a necessary pre-
requisite for seducing a potential one-night stand in
the local singles bar. Finally, as the push to find a
cure accelerates, research dollars will be drained from
other important disease research to promote a quicker
cure for AIDS. It is readily apparent why a fatal disease in the public spotlight, like AIDS, will receive
more research funding than an obscure disease. Media
hype has turned the controversial issue of AIDS into
the modern day black plague. Finding a way to reduce
auto accidents would save more lives than would a cure
for AIDS. But fear breeds hysteria, and placating AIDS
hysteria will be a top priority as AIDS becomes more
commonplace.

Therefore, AIDS has made Americans, drunk with sexual
indulgences, take a sobering look at the risk of leading such a lifestyle. AIDS has seriously undermined
the efforts of equality-seeking homosexuals, while in
the shadows the condom industry silently shrieks with
joy. Most of all, however, AIDS has made us aware of
the fact that medical science really doesn't have all
of the answers, and maybe it never will.

Source: Diane Jarrell. Printed with permission.

■ A Sample of One Student's Application of Revision Guidelines

If you responded to the revision-guideline questions, you'll be especially interested in seeing what the student writer said about her own
paper. Read through the questions and responses below, noting the
writer's honesty in evaluating her own writing. We should note that
the student revised this paper several weeks after writing the first

draft, a factor which no doubt helped her look at her own writing objectively.

Consider Reader Response to Your Paper

1. First read your paper as if you hadn't written it. How do you feel as you read it? After you've read it?

   I like it, but I'm not quite as happy with it as I thought I'd be. I think that there are some parts that don't fit.

2. What do you like about the draft overall? What disappoints you about it?

   I think that I am making a basically unified statement about the magnitude of the AIDS problem. But I think that I get carried away with a few ideas at times and lose sense of my main points.

3. Do you notice gaps in your thought processes? Do you notice parts that seem confusing?

   I want to stress that everyone is affected by AIDS. But when in the conclusion I say that ". . . , AIDS has made Americans, drunk with sexual indulgences, take a sobering look at the risk of leading such a lifestyle," it sounds as if AIDS has only touched one kind of American—the kind who is "drunk with sexual indulgences."

4. If you want, ask someone else to read your paper responsively. Ask for overall, general reactions before moving on to the more tangible concerns that follow.

   No one seems to be available this weekend to read my paper, so I'm trying to revise it myself.

Review the Overall Organization of Your Writing

5. Check to see if you have an interesting opening.

   I think that I need an introductory paragraph to attract a reader's attention.

6. See if you can identify a clear, unifying idea that is limited, significant, and appropriate to the assignment.

   I need a clearer thesis statement. None of my current sentences seems to be just right to give the overall idea of what I'm saying.

7. Note whether you have discussed any subpoints (from your introduction and thesis statement) in the same order in which you introduced them.

   It's not easy to locate my subpoints in my thesis statement. My subpoints are introduced in the same order, but one of my subpoints—the effects of AIDS on the future—isn't even mentioned in my topic sentence. I think I need to straighten out my thesis statement and my subpoints.

One problem with my topic sentence, and with the whole first paragraph, might be that I mention that AIDS makes herpes seem trite in comparison, in the same paragraph where I introduce my main points for the paper: slowing down of the sexual revolution, more problems for homosexuals, increased need for condoms.

8. Check to see whether you have a satisfying conclusion.

My ending seems to add an idea that I haven't really developed in the paper—the idea that Americans have been "drunk with sexual indulgences." I need to change my ending.

9. Determine whether you have maintained a smooth flow of ideas through the paper. Note where you need to improve the flow.

When I start speculating about the future—that AIDS has an unknown influence on the future—I seem to be digressing.

Maybe all I need to do is add that idea to my thesis statement; then the paragraph about the future won't be a digression.

Consider the Tone of Your Paper

10. Read your paper objectively. Do you seem to have a genuine interest in the subject and a good grasp of the subject?

I think that my interest shows, but when I say things like "virgins aren't prudish, they're proud" I may seem to be just playing with words instead of being sincere.

11. Pretend you just came across your paper and that you do not have any idea who wrote it. Does it sound as if the paper is written for a real audience? What particular kinds of readers would be interested in the paper?

I can imagine my paper as an editorial on the feature page of a newspaper. So any interested, intelligent reader might want to read my writing—I hope!

Analyze Your Paragraph Organization

12. Does each paragraph "in the middle" of the paper relate to the main idea and to a specific subpoint?

Some do and some don't. I need to make revisions and then return to this question again.

13. Is there adequate support for generalizations and assertions in each paragraph?

Not yet. I need to return to this question after I do some revising.

I need to do some revising before I go any further with these questions. I think I'll be able to answer them after I straighten some things out that I've determined I need to do.

■ Sample Student Revision

Just as writers draft differently, so they revise differently. In this case, the student writer, Diane, did a lot of revising during her drafting sessions. She felt that she could profit more by getting some of her revision done before devoting an entire writing session to revising. But she hasn't straightened up some overall problems at the paragraph level. Here is Diane's revision. Note the changes she has made in her draft as a result of answering some of the revision-guideline questions earlier.

THE CELEBRITY OF THE 80's

[Paragraph 1]

There's a new star that has been featured on the cover of almost every major periodical publication in the country. For at least two years this reigning celebrity has dominated conversation everywhere, from streetside coffee shops to nationally televised documentaries. Even <u>Dallas</u> and <u>Dynasty</u> have taken back seats to this current news gem. Any well-known individual would kill to have this kind of media coverage, if it weren't for the horrible certain-death associated with this celebrity. It's not a hit man or a Nazi fugitive or even a politician. It is Acquired Immune Deficiency Syndrome (AIDS).

[Paragraph 2]

Millions of people have been affected by this celebrity in unusual ways. AIDS has threatened their health and well-being, it has added a whole new dimension to the term "homophobia," and it has slowed down the "sexual revolution"—making people much more cautious about sexual behavior. But these changes are only the beginning. AIDS may have an even greater effect on society in the future.

[Paragraph 3]

Aids has been the hottest news topic around because it has affected many more people than just those afflicted with it. Short of nuclear holocaust, AIDS is perceived as being the greatest health threat to millions of people. It has made herpes, the only other incurable sexually-transmitted disease, seem trite in comparison. (After all, herpes is an occasional bout with blisters; AIDS is an almost certain bout with death.) Just as the polio epidemic in the fifties touched almost everyone in some way, so AIDS has made people realize that it can happen to them, too.

[Paragraph 4]

Never before have staunch haters of homosexuals been given a better excuse to publicly express their views than now, when homosexuals, along with Haitians and drug abusers, have been distinguished as the primary carriers of the AIDS disease. Although its ranks are growing in the heterosexual population. AIDS is still perceived as a homosexual disease, and has given rise to extreme prejudice against gays. For example, declarations by religious leaders attesting to this "divine revelation" of the evil of homosexuality have not been uncommon in recent months.·

[Paragraph 5]

The most obvious effect of the controversial AIDS threat is a slowing down of the rapidly growing sexual revolution. The "Love the One You're With" attitude of the sixties and the "Dating Game" mentality of the seventies have given way to the AIDS-plagued eighties. The price tag for promiscuity may be much higher than an unwanted pregnancy, or a shot of penicillin for an episode of gonorrhea. Cautious sexual behavior has taken on a positive connotation rather than a negative one. As a result, the old teenage standby contraceptive, the condom, has seen a new popularity. Touted as being the only form of birth control that can reduce the risk of AIDS, condoms may well become the preferred contraceptive. "National Condom Week" in February of 1987 kicked off a drive by government officials and health practitioners to promote condom use. Condoms aren't kid stuff anymore.

[Paragraph 6]

The effects of AIDS on society has now given rise to speculation as to its effects on society in the future. As U.S. News & World Report (February, 1987) predicts, the number of individuals expected to succumb to AIDS should rise to a yearly toll of 54,000, nearly equivalent to the number of casualties in the Vietnam War. If a cure is not forthcoming, we may see blood tests that screen for AIDS become mandatory. The time may come when dating services advertise disease-free dating partners; anyone over 12 may be required to carry wallet-sized certificates declaring a clean bill of health. As the push to find a cure accelerates over the years, research dollars will be drained from other important disease research to promote a quicker cure for AIDS. It is readily apparent why a fatal disease in the public spotlight, like AIDS, will receive more research funding than an obscure disease.

[Paragraph 7]

Media hype has turned the controversial issue of AIDS into the modern day black plague. Fear breeds hysteria, and placating AIDS hysteria will be a top priority as AIDS becomes more commonplace.

Source: Diane Jarrell. Printed with permission.

As you read Diane's first attempt at revising her essay, you may have been surprised to discover that she changed more than she planned to change—more than she had decided to change as a result of responding to the revision questions, that is. Here is Diane's record of her revising session as recorded in her notebook:

As I began revising, an idea for a catchy introduction hit me. I remembered that Time's "Man of the Year" was a computer one year and that made me think of AIDS as being the "Celebrity of the 80's." With that idea, I was off and running to write an introduction.

Next, I started looking for my thesis statement. I couldn't find one, so I wrote a new one. With a new sentence, I identified what I saw as my subpoints. I rearranged the order in which I'd cover them. Then I wrote a sentence in which I added the idea about the future to the list so that it wouldn't sound like a digression.

I worked pretty quickly—changing a little here and a little there in sentences to make them fit my new version. Since I had rearranged the order in which I covered my points in my first paragraph, I had to rearrange my paragraphs, too. Then I worked my way through my paragraphs, with my main idea statement in mind ("Millions of people have been affected by this celebrity in unusual ways"). I rearranged the order of the points presented by my paragraphs so that it would match the order I said I would cover them (in my thesis statement).

When I reread my last paragraph, I didn't like it. I decided to eliminate it. Then I read through my essay to see how it sounded with what had been my "next-to-the-last" paragraph as the last paragraph. I decided that it might work. Then, I had an idea. I could split it into two paragraphs. I did that, reread my paper, and decided that it seemed okay for now.

I still need to look this paper over one more time. Before I do, I'll respond to the rest of the revision-guideline questions; and I'll proofread, too. I usually catch a lot of errors as I draft, though, so I don't think I'll find too many through proofreading.

Source: Diane Jarrell. Printed with permission.

Diane made some more changes after completing the rest of the revision questions. But basically, she had done most of what she needed to do as a result of getting a handle on the problems in her draft. Before reading on, why don't you complete the revision-guideline questions on paragraphing and mechanics (p. 106) to see what additional changes you think Diane should have made in her paper. We won't bother to show you Diane's final version, because she made only a few surface changes after doing the extensive revising that you just saw. However, you might want to share your revisions of her draft with one another.

IDEA FILE: COMPUTER WRITING

Peer Review File

The next time you ask another student to read over your rough draft and suggest changes, you can use the following peer review file to help channel your reviewer's comments. Don't feel that you have to use the questions suggested. Substitute questions that you want your reviewer to answer. As the semester progresses, you might want to add questions to this list. Just add questions to your master file whenever you want. As the list is "recalled" and used by various students, be sure that you save it under a different name each time it is used. That way you'll always have your own "template" version of the file.

Review Questions

1. What do you like most about my writing?

2. What would you like to know more about?

3. How could I improve my writing?

4. What could I do to improve the organization?

5. What sentences need to flow more smoothly?

Different Ways of Revising

When you revise, you can limit your focus to a few things at a time, as the student who wrote and revised the preceding essay did. Sometimes, though, you may find that you can revise for many features of your text at once, without the Revision Guidelines. When that happens, respond accordingly.

As you develop a sense of what you want your piece to sound like, how you want readers to receive your words, you may discover that you can get inside your writing and rework it almost as organically as you wrote it. You can start reshaping it and resculpting it, almost as a sculptor shapes a piece of clay. It may not always be possible to sort out content, organization, and sentence structure when you try revising one thing at a time, because, in a good piece of writing, everything works together to create the desired effect.

Just as writers compose differently, so writers revise differently as well. Some writers continually change their words, sentences, and paragraphs as they draft. Other writers compose in a more linear way, waiting until late in their writing to focus on syntactic changes. Generating and drafting style determine, to a certain extent, what a writer's revising style will be.

The amount of revising that writers do often varies with the nature of the assignment. If you are writing about something that you know well, your sentences and paragraphs will probably flow smoothly as you draft. Formulaic writing, such as reports, case studies, and reviews, frequently need less revision than opinion or research papers. And in the case of in-class essays or on-the-job memos, you don't have time for much more than proofreading; you have to revise *as* you write. Remember, writing processes are different when a deadline is imminent rather than remote (as we discussed in Chapter 2). On the other hand, if the topic that you are writing about is one that forces you to struggle to capture your thoughts, you may find that your sentences and paragraphs need significant late-stage revising.

Sometimes, too, only part of a piece of writing needs to be revised significantly. Interestingly, researchers have found that often the "best" parts of student writing are in the greatest need of revision. This occurs in sections where the writer comes closest to what he or she really wants to say, but garbles the sentence structure in the effort to get the thoughts out. When writers truly struggle with complex thoughts, the sentences show evidence of that struggle. Sentences from difficult sections need to be reworked extensively until they convey their intended meanings.

No matter what kind of reviser you are, you will discover that there is a revising mind-set—a way writers feel when they revise—just as there are generating and drafting "modes." Here's how two students experience their revising mind-sets:

> JON: I know it sounds strange, but sometimes I just get into the spirit of revising. I tune in and all of a sudden I seem to know what to change. I feel close to the meaning of my words yet distant from the actual words. I don't mind changing them. I know how I want them to sound, so I can hammer away until they sound the way I want.
>
> MARY ANN: I kind of know what you're talking about, but you sound so mystical. I only feel that way when I really care about a piece of writing. Most of the time, I just need to get a job done.

Then, I look at my writing kind of distantly. I want to fix it. I'm done with it and I want to get it over with. But I guess I only feel like this when I've done a pretty good job drafting, and don't need to worry about much more than prettying it up.

When you feel ready to leave a party, you've had enough. No matter whether you've had a good time or a bad time, there's a point at which you're ready to go. In a similar way, writers know when they are ready to shift intentions in their writing. They have done what they can do to draft and redraft. They are ready to move on.

How do you feel as you revise? How do you feel when your intention changes from drafting to revising? Put the tape recorder on while you talk with someone in your class. Type up portions of your conversation to share with your classmates.

Proofreading

Most writers like to wait until they are completely finished revising their papers to do some careful, tedious proofreading and copyediting. Even though you probably won't like doing it, if you've put a lot of time and energy into your paper, you should force yourself to examine your paper for typos, mechanical and grammatical errors, and usage problems.

We've collected some of our students' favorite strategies for proofreading their papers. Perhaps you or your classmates can add some of your own ideas to this list:

■ Strategies for Proofreading

1. Start with the last sentence and read it. Correct any errors or note any questions you have. Then read the next-to-last sentence, and so on. Reading your sentences in this way helps you focus on their structure, not on their content.

2. Ask someone to read your paper to you as you focus on the words on the page. Ask your partner to stop whenever you need time to correct an error you have detected.

3. Use a marker of some kind to guide you as you read—a ruler or a note card will do. Computer writers sometimes move their cursor word by word or sentence by sentence through their writing, stopping only long enough to make corrections. Some computers will highlight a sentence at a time. This feature helps writers examine their sentences and words critically. Other computers have SPELL-CHECK features that will scan your writing for misspelled words. But be careful: a mistyped word (such as *it* instead of *at*) will not be caught using a computer SPELL-CHECK feature.

4. Read over your writing several times—sometimes moving forward in the text, sometimes moving backward. Often your eyes will miss something on one reading that they will pick up on the next.

IDEA FILE: COMPUTER WRITING

Strategies for Proofreading

1. When you have finished revising, you may want to get a printed copy of your draft so that you can proofread it from the paper. Many writers have difficulty proofreading on screen.

2. After you have determined what changes you need to make, and have noted those changes on your paper copy, load your computer file. Then use the SEARCH feature of your word processor to move quickly to each place where you need to change something. For example, if you have typed the word computer as "compuer," you can SEARCH for "compuer" and then make the change. If you have a need to rephrase a sentence in another part of your paper, just type in a few words from that sentence and again tell the computer to SEARCH for your words. Finding a place in your text is much easier when you search with the SEARCH feature than when you try to visually search by scanning with the cursor.

Summary

Our goal in this chapter has been to stress the importance of revising completed drafts. In particular, we want you to experience revising and to work with different revising strategies so that you know how revising after drafting *feels*. Basically, it's a matter of focus. When you finally have a completed draft to work with, you can focus your complete attention on revising. When you're drafting, you focus your attention on producing a draft. You try to stay with your main idea, but as your paragraphs develop, you don't worry if, at times, you write something that doesn't fit perfectly. Occasionally, you may choose to reread and recast sentences and paragraphs. But if you are "on a roll," and feel that you are drafting well, then you don't want to interrupt your concentration or interfere with your writing processes by checking for every inconsistency. When you're determined to revise, however, you focus on making what you've produced better. You let your writing processes work differently as you rescan and reread your text.

When your intention is to revise, you focus on reviewing completed text and preparing it for readers; you no longer focus on revealing your evolving meaning. You deliberately choose to think almost exclusively about revising. And so, you do little redrafting and generating as you proceed. You *try* to rework your draft, even though you recognize that to solve the problems you discover, you may need to shift intentions and return to generating or drafting.

In this chapter, we have also presented some strategies to use as you revise. It might be a good idea for you to record your experiences with these strategies—your successes and failures—in your Writing Processes and Intentions Log. In that way, you will be able to keep track of your development as a writer and as a reviser. You will be able to experiment with new strategies when you recognize that previous strategies have not been effective for solving specific kinds of problems in your drafts.

In Chapter 5, you will learn about attitude and audience, and ways that these concepts affect writers throughout the life of their writing projects. Try to keep some of the ideas that you contemplated in this chapter fresh in your mind as you read Chapter 5.

TEAMWORK WRITING

Teamwork is invaluable for revising. By having others ask questions about your work, you learn gradually how to ask these same questions yourself. You develop an inner-voice, an alter-ego who questions you just as your peers question you in teamwork sessions.

The writer of a draft is so close to the writing project that he or she can read right over problems, filling in meaning and jumping over logical gaps. But five sets of eyes and five inquiring minds working together on a draft can spot problems that are invisible to the writer. Also, the writer trying to determine how readers are going to react to his or her paper can learn a great deal from listening to a small group discuss a draft of the paper. For such reasons, revising in groups can be a very helpful strategy for student writers.

The Revision Guidelines (see pp. 105–106) can be applied by several students who work, one paper at a time, through the drafts of all the group members. But there are so many questions addressed by the guidelines, that no single group session could get through all of them. So, if you are setting up a revising group, you might like to follow one of the following agendas for group revising.

Teamwork Agenda A

1. Elect a workshop-coordinator.

2. Does the paper have a clear main point, or *promise,* that fits the assignment and seems reasonably original?

   a. Select one person to explain what he/she thinks the main point is.

What are your group reactions to this analysis? Decide, as a group, on a statement articulating the paper's main point.

b. If the writer disagrees with the group's statement, discuss (as a group) what may be preventing the intended main point from coming across in the paper.

c. As a group, discuss whether the paper's main point is original or if it is a rehash of ideas from other people, and whether the main point fulfills the requirements of the assigned paper.

3. Does each paragraph relate clearly to the overall promise of the paper?

a. Have different people check different paragraphs. As a group, discuss any problems individual members find within the separate paragraphs.

b. How can the paragraphs be made to more fully support the overall promise?

4. Are specific transitional devices used to emphasize key points and to clarify the relationships between the various paragraphs?

a. Have different people check different paragraphs for *transitional words*—still, secondly, in addition, on the other hand, and, but, etc.

b. Check for *transitional repetition* of words, phrases, or ideas in the last sentence of one paragraph and the first sentence of the next paragraph.

c. Discuss how transitions could be added to make the flow of ideas smoother and clearer in the paper.

Teamwork Agenda B

1. Elect a timekeeper-coordinator.

2. Does the paper have a single promise?

a. If not, suggest, as a group, how promises that compete as the main idea could be dropped.

b. As a group, discuss how competing promises could be refocused into a single promise.

3. Are there a number of subpoints that are used to back-up or illustrate the overall promise of the paper?

a. As a group, decide what the various subpoints are.

b. If the writer disagrees with the group's analysis, discuss the differences between the writer's intent and the group's perception of the various subpoints.

4. Is each subpoint of the paper developed in at least a full paragraph?

a. Have different people check for different subpoints.

b. As a group, decide on subpoints of the promise that need to be more fully developed.

5. Are there sections of the paper that contain assertions that are not supported with specific examples, statistics, quotations, or other evidence?

   a. Have different people check different paragraphs or pages for supporting examples, statistics, etc.

   b. Together, decide on areas that need more development (more support).

Teamwork Agenda C

1. Does the introduction of the paper prepare the reader for all of the subpoints that come up later?

   a. If not, decide whether the paper is weakened by not mentioning the subpoints in the introduction. (Are topic sentences and transitions so clear that the reader has no trouble following? Are the promise and various subpoints made clear in the conclusion?)

   b. If the group thinks the introduction should deal more fully with the promise and the various subpoints, make specific suggestions for accomplishing this.

2. Is the promise too broad? That is, does the paper seem "spread thin," by using lots of general words, by shifting from point to point with each new paragraph, by not giving enough evidence for subpoints?

   a. If so, decide which points are central and which are minor.

   b. Suggest sections that could be chopped out so that other sections can be given more development.

3. If there are assertions or conclusions in the paper that seem illogical, contradictory, or silly, point them out and make suggestions on how this might be avoided.

4. Are there places where short, choppy sentences can be combined to make the paper flow smoothly? Are there long, complicated sentences that would be clearer if they were broken into two parts?

   a. Have different people analyze the sentence structure of different sections of the paper.

   b. As a group, discuss any sentences that look as if they could be combined for smoothness, or divided to increase clarity.

Writing Exercises

1. Collect information on how different people you know revise their writing. Then do some library research to find out how various novelists and poets feel about revision. Jot down notes from your read-

ing. Which of these strategies that you have read about or learned about seem most useful to you? Which of these strategies do you already use? Which strategies would you like to begin using?

2. Not every writing assignment can or should be revised extensively. Consider the different writing situations and tasks listed below:

    a. an in-class essay test

    b. a response to an electronic mail message

    c. a memo intended to explain your writing problem

    d. an application for a semester abroad

    e. a paper for a college political science class

    In your log, describe how you would go about revising each of these assignments, and rank them in terms of how much revising each would probably require.

3. Try role-playing the following situations.

    a. You are Lisa, a student in a literature class whose paper needs to be reworked substantially. In fact, after a peer revising session, you feel that you need to start all over again. But you've only got two more days left before the paper is due. What should you do?

    b. You are Kevin, a student in another freshman composition class. You have just been through a peer revising session and you are upset. You don't feel that your classmates have given you good advice. You are used to positive remarks about your writing and this time all you seem to have heard were complaints. What do you do?

    Write your responses to each of these situations in your notebook.

4. Wilfred Owen, a World War I poet, revised his poems considerably before finishing them. Read the rough draft and final version of this poem, then see if you can account for the changes he made. Is the revision an improvement? Jot down your observations so that you can share your response with other students in your class.

■ Rough Draft

Last Words

"O Jesus Christ!" one fellow sighed.
And kneeled, and bowed, tho' not in prayer, and
died.

And the Bullets sang "In Vain,"

Machine Guns chuckled "Vain,"
Big Guns guffawed "In Vain."

"Father and mother!" one boy said.
Then smiled—at nothing, like a small child;
being dead.

And the Shrapnel cloud
Slowly gestured "Vain,"

The falling splinters muttered "Vain."
"My love!" another cried, "My love, my bud!"

Then, gently lowered, his whole face kissed the mud.

And the Flares gesticulated, "Vain,"
The shells hooted, "In Vain,"
And the Gas hissed, "In Vain."

Wilfred Owen

▪ Final Draft

The Last Laugh

'O Jesus Christ! I'm hit,' he said; and died.
Whether he vainly cursed, or prayed indeed,
The Bullets chirped—In vain! vain! vain!
Machine-guns chuckled,—Tut-tut! Tut-tut!

And the Big Gun guffawed.

Another sighed,—'O Mother, mother! Dad!'
Then smiled, at nothing, childlike, being dead.

And the lofty Shrapnel-cloud
Leisurely gestured,—Fool!
And the falling splinters tittered.
'My Love!' one moaned. Love-languid seemed his
mood,

Till, slowly lowered, his whole face kissed the mud.
And the Bayonets' long teeth grinned;
Rabbles of Shells hooted and groaned;
And the Gas hissed.

Source: Both poems—Wilfred Owen, "Last Words," in Barry Wallenstein (ed.) *Visions and Revisions: An Approach to Poetry* (New York: Thomas Y. Crowell Co., 1971), pp. 93–94.

5. What changes would you make in each of the following rough drafts?

a. Pretend that you are the writer of this essay. Decide what changes you need to make, then rewrite the paper in your notebook, incorporating those changes—use the Revision Guidelines (see pp. 105–106).

UTOPIA IN 1984

". . . Alone--free--the human being is always de-
feated. It must be so, because every human is doomed
to die, which is the greatest of all failures . . ."
(George Orwell, 1984). According to O'Brian in Orwell's 1984, this is the power behind the party,
(Oceania's ruling elite)--its negative Utopia. Orwell's negative Utopia contrasts a positive utopia
in the way it affects the public, how it's run and what
supports it.

The negative influence of the Utopia found in 1984 is
reflected in the bondage that its citizens are forced
to endure. These people have nothing secret from their
government--even their thoughts are a crime; "thought-
crime." They can only do what their government allows
for them: patriotic activities like the "hate sessions." They really do not have a life of their own.
For them to succeed in their community depends on devoting their life to Big Brother (the government). A
Utopia is usually defined as a heaven on earth. As de-
picted in 1984, however, it would more accurately be
described as a hell on earth. The party's Utopia only
benefits the very few belonging to the "inner party."
These chosen few have privileges in their choice of
food and a general freedom in their lifestyle. For the
rest of Oceania there's a constant fear of failing to
measure up to Big Brother's standards and therefore
being removed into a nonexistent state. Fear is the
true governing force behind their activities. A positive Utopia reflects freedom, and what will be beneficial overall. It centers on how society will be benefited as a whole rather than one particular minority.

How a government is run determines its success. How
success is measured depends on the goals involved. In
the case of 1984, the primary goal was obtaining and
maintaining power; "The Party seeks power entirely for
its own sake. We are not interested in the good of
others. We are interested solely in power. Not wealth
or luxury or long life or happiness; only power pure
power . . . " (Orwell, 1984 p. 217). Because power was
the main goal of "the party"--to maintain it--meant
constant monitoring against any threat that might hinder their purpose. A positive Utopia focuses on people,
how to better serve and benefit them. It does not need
to destroy them in order to maintain their goals, because the people are included into it. There is not
one elite class dictating over others. Instead the
people are represented by those people they agreed
on and are able to have some communication with.

Maintaining a purpose or direction in Utopia depends

on a type of support. Big Brother's support consists of a constant manipulation over the people, controlling every aspect of their life. A positive Utopia would be supported by people, because of this unifying element it could succeed in maintaining a sense of order. The government would not have to be fearful of its people, instead it would be supported by them.

Source: Lauren Howard. Printed with permission.

b. Assume that one of your classmates has asked you to help him revise the following draft of an essay. What advice would you give the writer?

IS A SLEEPING DOG APATHETIC?

College. To many it is considered as the final educational frontier, representing an unparalleled opportunity to broaden existing mental horizons. This time is essential for students to evaluate and compare cultural beliefs with their peers and thereby strengthen the values necessary for later life. In the past five years, young adults aged 16–22 have come under fire for supposedly possessing a strange disease that strips them of their will, ambition, and social worth. This crippling malady is called "student apathy": a self-perpetuating downward spiral that, if left uncorrected, will forever change the face of American society. Our critics, while projecting their antiquated values on modern students, make comparisons to ostriches in the sand by calling us the "Re-Run Generation." In actuality, apathy does not exist and these decadent labels only serve to create an ironically intriguing oxymoron because we are the first generation in history to successfully execute the "silent protest."
Misinformed older adults are quick to point at the alarming "regression" in academic standards (as published by Reagan's Department of Education) as undeniable proof that apathy exists. Declining performance statistics such as SAT/ACT scores prompt studies like "A Nation at Risk" to conclude that if the American educational community is not quickly overhauled, America is doomed to finish haplessly last in world technological markets. While competent education is important, these reports seem to, more often than not, resemble a little boy crying wolf. On college campuses today, professors are carrying the same yellowing lecture notes that they have been using for the last twenty-five years. This demonstrates that education hasn't radically changed. What has changed, however,

is the American bureaucracy's ability to figure out
where people are falling between the cracks.

For example, twenty years ago, young adults were
faced with the options of staying in school or being
drafted into the Vietnam conflict. This was a choice
slightly above life or death. For many years, the U.S.
military was a dumping ground for thousands of under-
educated, unemployed, and emotionally unstable individuals. At the time it was considered "okay"
because, instead of being dregs on society, they could
be channeled into a meaningful cause. There are no
distinct paths in today's world, which explains why
the decision to pursue an education is a bit more in
the grey area, nor is there a shelf to put unsuccessful
people on when they need it. It is the tide of malad-
justed citizens washing on the great society that is
causing people to see the flaws in the status quo that
have always existed.

The reason why the scholastic dropout rate is significantly higher than before is actually a combination of
two important factors. The first being the onset of computers, which have provided additional obstacles that
were undreamed of twenty years ago. Where the definition of "literate" before was the ability to read and
write, it has expanded to the ability to read, write,
and work a computer keyboard. To save time and personal
effort, many educational facilities are run by ma-
chines, which allows the learners to become more
easily intimidated. Because of this irrational, but
very real fear, many young people are jumping into a
hole in the hopes that this is merely a passing fad. To
counterbalance that, many educators are shifting computer literacy down to the elementary level. Secondly more students are finding their way into the
educational community from minority backgrounds. Inner
city pressures and lack of money are forcing students
to get an education via night school—and financial
prosperity from crime, if they are unsuccessful in
the classroom.

Over the past few years, organized student protests
on college campuses have dwindled off. This is a difficult pill to swallow for the survivors of the late
1960s when protesting was in vogue. It is an irrelevant
point that many of those protesters did not even know
why they were protesting, but they can say they tried.
The underlying causes of the sit-ins are twofold.
First, it was popular for people to become "martyrs."
Men with vision, such as Martin Luther King, Jr., and
Robert F. Kennedy, were being killed during the prime
of their campaigns and leaving long lines of fear and

frustration in their wake. The "protest" movement was just another way of saying misery loves company. Secondly, birth records show that more babies were born in 1946 than at any other point in previous history. It is suspicious that twenty-one years later (when these U.S. citizens were considered "legal" adults) Summer of Love (1967) sparked the anti-war movements. It may be concluded that 1967 was a giant birthday party that many would not live to see because of the war.

There is a feeling of futility among students when they attempt to concentrate on matters as a group. This is because any formal gathering by students that is unchaperoned, even with the most benevolent of intentions, is looked upon as a riot. Law enforcement departments view riots as serious matters and, particularly in the state of Colorado, put them down with excessive force. A recent popular example of this is the University of Colorado's Shantytown, a protest against apartheid in South Africa. Shantytown involved a group of students and their mimicry of the plight of the black people by living in wooden shacks on campus. CU's administration saw this as an embarrassment and forced Shantytown to be disassembled. A few weeks later, it reappeared in an area off campus. The police arrested everyone they could get their hands on, roughing up many who had surrendered in the process. These people who participated in this demonstration now have a police record, which will make it more difficult to get respectable jobs in the workforce. Simply, the majority of today's students do not feel the rewards of protesting outweigh the opportunities of changing the system from within.

American students today are of a different breed than they were twenty years ago. We come from a childhood that has seen the past generation stand up for what they "believe" in and still fail to change the world, even though they had superior numbers and opportunities. We live in an era where conservatism is at the heart of what we are, and that means taking each day and each event one step at a time. It is unjust that we have to be criticized for situations that we have no control over, yet that criticism only serves to make us stronger. Apathy in American society exists only in the broadened statement that we cannot cure everything overnight. Given time, who knows what we can change? Our strength lies in "overcoming the things we can, accepting the things we cannot . . . and the wisdom to know the difference."

Source: Glenn Smith. Printed with permission.

Suggestions for Writing

1. Since revising means re-seeing, writers occasionally choose to re-see by starting all over. [Donald Murray chose to start all over when he rewrote his text *A Writer Teaches Writing* (Boston: Houghton Mifflin, 1968).] Look over the essays you have done in the past and select one to use as the basis for an entirely new paper on the same subject. If you have saved essays from high school, you might want to choose one of those. Reread the paper, trying to remember the assignment, the issues you were confronting at the time, and so on. Then redraft the paper until you are satisfied that your new draft presents an accurate statement about how you currently feel about the topic. Then revise your new version of this paper.

2. Choose a paper that you wrote several weeks ago. Revise this paper using the revision guidelines suggested in this chapter.

The Writing Situation

5

Overview of Writing Strategies

In this chapter, we will introduce four important strategies for exploring the relationship between a writer and his or her subject and audience:

1. Determine your purpose for writing.

2. Explore your attitude toward your subject.

3. Use language to imply attitude.

4. Explore your attitude toward your audience.

Understanding the Writing Situation

Writers are a lot like jugglers. Sometimes, everything proceeds smoothly—the balls stay in the air, the words say what the writer wants them to say. But other times, both jugglers and writers lose control. The balls fall to the ground; the words fail to communicate the writer's purpose. Jugglers and writers have so much to attend to at once that it's no wonder when, occasionally, they lose control of some facet of their task.

We'd like to use the term *writing situation* to describe the predicament writers find themselves in with each new writing task. At some point, they need to make decisions. What is their precise topic? What is their attitude toward that topic? What is their purpose for writing? Who is their audience? What is their attitude toward their audience? What is their writing environment? (In other words, what circumstances surround their writing?) By answering these questions, writers learn how to get a clear perspective on their writing. They learn how to adjust their text to the particular demands of their assignment. How successfully they assess their writing situation can make the difference between a poor paper and an excellent one.

No matter what kind of paper you are writing, you need to clarify your purpose for writing and your attitude toward your subject. If you don't have an attitude, you should work hard at finding one. You're not going to write a good paper for any subject without some obvious interest in it, some personal connection to it. You should find a topic that intrigues you or you should try to customize an assigned topic so that it fits your interests. If you don't have a purpose, you need to create one. You won't be able to communicate with your readers if you haven't established a reason or purpose for writing.

As you know, most writing isn't exclusively for you. College assignments and writing you do on the job are inevitably directed to others—an audience whose attitudes toward you and your subject can vary from sympathetic, to hostile, to indifferent. Getting a grasp of that audience and of your entire writing situation can help you make accurate decisions about how to approach your subject and your audience—how much to tell them about the subject, how you want them to perceive your attitude toward the subject, how you want them to perceive your attitude toward them, and how you want them to perceive you.

As you also know, you can't focus on everything at once as you write. The various components of writing overlap and interweave, so it sometimes seems that everything is happening simultaneously. Writing is a land with indistinct and shifting borders. And nowhere are these shifting borders less sharply defined than in the subject of this chapter, the complex relationship between subject, audience, writing environment, and writer.

You can think of the relationship between subject, audience, writing environment, and writer in terms of the diagram of the *writing situation* provided by Table 5.1. Each arrow in this diagram points to one factor the writer must consider in a writing situation. The text that results from any writing situation is the result of the writer's assessment of the entire writing situation. To help you understand just how each part of this situation affects the other parts, we'd like to define the *writing situation* and its components.

1. *The writer.* You, with your personality characteristics, your purpose for writing, your knowledge of the subject, your attitudes and feelings about the subject, and your relationship toward and feelings about the audience.

TABLE 5.1   *The Writing Situation*

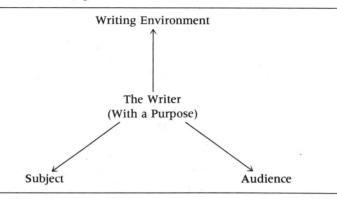

2. *The subject.* What you are writing about. The subject matter in general, the specific segment of the subject you are dealing with in a writing project, the main point you are working to prove.

3. *The audience.* Your readers—the people you expect to read the writing project, with the knowledge and feelings they have about the subject and about you. The obvious target audience (such as the teacher who assigns a paper), as well as other people who may read the writing.

4. *The writing environment.* The circumstances surrounding the writing—including specific requirements of the assignment, either self-imposed or established for you by someone else; the physical conditions and the time constraints under which you work; the historical era or political environment in which you work; the language you use to write.

Each component of the *writing situation* can change, slightly or significantly, from one writing situation to another, or even from one point in a writing project to another. Consider how various factors of the writing situation can change:

1. The subject alone can vary from one writing situation to another.

2. In different situations (a variation in audience or purpose, for example), a single subject may be written about in different ways.

3. Within one subject, your focus often changes as you draft (as your *purpose* changes and you work toward a final draft).

4. What you know and how you feel about your subject—your attitude toward the subject—changes over time, as you discover more about the subject, and influences the *purpose* of your writing.

5. Various readers (a teacher, students in your class, students and professors in your major, the campus paper, the local town paper, your home paper, your family) could appreciate the same subject, but

each of these readers would come to the subject with different interests, backgrounds, and reasons for reading.

6. Your attitude toward the same audience may differ from one writing situation to the next. Your feelings toward some of these readers may change according to the situation, so that you feel more or less comfortable, fearful, confident, insecure, able to offer information, etc.

7. Readers' attitudes toward you could vary from consideration, friendliness, and agreement with your views to criticism, apathy, and disagreement with your point of view.

8. The writing environment could change. You may transfer to a different university, you may change majors, local politics may change, or national trends may affect you and your attitude toward your topic.

Each part of the communications situation influences all the others. That is, changing one factor in the relationship between writer, subject, environment and audience changes the whole relationship.

▪ Exploring the Writing Situation

Not taking time to explore the writing situation can lead to fuzzy or blocked communication. Misunderstanding or misinterpreting your writing situation can result in writing that fails to communicate. In the following memo to his faculty colleagues, John Eisenberg, a professor in the College of Agriculture, has not analyzed his communications situation before writing. Read this memo carefully so that you will be able to discuss it with your classmates.

An Example of a Message That Fails to Communicate

```
MEMORANDUM

TO: Faculty Colleagues

From: John Eisenberg

Subject: Institute for Distribution and Development

Let me introduce the concept and purpose of the Insti-
tute for Distribution and Development. I look forward
to the Institute emerging as a significant university
resource and hope that you will share my optimism.

The Institute's goals are (1) to create a true center
for excellence at XYZ University in this important
field, (2) through this center to link XYZ University
to a wider global community of scholars and practition-
ers interested in the distributional dimensions of eco-
```

nomic growth, and (3) to advance the state of knowledge and the range of its applications in this arena.

In pursuit of these goals, the Institute is authorized to seek the following objectives:

1. Conduct basic and applied research.
2. Develop and deliver educational programs.
3. Provide technical assistance and consultant services.
4. Stimulate and nurture a global community of interest.
5. Maintain a library and other resources in support of the above objectives.

Each of the above assumes an explicit, if not dominant, focus on the distributional and poverty dimensions of growth. The twin razors of scholarship and a commitment to improving the human condition will prioritize the Institute's activities. Research will dominate. Also important will be the dissemination and/or policy or program application of knowledge. Technical assistance activities, when they are undertaken, will be clearly related to the Institute's chosen field of specialization.

I expect the Institute's research activities to be multidisciplinary, as opposed to interdisciplinary. Several disciplines have a great deal to contribute in this field and the Institute will be eclectic in soliciting these contributions. There is a vast unfinished research agenda of issues relating distribution and development. The Institute seeks to advance the frontiers of knowledge in these areas. And, to my way of thinking, this requires the power and depth of disciplinary paradigms and methods.

Within these guidelines, if there are ways that the Institute can work with you, to strengthen, facilitate or highlight your program, I would like to hear from you. In the near future, we may be able to assist with the following:

1. Conceptualization and program definition
2. Proposal preparation
3. Management and/or administration of sponsored research
4. Contacts with other interested scholars
5. Publication

The Institute will be in a formulative phase for its first year. Suggestions, ideas, or constructive criti-

cisms are welcomed. We will issue a newsletter covering the Institute's program and significant events
beyond XYZ University in the field of distribution and
development. If you would like to receive copies, let
me know.

If you were a faculty member, how would you respond to this
memo? Why does the author's message fail? As you've probably already determined, the author's message fails because he has not as-
sessed his audience's knowledge of the subject. As you began reading
the memo, you probably got lost as soon as the writer failed to explain
what the "Institute for Distribution and Development" is. Because the
author knows what it is, he assumes others know about it, too. He is
wrong. As a result, the entire message—his attempt to explain the Institute for Distribution and Development studies—is lost on his audience. No one can understand a writer's explanation of a subject if they
don't understand the subject in the first place.

The *writing situation* in the above memo can be explained as follows:
The writer's *purpose* is to let other faculty members know about a new
institute that he is in charge of. He is proud of the institute and wants
to encourage faculty to write to him if they can think of ways that the
institute can work with them. The *subject* of the memo is the Institute
for Distribution and Development. The author never defines or explains his subject. The *audience* for the memo is the writer's "colleagues," other faculty. The *writing environment* is the university—with
many different colleges. The *writer* has obviously failed in assessing
his readers' knowledge of his subject. He seems to expect his readers
in different colleges to know exactly what he is talking about. He assumes they are following his points. But unless they, too, are in the
College of Agriculture, they probably won't know what the subject is;
they probably won't be able to follow his discussion of the objectives
for the Institute, which, by the way, is an organization devoted to
helping Third World countries improve their economies.

■ Writing for Different Audiences

Not all writers are as unskilled as the author of the preceding memo in
assessing their writing situations. Effective writers take the time to assess their purpose for communicating, and thus are able to decide not
only why they are writing, but what they want their audience to know
about the subject, and how much they need to tell them. Looking at
how a writer effectively shifts from one audience to another can help
you understand the power you have as a writer when you fully understand your writing situation.

A student in one of our classes borrowed his friend's new motorcycle—a shiny, new machine that his friend had saved money to buy.
Driving near the campus, he went through an intersection on a green
light and hit a car. As it turns out, the other driver also had a green

light; some sort of malfunction was at fault. The student wound up in the hospital with a broken leg, as well as other injuries. The motorcycle was a total wreck.

This student had to write three *different* letters describing the accident, his injuries, the condition of the motorcycle, and other necessary information. He used many specific details to help his readers "see" what took place. Most important, as he wrote each letter (describing the same accident), he had a different reader in mind:

1. His friend—The person who saved money from a part-time job and cut back on cigarettes and beer in order to buy the motorcycle.

2. A relative—A "loved one," a person who cares a great deal about him.

3. The City Safety Director—The person in charge of traffic lights in the town and so, in a sense, the person responsible for the accident.

Here are the letters he wrote. When you finish reading them, compare them. Try to decide how the student's purpose varied in each letter. Note how he uses details differently in the letters. Determine whether there are different "sounds" or tones to the letters.

An Example of a Letter to a Friend

Dear Paula,

I'm sorry that this is so hard to read. You know that my handwriting is bad enough normally, but with my right arm in this cast and a splint taped to my "pinkie" finger it really gets ridiculous! That's right, my arm is broken! So are two fingers and my nose, and I've got a bruise down my right side about as purple as eggplant.

It all happened yesterday after you let me take your bike down to the carry-out. I was coming slowly down that curve above Fifth and Ash when the light turned green. So I coasted on into the intersection and WHAM! A blue Toyota grazed the rear wheel and flipped me over onto my right side. I was all scratched and bloody for a while, but luckily I was going slow and so was he, and I didn't really hit my head or anything. So I should be out of the hospital in another day, and I should be out of the cast by July.

The guy's insurance is going to take care of the repairs—or maybe the city will. It seems that there was a short-circuit or something and we both had green lights. I was in the intersection first and had the right of way, the officer said. So if the city doesn't fix up the bike, the other company will.

I am sorry, Paula, and I'll ask my insurance agent how we can get you your money as quickly as possible.

Sincerely,

Mark

An Example of a Letter to a Relative

Dear Dad,

Thanks for your flowers and all the cards! Yes, I know you are worried about me, and sorry this had to happen at college and not back home. But you really don't need to spend the money to fly out here to be with me in the hospital. By the time you'd get here, I'll be back at the apartment with a cast covered with signatures, and maybe a little bit of a black eye.

I guess I bounce better than Paula's motorcycle. I just got skinned up some and cracked that one bone. The cycle looks more like it needs intensive care. The back wheel is bent so you can't even turn it, and the frame twists enough that you can see a slight curve. We were both going so slow, it's hard to figure how a little Toyota could do that much damage. I'm just glad it did the damage to the bike and just bumped me around some.

Give my love to Mom. And tell her, yes I will stay off "those two-wheeled contraptions." See you soon for a good long summer vacation.

Love,

Mark

An Example of a Letter to the City Safety Director

Dear Mr. McGuire,

At 4:15 p.m. last Tuesday, I had an accident at the corner of Fifth and Ash. As you can tell from the attached letter from my physician and the two repair estimates, this was a serious accident. Because I have to wear a cast for the next two months, I will not be able to keep my summer job as a lifeguard at Central Pool. It is possible that the broken nose and damage to my right cheek will require plastic surgery later. And, of course, with a twisted frame, the new Yamaha 650 I was riding really can't be repaired and will need to be replaced.

I am writing you because, as you undoubtedly know

from Officer Sullivan's accident report, all of the injuries and property damage resulted from a malfunction
in your city's traffic light. My insurance agent has
already contacted the city attorney about this matter.
But I wanted to write you personally, to ask if you
could help speed up the settlement process, and
also to inquire at what level you may be thinking of
compensating me for my lost salary. I estimate that
the malfunction in your traffic light will cost me
$1500 that I need for my college expenses next fall.
     What I want is fair treatment, not a lawsuit. So I
thought I should contact you directly to find out how
the city plans to respond to this problem.

Respectfully,

Mark A. Donnelson

In the preceding letters, you can see some pretty sharp differences, and some patterns to the differences. For example, notice how the letters reflect

1. different purposes in writing. Writing to Paula, a friend and the owner of the motorcycle, Mark apologizes and works in different ways to keep a friendship intact. For his father, he tries to relieve anxiety about his condition. For the Safety Director, he tries to get the city to pay hospital and replacement expenses, and to reimburse him for lost salary.

2. different strategies in the selection of details. To his father, Mark says more about the motorcycle and less about his injuries, since he wants to downplay the injuries by contrast with the horrible condition of the motorcycle. For the friend, he reverses the strategy: telling details of his pain to deflect Paula's anger over the mangled motorcycle.

3. differences in the tone or flavor of the writing. For his friend and father, Mark writes conversationally and "person to person." But, for the Safety Director, he writes more formally, with bigger words and more official-sounding sentences.

The preceding letters reveal a good deal about the relationship between writer, subject, and reader. The writer changed *what* he had to say about the accident and *how* he said it, according to which audience he was addressing. Helping you make such changes—and so exercise effective control over the relationships of subject, writer, and reader— is the central goal of this chapter. In later chapters, you will have the opportunity to apply your understanding of the writing situation as you work on different kinds of writing assignments.

IDEA FILE: COMPUTER WRITING

Creating Letter Templates

Create a "template" (or *master*) to guide you when you write in a certain form (letter, outline, list). If you use the same form later, for a different subject, you can use your *template file* so you don't have to "reinvent the wheel" every time you work. To make letter-writing easier, consider setting up letter-template files. Create a separate file for a friendly letter, a business letter, a memorandum, and so on. If you have a way of organizing your disk by "subdirectories," you can create a directory called "letters" and then make a separate "subdirectory" for each specific letter format. Remember to save the letter you are writing with a name different from that of the original template. Then your original file will remain "clean" and you will be able to reuse it.

(Your Name)
(Street Address)
(City, State)
(Zip Code)

(Name of Addressee)
(Street Address)
(City, State)
(Zip Code)

Dear (name):

Sincerely,

(Your Name)

Strategies for Exploring Writing Situations

You can't avoid the fact that the relationships between writer and subject take a good while to grow. When the relationship will begin to grow is not always predictable. But you can speed up this evolutionary process a bit by consciously controlling your *intentions* for different parts of your writing sessions. Even if your primary intention is to *draft,* you can consciously decide to *generate* ideas for awhile. But instead of generating ideas about your topic or about the content of the paper, why not generate ideas about your audience and your attitude? Rapid writing strategies can give you time to explore your relationship. You might decide to think directly about your attitude toward the subject each time you begin or end an especially effective drafting session.

We can't help you with your specific writing situations, but we can give you some guidance. The following strategies can help you assess your assignments.

■ Strategy 1—Determine Your Purpose for Writing

You don't have to explore your writing situation before you begin an assignment, but at some time in the life of your writing project, take time to think about your purpose for writing—the reason you are committing words to the page. In your writing, make sure that you provide your readers with some way of determining your *purpose* for communicating with them.

Consider the writing situations and the purpose in each of the following statements:

> **Statement 1:** "We need to control the amount of carbon monoxide that pollutes the air. Using ethanol instead of gasoline would help the situation quite a bit."
>
> *Writing situation:* Letter to constituents
>
> *Writer:* Colorado legislator
>
> *Purpose:* To demonstrate a commitment to the governor's plan to require Coloradoans to use ethanol-based fuel.
>
> **Statement 2:** "The idea of using ethanol is just an attempt to give money to a special interest group, the corn producers, who supply much of the ethanol in use today."
>
> *Writing situation:* Newspaper editorial
>
> *Writer:* Newspaper editor
>
> *Purpose:* To convince readers that the real idea behind using ethanol is a plan to help one special interest group—the corn producers.
>
> **Statement 3:** "Ethanol fuel may be acceptable, but until I know that it won't harm my fuel tank, I won't use it."
>
> *Writing situation:* Letter to editor of local newspaper
>
> *Writer:* Concerned citizen
>
> *Purpose:* To object to the proposed policy of requiring motorists to purchase ethanol-based fuel in the winter.

When you formulate your purpose for writing, try to establish an authentic purpose, such as those indicated by the preceding statements, not just a matter-of-fact purpose, such as "to complete this assignment." And even though you probably won't state your purpose directly to your readers, try to make your purpose readily apparent. Having a distinct purpose in mind as you draft will add power and conviction to your writing. Answer the following questions in order to clarify your purpose:

Establishing Your Purpose for Writing

1. Why are you writing? (To express outrage, to explain, to entertain, etc.)

2. What do you hope to accomplish as a result of your writing? (To change your readers' opinions, to help your readers understand your situation, to show your readers that you understand their situation, etc.)

IDEA FILE: COMPUTER WRITING

Role Playing to Clarify Purpose and Audience

You'll need a partner for this exercise. Before you begin, explain to your partner that you want him or her to assume the role of one of your readers—either someone who agrees with you or someone who is likely to disagree. Type the following into your computer:

Writing Situation:
Subject:
Audience:
Purpose:

WRITER:
READER:

WRITER:
READER:

Next, *save the entire file* and call it something like "reader. (You'll be able to use it again for another topic.) Then, using the COPY command of your word processor, copy the "WRITER" and the "READER" tags about twelve times. Take turns filling in the blanks as you "talk" in writing with your partner. When you finish, save your file under a different name. *Remember,* all your writing should be done on the computer screen. Then you'll have a record of how your audience might respond to your ideas. Here's an example of how you could use this technique:

Writing Situation: Letter to editor of campus paper
Subject: Student Attendance at Football Games
Audience: Students

Purpose: To convince more students to attend sports events

WRITER: I think it's a darn shame that students only support the football team when the team is winning.

READER: Don't expect me to waste my time when I've got other things to do. I don't even like football.

WRITER: Whether you like football or not isn't the issue. I think that if you like your school, you should show up at the games.

▪ Strategy 2—Explore Your Attitude Toward Your Subject

It is important, in effective college writing, to discover your attitude toward your subject, and to project it in your writing. Usually this discovery evolves slowly as you

1. dig beneath the surface of a "general" subject and discover a more sharply focused "real" subject.

2. develop feelings about your subject in the process of drafting.

3. try to anticipate how different readers might respond to your words.

4. share your writing with other students, listen to the kinds of specific responses they have, and learn what they think you might do to make your writing clearer and more interesting.

Early in the drafting process, you should take some time to explore, directly, how you really feel about your subject. Here is one way to use rapid writing when your *intention* is to explore your attitude toward your subject:

Using Rapid Writing to Explore Your Attitude

1. After you have completed a draft, or after a good drafting session, shift intentions. Try to generate ideas about each of these questions:

   a. How do I feel about my topic?

   b. Can I be coolly rational about the subject, or does it make me mad, sad, bitter, fearful, nostalgic, resentful, happy, etc.?

   c. Have my experiences and beliefs colored the way I feel about this subject? Which ones?

   d. Are there specific things I have discovered about the subject, so far, that really grate against values of mine? What?

   e. If I wanted to attack this subject in some way, would I be likely to do so respectfully, sarcastically, as quickly as possible, emotionally, humorously, etc.? What about the subject makes me think this might be my approach?

   f. If I were going to explain the topic or argue in favor of it, would

I be likely to do so with objectivity and detachment, or would my feelings show through? What about the topic makes me think this might be my approach?

2. Read over your answers to those questions. With this information in mind, write a *Statement of Intended Attitude* for your writing project. In several sentences, set down what the attitude is (at the current moment) that you want to express in your paper. Include a good sense of what your project will "be about," what sort of attitude you want to express, and how you now think you could project this attitude. For instance: "It really irritates me to see other students oversleep and drag into class five minutes late every day. I plan to express my anger by showing just how discourteous it is to come in late. But I think I can do this in a funny way by showing how silly these students look when they bustle in, out of breath, looking like they had just made some superhuman effort to get to a ten o'clock class at all."

3. If you have confused or divided attitudes toward the subject, you could write several different Statements of Intended Attitude in order to try to discover how you really feel about it.

Completing a Statement of Intended Attitude will not, by itself, work any magic on a project you are drafting. But the effort you expend in writing it—the thought focused on subject and attitude in the process of writing about them—may pay off when you begin your next drafting session on the project. Remember the significance of your *intentions* as a writer? Well, if you stir up thoughts and feelings toward your subject and if you think about how you might express those feelings, you will be putting yourself into a good frame of mind for writing. Because your *intentions* for your writing sessions have changed, your mind may shift gears. When you decide to stop drafting and start generating ideas, your hands, eyes, and brain have a chance to actively work together and you may find *shades* of your attitude beginning to emerge as you write. That attitude may continue to develop (or even change) during your drafting sessions. In some cases, you may not begin to develop an attitude toward your subject until you've begun drafting.

■ Strategy 3—Use Language to Imply Attitude

It may trouble you to think that *"shades* of your attitude" can show in your writing. Doesn't that seem awfully vague—that attitudes don't show up, just their formless *shades*? Isn't it possible to be more direct? Yes it is, and in much of the writing you will do in college and in your career, you probably should work to be more direct. But imagine how you would react if you opened a magazine, spotted an interesting sounding article on the eccentric behaviors of college students, started to read, and found a first paragraph this direct:

> It really irritates me to see other students oversleep and drag into class five minutes late every day. I think this is just plain discourteous. Not only that, but the people who do it usually look downright silly—bustling in, out of breath, looking as if they had just made some superhuman effort to get to their ten o'clock class at all.

If you were to read much further into that article, we would be surprised. That opening is true to its writer's Statement of Intended Attitude. But such an explicit and obvious treatment—sort of beating the point with a heavy club the way newspaper letters-to-the-editor often do—can be just as dull as it is clear.

The blunt, dull statement of attitude can be important when you use it—between drafts or at the end of a productive drafting session—to sharpen your sense of your subject and how you feel about it. But as you move toward complete drafts, you should try to submerge your Statement of Intended Attitude in specific details about your subject so that readers understand your attitude without feeling that they are reading an editorial on the subject. In the following example, the writer does not state a disapproving attitude too directly, but still communicates a judgment about the discourteousness and silliness of some students:

CLASS TIME

10:05. I'd just started the daily-quiz problem in Statistics when Marv blustered through the door five minutes late—unshaven, out of breath, and carrying a Wendy's carry-out cup of coffee. "I had to stop to get a 'transfusion,' he whispered, wiggling the cup at me as he passed. "Did I miss anything?"

He'd missed the daily-quiz assignment, of course—for maybe the tenth time that term. I'd been interrupted, and lost another couple of minutes rereading the story problem. Julie had to duck to avoid Marv's backpack as he moved past her, and Tim had to stop to move his coat so Marv couldn't splash coffee on it while he was rummaging for a pen and notebook.

Marv is a fictitious character. Rather, he is a composite of students who can't seem to make it to class on time (even though they'd never think of registering for any course that met before ten), and who never seem to think about how irritating they are to students who do manage to get their alarms set, to get to breakfast—even to get to class on time.

Campus legend has it that there once was a history professor who liked teaching eight o'clock classes and

```
deliberately locked the door at 8:01. Maybe we should
try that on Marv and his buddies--only with ten o'clock
courses.
```

In some kinds of writing, you may want to keep your Statement of Intended Attitude even more to yourself and try to imply for your readers how you feel by the details you select about your subject and the words and phrases you use. Think of it, if you want, as the old game of Twenty Questions in which you give clues and the reader tries to guess what you feel about your subject. In this attitude game, of course, your goal is not to stump your readers, but to help them guess correctly. With each succeeding draft, you should try to eliminate false clues and to sharpen the precision of your words so that readers do not feel that they are guessing about your ideas and attitude—even though they do not have to put up with dull, direct statements of attitude.

The following short sketch implies the author's attitude toward carnivals, but never states her attitude directly. You won't find any blunt-object statements about carnivals—statements like, "In this paper I plan to show that I think carnivals are . . . ." On the other hand, you won't have any doubt how the writer feels about carnivals:

```
                        CARNIVAL

    Someone is dead because of the carnival--dead
because one of the rides broke and dead because the
barker wheedled him into buying a ticket. And you
heard the screams and the horrible shattering crash as
the car hit the earth. And he was dead, his last mo-
ment lived in a frenzy of horror, feeling himself fall
lower and lower, helpless, for he couldn't stop his
own momentum.
    Now the winking rainbow lights of the carnival seem
to be the eyes of a person hiding something ugly inside
himself. They seem beautiful if you don't look
closely, but if you do, you see bare bulbs covered
with dirt, blinking as if they can't stand your close
scrutiny.
    Look at the barker and what do you see? A middle-
aged man who is cynical and has very dirty hands. He
grins, beckons, calls, and cajoles. He wheedles,
smiles, begs, and sells. A ticket to death. You tell
yourself that he didn't know what was going to hap-
pen. But his eyes seem cold, almost sinister, as he
takes your money and directs you onto one of the
monster's appendages. He grins as he places the bar
across your lap, but the grin seems more leering than
friendly.
```

> The rides look beautiful because of the use of lights.
> The ride's motion carries you to new heights: a deli-
> cious, flying feeling, with maybe a little fear for
> spice. You laugh and scream, clutching the handle for an
> ounce of security. At least that is what you usually do.
> But tonight is different.

Your attitude toward your subject, as we have said, can come through, by implication, in the words you choose. "Carnival" shows this in its repeated use of words and phrases that connote the sneaky or the sordid or the horrifying: "wheedled," "horrible shattering crash," "frenzy of horror," "bare bulbs covered with dirt," "blinking as if they can't stand your close scrutiny," "cynical and has very dirty hands," "his eyes seem cold, almost sinister," etc. Such language works to imply the writer's attitude toward carnivals, after she had witnessed a shocking accident on one of the rides. Since the emotion was so strong in the writer, the use of language to convey the emotion is strong—probably too heavy-handed for most writing projects you will have in college or in your career. But "Carnival" is a good model for you to work with as you explore how to use your language to imply your attitudes.

Probably, there will be few times you want to write an emotional sketch like "Carnival" unless you are working at fiction writing. But the principle of finding and using the right word for your attitude— for instance, *wheedled* rather than *persuaded* to describe how the carnival barker sells tickets—is important in any writing project. A feel for the right words and phrases is something you need to develop as you move through the remaining chapters in this book and as you move from purely personal exploratory drafting toward drafts intended for other readers.

After you have written a Statement of Intended Attitude, you might begin a drafting session by asking and answering the following questions (either on paper or on a computer monitor):

Expression of Intended Attitude

1. What examples would best suggest my intended attitude to my audience?

2. What specific words and phrases would imply this point of view toward the subject?

3. Could I, and should I, try to avoid all direct statements of attitude and to rely on words and phrases to imply my attitude?

4. If some more direct attitude statements are necessary, how can I avoid being blunt, obvious, and dull?

In trying to get the "feel" of how words may imply your attitude about your subject, what you are really doing is trying to sense how readers may respond to your words. The writer of "Carnival" knew what she thought about carnivals. She did not need to pay attention to her words to imply anything to herself; she groped toward words that would suggest to readers the attitude she wanted to suggest to them. The same thing will be true of your writing projects. Exploratory drafting and other activities will take you into your subject so that you can begin to understand your attitudes toward it. But in working on later drafts, you will need to pay attention to your readers. And that is one of the reasons we urge you to work collaboratively with other students in your class—to gain experience sensing how other people react to the words and phrases that you have chosen to communicate your ideas.

■ Strategy 4—Explore Your Attitude Toward Your Audience

Your relationship to your subject is quite important to the shape and effectiveness of your writing. Exactly the same thing is true of the network of relationships between you, your subject, and your readers. What you understand and how you feel about your readers is part of the picture. Just as important is what your readers understand and how they feel about the subject and about the image of you they see reflected in your writing. The effectiveness of your writing depends to a considerable extent on what you do to write "for your readers"—to let your understanding of your readers' attitudes and familiarity with the subject shape how you write.

It is not enough to decide that the audience for a paper on "Why I Want a Career in the Navy" is going to be a teacher who has assigned a paper on the broad topic of "Careers," or that it is going to be the Admissions Board of the U.S. Naval Academy. You must define your audience more clearly by considering its assumptions and attitudes, its interest in the subject, and its general knowledge of the subject. The Admissions Review Board, for example, would have a positive attitude about naval careers and would be sympathetic with your career plans. But, knowing a great deal about the subject and facing the tough job of evaluating hundreds of applications, the Admissions Review Board could be very exacting as it studied your essay. On the other hand, your writing teacher's limited knowledge of work in the Navy might make him or her a less demanding reader. But if the teacher's religious beliefs made him a confirmed pacifist, or if her politics had a definite anti-military bias, you could find yourself writing to a skeptical or even hostile reader.

If you are writing a paper for a college professor (or a report for an employer, a funding proposal for a community project, or a job-application letter), you do not want hostile readers. You do not want to write so that you anger or alienate readers. And so you should try to avoid approaches that will bore, puzzle, or insult readers, or otherwise set up barriers between your writing and the people you are writing for. This does not mean that you should hide your attitude toward the subject or adopt a phony attitude with which you think your readers will agree. It does mean that you should handle examples and language so that your readers can understand your attitude and why you hold it, even if they do not share your view.

For instance, you probably do not agree that carnivals are sleazy and treacherous, but as you read "Carnival" you probably could understand the writer's attitude. Knowing that most of her readers would not share her attitude, the writer avoided making a direct statement that would challenge you to disagree: "Carnivals are terrible places, deadly places! They should be outlawed and the people who run them should be imprisoned as the thieves and murderers they are." Instead, she gave examples of surface glitter over deeper dirt, and she described the accident in emotionally charged language. So rather than being an argumentative or hostile reader, you probably had a more positive feeling of understanding how a witness to a terrible accident could have negative feelings about carnivals.

In order to develop this positive sort of relationship with readers, you should try to create a mental image of the readers for whom you are writing—their attitudes and assumptions about your subject, their knowledge or interest in the subject, their likely responses to the various images of you that might slip between the lines of your writing. So as your writing project approaches its final drafts, you should try to create a picture of the readers you expect to read your words.

After you have finished a draft or a good drafting session, write rapidly as you spend a couple of minutes answering each of the questions in the following questionnaire:

Questionnaire for Assessing Your Audience

The Environment of the Audience

1. What is his/her physical, social, and economic status? (Age, environment, health, ethnic ties, class, income.)

2. What is his/her educational and cultural experience?

3. What are his/her ethical concerns and hierarchy of values? (Home, family, job, success, religion, money, car, social acceptance.)

4. What are his/her common myths and prejudices?

The Subject Interpreted by the Audience

5. How much does the reader know about what I want to say?

6. What is the opinion of the reader about my subject?

7. How strong is that opinion?

8. How willing is he/she to act on that opinion?

9. Why does he/she react the way he/she does?

The Relationship of the Audience and the Writer

10. What is the reader's knowledge and attitude about me?

11. What are our shared experiences, attitudes, values, myths, prejudices? In other words, what kinds of experiences have I had that my readers might have had, too?

12. What is my purpose/aim in addressing this audience?

13. Is this an appropriate audience for my subject?

14. What is the role I wish to assign to the audience? What role do I want to assume for the audience?

Source: Adapted from Fred Pfister and Joanne Petrick, "A Heuristic Model for Creating a Writer's Audience," *College Composition and Communication*, 31 (May 1980), pp. 214–215.

IDEA FILE: COMPUTER WRITING

Audience Information

If you want, you can create an audience-data *template* in your computer disk. Then, whenever you feel that you need to get a clearer picture of your "typical" reader, you can fill in the blanks on your chart. Remember to save your filled-in file with a new name so that you can keep your original template file clear and ready to reuse.

Audience Data

Age: Health: Ethnicity:

Educational Background:

Religion:

Occupation:

Honors or Awards:

Preferred Cultural or Educational Activities:

Type of Car:

Approximate Cost of Home:

Other:

You can use the preceding questionnaire any time you feel you have finished a draft or an especially effective drafting session. The first time you use it, you might work systematically to answer each question as fully as possible. Later, you might skim the list, looking for questions that strike you as useful to whatever stage you are at in your work. You can also use the questionnaire in your writing group, during class time or less formally.

We hope you now understand that sorting through the relationships between subject, writer, reader, and environment is a necessary part of completing most writing projects. After all, analyzing these relationships

1. gives you a better sense of your subject by letting you see it from perspectives other than your own.

2. helps you avoid irritating or insulting your readers unnecessarily, and so removes some large blocks to effective communication.

3. allows you to imply an attitude toward your subject that is consistent with your stated purposes.

4. helps you revise drafts by making you more sensitive to the needs your readers may have as they try to follow the track of your logic toward your conclusions.

These qualities are important to achieve in most of your college writing. But this does not mean that you must use strategies from this chapter at any definite point in a writing project. Often, it may make sense to use audience or attitude strategies from this chapter to help you change direction or emphasis between one draft and another. But you should also be prepared to just let changes in the relationships between subject, writer, reader, and environment take place naturally as your writing project moves toward completion. For instance:

1. Worrying about your reader does not make sense when you are just trying to get words down so you can see what you think about the topic. But there may be times (such as an "irate citizen" complaining about a faulty traffic signal, or a person sending a friend a sympathy note after a parent's death) when a sense of the reader out there seems to take care of itself and can even help the words flow.

2. Your sense of your audience may change as you write. For example, many students think, incorrectly, that they should write for a teacher-grader, when most composition teachers would prefer to let students develop projects for a writing environment a lot more "real" and natural than the artificial situation that exists in a writing class. As you progress through a few drafts in a writing project—or through several papers in the course—you may find yourself

shifting from your teacher as the only reader to a more useful audience: your classmates and the teacher, other students in your major as well as your teacher, the broad range of students and teachers who read the campus paper, etc.

3. Your sense of your subject will change the more you write about it, narrow your topic, clarify your main point, and find new information through research and your personal observations. So committing yourself too soon to a specific audience or attitude may make less sense than planning to focus on these things after you feel you have completed a full draft. Frequently, in college writing, you do not know enough about a subject early in a writing project to decide what your role in writing will eventually be. That is, when you just begin a research project you know so little that the roles of *expert* or *peer* are probably not possible for you. As you learn more about your subject, though, your growing confidence may be reflected in your writing and you will find it easier to choose which type of tone or identity you want to adopt as writer.

4. Your role may change, too, as you come to know your readers better. For instance, as you work through early drafts of a paper, you may be able to tell from your teacher's comments that you know more about the subject than you think—that, compared to the teacher, you are an expert on your subject. But as you broaden your readership to include other students and other professors, you probably would sense that, within the wider audience, there are enough people more expert than you that it makes more sense to present yourself as a *peer* in your writing.

Summary

■ Audience Response and Readable Writing

This chapter has suggested several strategies for developing a sense of your readers that can keep you from setting up unnecessary barriers between your writing and your audience. As you work with these strategies, you may feel that you are analyzing your readers in order to reduce friction that could reduce the effectiveness of your communication. But such public relations work is only part of what you were doing—and not the most important part, at that.

Think back to the Questionnaire for Assessing Your Audience (pp. 147–148). Those questions did not just deal with attitudes, assumptions, prejudices. There were also questions about your readers' educational background and their familiarity with your subject. Such questions can help you improve the clarity and readability of your writing, by helping you sense how much background information your audience may need to understand your ideas. For instance, if you were writing a paper about the common cold, once you realized that your readers had very little medical information about the common cold, you would sense intuitively that you should provide a fair amount of general background information if you want to use technical details as well as personal experiences in an article on the common cold. Once you understand that you are writing about the book *Megatrends* for the general group of people who read the campus paper, rather than for the professor who assigned the book, you will know it is important to write clearly, with plenty of examples and as little specialized jargon as possible.

Readers who know a lot about your subject may be able to find their way to your point in spite of organizational tangles or a lack of clarifying examples. But other readers can't. Even readers who know your subject very well—including professors—still prefer writing with clear organization, widely-understandable vocabulary, and plenty of examples. And they are likely to be irritated and put-off when they have to struggle through writing filled with

1. complex ideas and details that you do not understand well enough to explain to others.

2. inconsistent logic and disorganized presentation of ideas.

3. lack of clear, smooth transitions from one point to the next.

4. few or ineffective examples and supporting evidence.

5. awkward, tangled, or overly complex sentences.

6. vague, abstract, or unnecessarily technical words.

To write clearly and avoid confusing your reader requires that you pay attention—especially in the final drafts of a writing project—to ideas and evidence, to organization, and to the readability of sentences. Helping you to pay attention to these features of your writing, in different kinds of writing assignments, is one of our purposes in the final chapters of this book. Chapter 6, Writing Projects Based on Personal Experiences, will help you explore these and other concerns as they relate to personal writing topics. Chapter 7, Writing Projects Based on Reading, will demonstrate how audience and attitude affect writing about reading. Finally, Chapter 8, Writing Based on Reasoning, will help you achieve readable writing by focusing on the presentation of clear logic and relevant examples in your papers.

As you work on your writing, remember: while you may write early drafts just for yourself, your later drafts are for other people. You may find your ideas fascinating and perfectly clear—since they are yours. You may be willing to overlook fuzzy passages and dull phrases, but your readers may not. Unless your writing is clear to them, your readers may disregard, ignore, or misconstrue it.

TEAMWORK WRITING

The following teamwork activity can be used to help you and your classmates clarify your attitude toward the subject and audience of your writing. You can complete this activity before you begin drafting or before you begin revising. Or, you can sharpen your understanding of audience by using the activity to analyze a sample essay or magazine article in order to determine the writing situation.

1. Get together with your writing group for some brainstorming after all of you have written a Statement of Intended Attitude on an assigned project. Or, if you are analyzing a published article or essay, imagine what the writer of the essay would say. Each person should clarify his or her intended attitude. If the group is analyzing a published essay, each student should suggest what the writer's attitude probably is. Discuss the following questions as a group:

   a. What examples work best, or would work best, to suggest the writer's intended attitude?

   b. What specific words and phrases does the writer use to suggest his or her point of view? Or, if you are helping one another revise, what changes in wording might help the writer clarify his or her point of view?

   c. Does the writer need to directly state the attitude? How can the attitude be revealed? If you are helping one another revise, find places where the writer is too explicit in revealing his or her attitude. Also find places where the writer might be less explicit.

   d. If the writer really should have a more direct statement of attitude, what should he or she do to avoid being blunt, obvious, dull?

2. If your college has a computer lab where your group's members can work near each other, try some electronic collaboration. Working at separate computers, each of you can put your current Statement of Intended Attitude on the screen, along with other details about what you want to do with your project or about what you hope you have accomplished in your draft. The group can circulate this material, each stopping to add his or her ideas and comments to each person's work. You can save this information under a distinctive title, if you want to keep it for later use.

Writing Exercises

1. Don Novello, who some of you may know as Father Guido Sarducci on the television show "Saturday Night Live," enjoyed writing letter to celebrities. In *The Lazlo Letters,* he assumes the role of Lazlo Toth, American. The book includes letters that Novello wrote to politicians, business executives, and celebrities between 1973 and 1976. Examine the writing situations in the following letters and replies, attempting to identify the writer's purpose, his attitude toward his subject, and his attitude toward his audience in each letter. Then analyze the writing situations from the point of view of the recipient of the letter, Gold Seal Company.

■ Letter 1

```
                            164 Palm
                            San Rafael, Calif.
                            February 18, 1974

    Mr. Bubble
    Gold Seal Co.
    Bismark, N.D. 58501

    Dear Gentlemen:

        I want you to know first of all that I enjoy your
    product. It's always refreshing to spend some time
    in the tub with some bubbles.
        However, I must confess I am puzzled by some of the
    instructions on the box. It says: "KEEP DRY." How
    can you use it if you keep it dry?
        Thought you'd be interested to know someone like me
    caught the mistake.
        I thought you'd like to know.

    Sincerely,

    Lazlo Toth
```

■ Reply to Letter 1

```
                            February 26, 1974

    Lazlo Toth
    164 Palm
    San Rafael, Calif. 94901

    Dear Friend:

        Thank you for your recent letter regarding "MR
    BUBBLE," which has been referred to this Consumer
    Relations Department for reply.
```

We are pleased to know that you enjoy using "MR BUBBLE" and that you find it refreshing to spend some time in the tub in a bubble bath.

It is true, we do say on our box: Free Flowing "MR BUBBLE" must be kept dry. By this statement we mean that the box of powder should be protected against dampness, such as moisture in the bathroom if the box is not put away. The box of "MR BUBBLE" should be closed and placed in a cabinet until the next use.

Some people tell us they transfer the "MR BUBBLE" powder to a plastic container, or even a large coffee can, to keep dampness out of the powder. Some have mentioned they keep a measuring scoop in the can for convenient measuring of the proper amount of powder to use in each bath. Overuse is only wasteful.

Our other products are listed above in our letter-head. We are enclosing an educational bulletin based on our "SNOWY" BLEACH, which we would appreciate your giving to your mother. Perhaps you already use "SNOWY" in your home. "SNOWY" is the safe oxygen-type bleach for all washable fabrics and colorfast dyes. When regular laundry such as sheets, towels, underwear, and linens are washed with "SNOWY" from the very beginning, and in each wash load, these items will have stronger fiber strength, longer life, and better appearance than when harsh chlorine bleaches are used.

Thank you again for writing to us.

Yours very truly,

GOLD SEAL COMPANY
M. Hershey,
Consumer Relations Dir.

Encl.

Bulletin #22
"SNOWY" & "MR BUBBLE"
Coupons

Letter 2

[Note how Lazlo Toth has changed his attitude toward his audience.]

Dear M. Hershey,

I was being nice to tell you about the error you have on your box and you send me coupons and tell me

to give an educational bulletin about stains to my
Mother.

To begin with, I wouldn't give your lousy educational bulletin #22 to nobody! Everybody I know
knows more about stains and that stuff than your
fancy company will ever know! Why you don't even
know how to thank someone when they offer you an intelligent suggestion! And then you have the nerve to
try to give me some pitch about your BLEACH!

I was writing about MR. BUBBLE, I don't care about
BLEACH! What does BLEACH have to do with it? Come on!

And how come the only words in capitals are your
SNOWY BLEACH and MR. BUBBLE while my Mother doesn't
even get a capital for her M!

This is a warning that I'm thinking of moving on to
another bubble bath.

Stand by our President!

With a right to be angry,

Lazlo Toth

■ Reply to Letter 2

[Note how the writer has changed his attitude toward his audience
in this letter.]

Dear Friend:

This is to acknowledge your letter of March 1st and
to say that we regret that our reply to your suggestion of February 18th was not satisfactory to you.

We certainly do appreciate your suggestion that we
eliminate the words "keep dry" on our "MR BUBBLE"
box. As mentioned in our previous letter, we say
"keep dry" for important reasons:

For instance, if the box is left on the side of the
tub, it could become wet, and the powder would no
longer be free-flowing.

If the box is left open in a bathroom that has much
moisture in the air, the powder could absorb the
moisture, and again would not be free-flowing.

Like other manufacturers of products sold in grocery stores and advertised on television, we receive
thousands of letters each year, some praising one
of our products, some complaining, and others with
suggestions. We answer each letter received as
courteously as possible, and in almost every instance we mention one of our other products and send

some of our advertising. We regret if we offended you
in doing so, but assure you this was only a friendly
gesture.

Thank you again for your suggestion, and naturally
we hope that you will continue to use and enjoy "MR
BUBBLE."

Yours very truly,

GOLD SEAL COMPANY
M. Hershey,
Consumer Relations Dir.

Source: Don Novello, *The Lazlo Letters,*
(New York: Workman Publishing Company, 1977).

2. Imagine that you have to speak to different groups of citizens on
   the same topic. How would your presentation change for different
   audiences? Choose a subject and several different audiences. Write
   separate notebook entries for each audience.

3. Examine several magazines in the library. Try to look at some that
   you normally wouldn't read. In your notebook, write a statement
   explaining the editor's view of the intended audience for each
   magazine. How can you determine the editor's view of the audience? (Consider ads, article subjects, letters to the editor, etc.)

Suggestions for Writing

1. Recall the worst cold of your life. Use rapid writing to discover—
   and capture on paper—details of how you felt, what you looked
   like, what you think was going on in your body to make you feel
   and look that way.

   a. Write about the common cold for a human interest column in
      your campus paper. The point of the column is to treat common
      occurences—things everyone has experienced—in such a way as
      to entertain a broad readership of students and faculty members.
      Work with rapid writing for awhile; draft for awhile. Get the
      project to the point that you are thinking of it as a second draft.

   b. Study your "Uncommon Cold" draft in light of the writing situa-
      tion. Write a brief analysis of the subject-writer-reader relation-
      ships in your article. Provide specific examples from your writ-
      ing to illustrate the statements you make.

   c. Read the following passage about colds. How would you de-
      scribe the differences in subject, writer, and reader between this

passage and your "Uncommon Cold" article? How would you describe the different emphases in your piece and this passage?

... the common cold, known in medical jargon as the "coryza" syndrome, is not a simple matter; rather it is a complex of symptoms. Caused by any one of a group of virus (currently estimated at about 100 in number), the common cold is primarily an infection of the lining membrane of the upper respiratory tract, including the nose, the sinuses, and the throat. This delicate membrane reacts to infection by swelling and by increasing the rate of mucus formation, leading to congestion, stuffiness, and probably a good deal of nose blowing. Due to loss of the nasal cavity as a resonating chamber, a characteristic change in voice quality also occurs. The increased mucus flow usually causes postnasal drip, which is irritating and contributes to the familiar "scratchy" throat and cough.

The sinuses, which normally empty into the nasal cavity, may become blocked by excessive swelling of the membranes. The resultant increase in sinus pressure may cause a frontal headache. In similar fashion, swelling in the upper part of the throat can block the Eustachian tubes—the two narrow canals that lead to the ears. This blockage can cause accumulation of fluid in the middle ear, which may be painful. Less commonly, an unpleasant spinning sensation known as vertigo may result.

A cold is usually self-limited, lasting about one to two weeks. At any time during the course of a cold, bacteria (such as staphylococci or pneumonococci) can be secondary invaders, bringing on debilitating infections of the sinuses and ears. However, the old warning that, if you don't take care, a cold will turn into pneumonia, is hardly ever true.

Fever above 101°F on a rectal thermometer is not usually part of an uncomplicated cold. Although mild elevation of temperature can occur, most people stay home from work or school because of generalized symptoms—muscle ache, weakness, and fatigue. The extent of these symptoms varies with the individual. If fever above 101°F rectally persists beyond two days, medical advice should be sought.

Source: The Medicine Show, Revised Edition (Mount Vernon, N.Y.: Consumers Union, 1974), pp. 27–28.

2. As you work on one of your current writing projects, follow the suggestions given earlier for exploring your attitude toward the subject (see pp. 141–142). Spend at least a half hour in rapid writing, answering questions 1a–1f. Then work at drafting a Statement of Intended Attitude that incorporates as many of your answers as possible. Rework the Statement of Intended Attitude to make it clear and precise. Try for a finished version that would let a group of students really understand what your attitude is toward your subject.

3. Write a three- or four- paragraph "emotional sketch" similar in approach to "Carnival."

   a. You might start by rapid writing on the general topic: "What events or experiences have I had lately to which I feel strong emotional responses?" Try to pick the target experience quickly, so that you can give most of your attention to finding the words to imply your emotional response and your present attitude toward the experience or event.

   b. When you have selected a target experience, jot it down at the top of a clean sheet of paper or a blank computer screen. Now list words and phrases that occur to you about the target. Concentrate on finding emotionally charged words.

   c. Go back over the list of words and phrases, changing and adding to increase or enhance the "emotional charge" of the list.

   d. With the target experience *and* the specific words on the list in your mind, write a Statement of Intended Attitude.

   e. Now write about the experience so that a group of students reading your draft in a "teamwork writing" session would have a good sense of what your attitude is toward your subject. But do *not* state your attitude directly.

4. Write an "emotional sketch" of an experience that had a great deal of emotional impact on you. This piece should be between 750 and 1000 words. Concentrate on selecting details and words that will convey your feelings to the other people in your class, but do not make many direct statements about your reactions or feelings.

5. Write an entertaining article about some simple, daily inconvenience everyone experiences—and is irritated about. This piece should be between 750 and 1000 words. Blend personal experience and facts to entertain and inform the wide range of people who read your campus paper.

6. Write an article (between 500 and 750 words) explaining what you sense are the important differences in editorial policy and readership of *two* of these magazines: *Changing Times, Consumer Reports,* and *Money*. As background for your writing, study two issues of each magazine you plan to write about. Answer the following questions twice—once about each of the two magazines:

   a. How long is an issue, and how long are typical articles?

   b. What types or subjects are treated most often in the magazine?

   c. How much use does the magazine make of photographs, comparison charts, statistics, colorful graphics?

   d. Do articles seem to have been written by "real" people—individuals with names and attitudes toward their material—or by committees? Why do you think this? How would you describe the attitudes the writers seem to have?

e. Is there an official editorial policy suggesting the "slant" the editor and publisher intend for the magazine? Summarize and quote selectively so that you have a compact statement of what you understand the editorial policy to be. Does the editorial policy have anything in common with the attitudes you noticed in question d?

f. Does there appear to be any similar structure or "outline" for full-length articles in the magazine? Can you find an introduction section? Is there a separate section on conclusions, or some other distinct ending section? Are subheading titles or other devices used to divide the article into sections? Do articles use the experiences of specific people to organize material and illustrate points?

g. What feelings do you have about the typical reader of this magazine? Who do you think reads the magazine? Why do they buy the magazine? What do they want out of the magazine?

7. Write a consumer-oriented article for readers of *Money, Consumer Reports,* or *Changing Times.* (If you have not written on the sixth writing suggestion, take a look at the "background" questions there before you start to work on this project.) Realistically, your article probably wouldn't be accepted by these national magazines. But the slant of an article for one of those periodicals would also be a good one for a piece in your campus or home paper, or a smaller local magazine. You could write about product safety, personal investment, over-the-counter medication, cosmetics, leisure products and activities, new products and services—in fact, any topic commonly treated in the magazines you are writing for. If you worked earlier on the first writing suggestion, you might like to keep the general subject of the common cold but alter your intended focus, as well as the audience, by writing about a topic such as effective and ineffective treatment, excessive cost of medication, losses in productivity caused by workers with colds, discoveries or breakthroughs in treatment. For some ideas and basic information, you might get *The Medicine Show* in the library and read the entries on "The Common Cold," "Coughs and Cough Remedies," and "Sore Throats." The public service librarian (or reference librarian) on duty in your library will be able to help you find other sources of information.

Writing Projects Based on Personal Experiences

6

Overview of Writing Strategies

In this chapter, we'll discuss, in detail, the following strategies, which you can use when you are assigned writing topics based largely on personal experience or personal knowledge:

1. Explore personal experiences.

2. Dissect the assignment.

3. Locate promising topics.

4. Create authentic writing situations.

5. Create a sequence of writing tasks.

6. Examine a model essay.

7. Use prewriting techniques to generate material and find a focus.

   • Answer "Who-What-When-Where-Why" Questions

   • Create and Shuffle Lists

   • Question Your Topic

The Value of Writing
from Personal Experience

Writing about your experiences, the people you have known, the problems you have confronted and solved, and other "personal" subjects can help you become more aware of yourself. Through the mental and physical processes of writing, you learn about yourself as you write about your life and your opinions. We live in a fact-centered age, an era of statistics and broad trends, where electronic media pull our attention outward to events around the world. Personal writing can provide a humanizing counter-pull, a fulfilling introspection. It can give you—as it did the students whose essays are included in this chapter—time to reflect on your nature, your chosen career, your connections with others, your relationship to events around the world.

Poet and textbook author Donald Hall says, "understanding the self allows us to move outside the self, to read, to analyze, to define." He adds, "Self-examination finds what we have inside us that is our own." [Donald Hall, *Writing Well,* Third Edition (Boston: Little, Brown and Company, 1979), p. 6.] We fully agree. And we'd like to help you find meaningful personal writing topics. When you write about yourself you have an opportunity to learn more about who you are and what you value. In the process, you can also learn more about your special needs as a writer.

Personal writing assignments will help you with assignments in other courses, too. Even when you have to write an essay or a midterm you will do a much better job if you care about your subject. Further, no matter what the topic, you may be able to include some material of a personal nature.

Earlier chapters have given you much information about writing processes and writing. By now, you should be able to tackle almost any assignment you get in college by using the strategies we have already presented. By all means, keep using the strategies that have begun to work for you. But the general strategies you learned about in earlier chapters may not be the best strategies for all kinds of assignments. In this chapter and in the remaining chapters in this textbook, we'll look more closely at specific kinds of assignments you'll get in college and we'll suggest ways to begin writing about these assignments.

Writing about your life, your ideas, and your experiences can help build your self-awareness and increase your personal insights. But just because you are "close to" your material in this kind of writing does not necessarily mean that personal projects are easy. Indeed, you may be so close to your material that you find it hard to get started on a personal project without working through some special exploratory strategies.

Essays Based on Personal Experiences

Personal experience essays come in all shapes and sizes. They can be long, intellectual discussions such as those in the *Atlantic Monthly*. Or they can be light, humorous sketches such as those you will find in your daily newspaper. If your English teacher or a teacher in another course assigns one or more personal experience essays, it doesn't mean that he or she is trying to prepare you for a career as a writer. What it probably does mean is that your teacher is giving you a chance to practice writing about a topic you know well before asking you to write about more remote ideas, events, or issues.

Just *how* you go about writing your personal experience papers will vary depending on the assignment you are given, or, if you have free choice of topic, on the topic you choose. Do remember, only *you* can determine what strategy will work best for you on each assignment. And remember, too, that each assignment may require a different strategy. By developing confidence in your abilities as a writer, you should also be acquiring the flexibility you need to respond to each new assignment on an individual basis. We invite you to explore the strategies in this chapter and use them as you see fit.

■ Strategy 1—Explore Personal Experiences

Personal writing, as you probably know from assignments in high school or college, can take many different directions and deal with many different subjects. Very often, though, personal writing projects involve one or more of these general subjects:

1. The writer's community

2. Family life and family members

3. Friends and acquaintances

4. Education and school experiences

5. Jobs and career interests

6. Hobbies and leisure activities

7. Personal attitudes and opinions

So if you are given a fairly general assignment, you might well begin by asking—and answering—questions about these seven subjects.

To practice this strategy, first select a subject you think you might be able to write about from the preceding list. Make this subject "it" as you write three-minute answers to each of the following questions. If you are writing about plural items, just use "their" or "them" instead of "its" and "it" when you ask and answer the question.

1. What are its most unusual or surprising features?

2. What are its most typical or characteristic features?

3. What are the most important things I got out of it?

4. How do I react to it?

5. What are its consequences for my life?

6. In what way would I change it if I could?

Understanding the Assignment

Some teachers like to assign specific topics to their students. Other teachers like to allow their students to find their own topics. Whatever your situation, begin by making sure that you understand what your assignment asks you to do. Read through assigned questions or topics slowly and carefully in order to be sure you understand all the parts of each assignment.

So that you can practice ways of beginning personal writing assignments, we'd like you to take a look at a few examples. Suppose you are given the following assignment:

Sample Assignment

> Write about a person or a place in such a way that others will enjoy reading about it. Include sights, sounds, feelings that will help your reader understand your person or place in a way that approximates how you feel.

When you get an assignment like that, what do you do? A good way to begin is to break the assignment into parts. First, you have to decide whether you want to write about a person or a place. If you decide to try thinking about a place, you might want to jot down some places you have visited. When you hit on the one place that you are motivated to write about, then you could try to list the sights, sounds, and other concrete details to see how much you remember.

Other assignments aren't quite as easy to dissect. Consider the following assignment:

Sample Assignment

> Write an essay in which you use examples from personal experience to demonstrate why you hold a certain viewpoint or belief.

In this case, you've got free reign to express one of your beliefs. But what are your beliefs? And which beliefs are fair game for this assignment? Can you write about convictions you have that are related to your major? Or does your teacher expect you to write about more general concerns? And which of these concerns do you want to write about? Maybe one of the best topics for you to write about is one that is most important to you right now. Do you think that faculty evaluations should be required? Do you believe that everyone should be involved in some kind of sport? Do you think that students should take part in campus organizations? Do you support the United States' involvement in Latin American governments? You can proceed by deciding what really moves you at the moment and then begin planning how you will write about your topic. But then what?

After you decide what you want to write about, you need to begin generating ideas. Sometimes thinking about what the finished paper might look like can help you come up with organizational strategies that might work for those topics. Do you want your paper to be one in which you explain your topic in a series of paragraphs, each of which gives an example of why you believe what you believe? Would you prefer that your paper take the shape of a comparison/contrast essay in which you explain your beliefs or ideas by comparing them or contrasting them with someone else's beliefs? By answering questions like these, you will have made some important decisions that should help you get started.

Sample Assignment

> Write a personal essay in which you tell an anecdote or a series of anecdotes about your family or your relatives. You can tell a favorite story, one members of your family enjoy telling and retelling. If possible, choose a story that has "a point" to make or a comment to make about life.

This could be an easy assignment—*if* an idea "pops" into your mind immediately. But if you don't think of anything right away, you need to determine how to proceed. You could begin working on this assignment by thinking about or listing several family "stories" worth retelling. Or, you might do some rapid writing about some family incident—*any* incident if a special one doesn't leap out at you. If one of the incidents you write about seems to have a point, then you might be able to move directly to drafting. If you are at a loss for a topic, consider calling a sister or brother or a family friend to chat about your shared experiences. Talk is often a useful way to prepare for writing.

Strategies for Understanding Assignments

In the preceding sample assignments, we tried to illustrate how you might deal with an assignment by examining it closely. If you can work out a way to generate and focus your ideas without using additional strategies, you may be ready to begin drafting without concerning yourself with additional strategies. But if you are stuck, then you might want to reexamine the assignment to be sure you understand it. Then, apply some of the following strategies, which should help you explore *any* personal writing assignment.

■ Strategy 2—Dissect the Assignment

Learning to dissect, or break down, your assignment will help you understand more clearly what you must do to fulfill the requirements of the assignment.

1. Jot the assignment at the top of a sheet of paper or on the computer screen, and use five minutes of rapid writing to explore this question: "What does this assignment *really* ask me to do?"

2. Read over your writing. Then try to write one-sentence answers to each of these questions:

   a. Does the assignment call for a particular "type" of development? (Summary, argument, comparison-contrast, analysis, description, research-based writing, humorous writing, etc.)

   b. Are there special requirements? (Length, typing requirements, quotations from library sources, style of documentation, more than one copy to be submitted, all drafts to be submitted, or any other details.)

   c. Does the assignment commit me to working with a very *precise* topic? ("Write about a specific person who influenced your life.")

   d. Can I come up with a plan for "attacking" the assignment?

■ Strategy 3—Locate Promising Topics

As you begin to understand your assignment, start thinking about how you can "customize" the topic, how you can make it your own. There is no *one* or *right* way to personalize topics. But here is a strategy that can help you early in your work on a writing project:

1. Refer to the questions suggested in Strategy 1. On paper or on the computer, write a few sentences that summarize answers to these questions (applying them to your assignment). For instance: "I need to write a 750-word paper related to the theme, 'A Responsible Education,' that we have been discussing for the past two weeks. The paper should draw on my experiences as a high school and college student—including my reading experiences."

2. Fill the sheet with a *list* of possible topics, ideas about those topics, or anything else that comes to your mind. For instance:

   a. Ethical consequences of career choices.

   b. Liberal education's role in shaping responsible professionals.

    c. Preparing to meet future needs of society with today's education.

    d. Preparing today to meet future needs.

    e. "Responsible" and "practical" education—must they conflict?

3. Look over this list of topic ideas. Mark on the page:

    a. Topic ideas that you "care" about, and how much.

    b. Topic ideas on which you have a pretty good general background, either through previous study or personal experience.

    c. Topics that you would like to learn something about, even though you do not know much about them now.

    d. Clusters of topic ideas (like the emphasis on the future in items c and d in suggestion 2.

Through this sort of review, you can eliminate unpromising topics from the list and try to arrive at one idea that you could begin to write about.

4. Write out several potential paper topics related to your most likely candidates. For instance, the cluster of ideas about "education for the future" might seem to suggest a paper with one of these topics:

    a. Education must anticipate the future.

    b. A "responsible" education cannot forget the needs of society in the future.

    c. A "practical" education cannot focus exclusively on contemporary needs of society.

5. Get a second (or third, or fourth) opinion from a group of other students in your class. Share your lists of potential topics with each other, so that for a few minutes at least, each list of topics becomes the target of the whole group's conversation. Here are some suggestions for group discussion:

    a. Is the topic interesting or important enough to make people want to read a paper on it?

    b. Is the topic too broad or too narrow?

    c. How could the topic be changed to make it more interesting? Of a more manageable scope?

6. Review your potential topics in light of the group discussion. You may find yourself being guided toward a topic. You may agree with the group's feelings about the possibility of dullness or excessive generalization in a topic and find ways to modify it. At any rate, you should try to reformulate the topic into a compact and clear statement that you can use as a topic in your later efforts to explore the subject. For instance, after a group discussion on the potential of "education" as a paper topic, you might decide to focus your writing project on this thesis statement:

"While a college education should prepare people to live and earn a living in the first few years after they graduate, it must also prepare them to live in a future they may, perhaps, be unable even to imagine."

Creating Your Own Writing Assignments

If a *writing situation* is not built into your assignment, see if you can create one. Or, if you have free choice of topics, consider creating a "real-world" group assignment for your entire class: write about situations that are authentic, that are related to your experiences, that you don't *have* to write about but that you want to write about.

■ Strategy 4—Create Authentic Writing Situations

Here are some suggestions for creating authentic writing situations.

1. Help the Admissions Office or whatever office handles Freshman Year Orientation at your college: Create a class booklet of "survival" essays for incoming students. This booklet might include essays or sketches about: restaurants to frequent; cultural events worth attending; extracurricular activities available to students; and recreational opportunities such as biking, skiing, hiking, and canoeing. Or, you might create a separate booklet on surviving the problems freshmen experience—loneliness, needing to make friends, getting lost in a new town or on a new campus, finding out how to drop or add a course. Students who are older than the norm might want to create a separate series of essays about their unique experiences in college, including such topics as returning to school, relating to younger students, relating to non-students—family and friends, and studying in the midst of chaos at home. Another booklet could also include sketches about favorite courses, favorite professors, favorite campus events. (An underground version of this booklet could include places and people to avoid—but it wouldn't be good public relations to suggest that your college advising office distribute it.)

2. Create travel guides for students at your university. Though college can put you out of touch with your human needs, remember that you and other college students "are people, too." You need breaks from studying. You need to travel and explore the world. Try to write up some accounts of where you've traveled so that others can get an idea of where they might want to travel, too. Perhaps the Student Government Office can make these guides available to other students. Write descriptions of places you enjoyed visiting in your state or in a nearby state. Write them in such a way so that stu-

dents who would like to take a weekend trip or a between-semesters trip will get an idea of what the place is like and how much it would cost.

3. Help one another. You've all got personal problems of different kinds. Assume a "Dear Abby" role for your peers. But do it anonymously. Here's how it could work. Everyone can put a slip of paper into a box, asking a personal question (an advice question) of some sort. No one need know who wrote the question. Next, your teacher should "publish" the list of questions. Students select questions they want to answer. Some questions may be answered by several people. Others may not be chosen at all. What about the ones that are left? Maybe your teacher can assign them as topic ideas for the next theme.

4. Write some personal remembrances. Instead of just writing home, why not write home with a special gift—a written account of a family memory. Write a family memoir or a family story. Write a biography of one of your relatives. Or do a series of family sketches. Dawn Rodrigues's mother gave us the idea for this assignment. Last year, she wrote and gave Dawn a gift of this kind—a booklet about her experiences growing up as a Pennsylvania Dutch girl. This gift will become a family heirloom. Dawn plans to give it to her child one day.

5. Write "letters to remember." Instead of just writing a totally casual letter to a friend, why not try writing letters that are records of your college years—carefully structured accounts of experiences you'd like to preserve?

   A friend of ours is writing letters to us and to other friends while she spends the year at Carnegie Mellon University in Pittsburgh. These letters are not ordinary letters. They are more carefully structured, filled with more details and observations than her usual letters. Why is she sending these detailed accounts? She wants to keep a record of all that she's doing and learning. And she's much more motivated to write if she thinks of a real person as she writes about her daily experiences.

6. Help yourself *and* the advising center at your college. One way to learn more about how people in your chosen career (or, if you're not yet committed to a career, in some career you'd like to know more about) feel about their jobs is to interview them. A way to make those interviews useful to your college would be to rewrite them as character sketches or "career profiles" so that the placement bureau can keep them on file. Students can read them as they contemplate their own job searches or as they consider choosing or changing their major field.

After you customize an assignment, try to create a sequence of tasks that might help you generate and draft ideas efficiently. Think carefully about the "steps" you want to take as you move through the beginning stages of your writing assignment. Try to sequence the steps you might take in completing the assignment. Ask yourself: "Where should I start?"; "What could I do that would help me get some idea of where to go next with my writing?"; "Does the assignment have a logical sequence?" No one but you will be able to determine just what sequence of tasks will be most helpful as you move from generating ideas about your topic to drafting.

■ Strategy 5—Create a Sequence of Writing Tasks

To get a sense of how to plan your own sequence of writing tasks, see if you can determine the sequence you might follow if you decided to write an essay about a person who has influenced your growth and development—a kind of customized thank-you note to someone who you respect and want to thank. Here's the sequence that one of our students, Chuck, created in order to help respond to this task:

1. First, I'd ask myself, Who do I know who's worth describing? I'd list the first people who come to mind. I'd select one or two and think more about the topic.

2. Then, I'd ask myself, What do I really value in this person? I'd list a few values. Maybe a few experiences, too. That might lead me to the values.

3. Next, I'd decide who to write about and I'd ask, Why am I writing this? What point can I make about this person? Do I remember an experience I had with the person?

4. By then, I'd probably be ready to draft.

Using these questions to guide him, here are the notes Chuck wrote to himself:

1. *People I could write about:*

   my Uncle Harry; my high school teacher, Mr. Law; the bowling coach, Jack Morgan; my friend, Sharon Cooper; my boss, Ross.

2. *What I'd say about each of these people if I focused on what I value in them:*

   Mr. Law—led me to my chosen career; believed in me; showed this on several occasions. Sharon Cooper—funny; encourages my sense of humor; helps me put things in perspective.

3. *Who I'll write about:*

   Ross, my boss, I've never seen this kind of honesty; I really admire his honesty.

4. *Situations in which he showed his honesty:*

> the gutter episode, the license plates incident, the time he underpaid me.

Read this early draft of Chuck's essay written in response to this assignment. Notice that he seems to have written this comfortably, with the preceding notes proving sufficient to guide him as he drafted:

HONESTY AND RESPECT

While I was growing up my Dad taught me to be honest, and at the same time he would say, "Chuck, don't believe anything you read and only half of what you see." He also would tell me, "Chuck, when you meet someone who is truly honest, they deserve your respect." Quite a few years later I was hired by Royal Heating in Castle Rock, and the owner, Ross Baumgarner, turned out to be the type of honest person my Dad was talking about. During the five years I worked for Ross I came to respect him because of the honesty he showed in dealing with his clients and his employees.

Ross's honesty was evident in the way he dealt with his clients. For example, in 1981, the first year that I worked for Ross, a coworker, Doug, and I were hanging seamless rain gutters on a new house. We were carrying a forty-foot section of gutter onto the roof when a gust of wind came up and blew it out of our hands. When the gutter crashed to the ground, it bent over at a forty-five-degree angle, which left a noticeable kink on the outside edge. Not knowing what we should do, we decided to fix the gutter. We were able to straighten it so that the damage was hardly noticeable; so we went ahead and hung it on the roof. About a week later the homeowner called Ross and asked him if he knew anything about the slight flaw in his gutter. Not knowing what had happened, Ross asked us. We told him the truth. Immediately, Ross offered to replace the gutter free for his client. Another example of Ross's honesty has to do with an order from the Denver Public Schools for fifty bus number-plates. I filled the order and waited for the plates to be picked up. When Jim, from the Denver Public Schools, came by to pick up the plates, he noticed that the plates were two inches too long to fit his buses. I showed him my list of specifications for the plates and he agreed that the dimensions on my list were the same as the dimensions of the plates I had built them. Jim figured that he had given the wrong dimensions to Ross over the phone and so agreed to pay a five-dollar charge for each alteration. Later that day, I told Ross what had happened, and he went and compared his note pad with the list he had given me. The numbers did not agree. Ross had made a mistake when he made up the list. Ross immediately called Jim and told him about the mistake he made. Afterward Ross told me to go ahead and alter the plates for no charge. Ross could have easily withheld the truth from these people for his own benefit, but chose to be honest with them instead.

Not only was Ross honest with his clients, but he also showed his honesty toward his employees. For example, in December of 1982, Ross came to me and told me that the projects we were working on would only last another month, and after that the company would be out of work until things picked up in March. Ross explained to me that he could not afford to keep me on through the slow period. He told me that he wanted to give me enough time to find another job, and that my job with him would be waiting for me if I still wanted it. Ross could have used me for a few more weeks, but didn't want to take advantage of me. By letting me know in advance I was able to find a temporary job the next day, leaving Ross without sufficient help. But because Ross had been so good to me, I went back to work for him as soon as he was able to rehire me, even though the second job paid more money than Ross would be able to give me.

Another example of Ross's integrity occurred in late 1983 when I received a promotion with the company to shop foreman. This promotion gave me authority over all shop business: purchasing, employees, and production. Along with the increase in responsibility there was an increase in pay. From the checks I was receiving, I figured my increase in pay to be about one dollar an hour. After a few weeks went by, Ross came and told me that the bookkeeper had made a mistake on my paychecks. My raise was supposed to be two dollars an hour instead of one dollar an hour. Ross told me that the back pay I had coming would be in my next check, and he apologized for the mix-up. Amazing! Not many people would be that honest.

My Dad, like so many other dads, used maxims as guides to help their kids in growing up. Sadly, it isn't until we're grown that these maxims become meaningful—that they become more than an accumulation of old sayings rotting around in our heads. Ross personifies those maxims about honesty and respect—and now I'm old enough to fully appreciate those virtues. From the dealings that I had with Ross I discovered that he

was the type of honest person that my Dad was telling
me about when I was younger. His honesty showed in all
situations that he dealt with, and because of this he
earned my complete respect.

Source: Chuck Alpert.

Certainly Chuck needs to revise this essay in order to improve it.
But he's off to a good start because he found a topic he wanted to
write about—a topic that seems to be an important memory for him.

Using Professional Models

Assignments that you receive in English classes might not always
sound like the kinds of assignments professional writers take on. But
you'll be surprised at how easy it is to find samples of published essays on the same kinds of topics that you write about. Sometimes
reading a professional sample can help you plan your own essay.

◼ Strategy 6—Examine a Model Essay

Your writing processes often work more efficiently when you know
what your finished product—your theme, your essay, your paragraph—might look like. So when you are given a general assignment,
it might help if you could find a professional sample that covers the
same kind of topic. After you locate the sample, read it carefully, analyzing the writing situation: the subject, the intended audience, the
writer's attitude, the purpose of the writing. Then plan a strategy for
writing your own essay in the same format as that of your model
essay.

One of our students, Kathy, chose the following assignment as the
basis for a personal essay:

Sample Assignment

> Describe a place that you have visited. Include sufficient information
> and details to let your readers decide if they would be interested in
> visiting your chosen place.

Kathy looked through several magazines before finding the following
account of the Albuquerque, New Mexico, balloon festival in an issue
of *New Mexico Magazine*.

Model Essay

CHASING THE CLOUDS

Neither words nor wide-screen TV can capture the magnitude of the
annual Albuquerque International Balloon Fiesta.

You have to be on the scene to feel the chill of the morning darkness and welcome the first rays of sun rising behind the Sandia Mountains to the east. You have to be there to enjoy the jostling of the crowd, the aroma of fresh-baked Indian bread, and other pungent foods sold at booths rimming the launch site.

And, of course, you have to be there to hear the whir of the big fans coaxing the balloons, lying shapeless on the ground, to rise like awakening giants for the ride to the sky. Camera bugs go bananas.

Most thrilling are the four ascensions on Saturday and Sunday mornings of the opening and closing weekends. For two hours after dawn, more than 500 balloons float over Albuquerque like an invasion of sugar plums—a palette of color across the sky.

Albuquerque, the Balloon Capital of the world, is especially suitable because of its high altitude, few obstructions, and October winds that are steady but manageable.

Besides the mass ascensions on weekends, military sky divers and acrobatic airplanes present shows. During the week, the balloon pilots take part in spirited competitions, highlighted by the key-grab, when balloon jockeys vie to snatch new car keys hooked atop a 25-foot pole.

Dates of this year's fiesta are October 4th through 12th. The fiesta is at a new site, between Paseo del Norte and Alameda Roads, just west of I–25. Public parking, through the Alameda entrance, is $1.00 per person.

Last year, more than 500,000 persons attended the launching, though, in a sense, everyone takes part merely by looking up.

Source: Rusty Brown, "Chasing the Clouds." *New Mexico Magazine,*
(October, 1986) p. 63.

Sample Student Response. After reading and analyzing the model essay, Kathy planned her strategy for writing her own essay:

1. First, she would look at the model essay carefully. When she did, she noticed that the first few words in each paragraph carry the reader along through the essay: "Neither words nor wide-screen TV can capture . . . "; "You have to be on the scene . . . "; "Most thrilling are . . . "; "Albuquerque . . . is . . . ." She noticed that the purpose of the essay seemed to be to attract readers of *New Mexico Magazine* to visit the balloon festival.

2. Next, she gave herself some time to just reminisce about the fun she had at the place she was going to write about—the Home Ranch outside Steamboat Springs, Colorado. Here are a few sentences from her rapid writing:

   "I think that the ride high up in the aspen-covered mountains, overlooking the green meadows below, was about the most beautiful scene I've ever seen. It was so exciting to get off my horse, tie it to a tree, and help the ranch-hands cook lunch."

3. After doing rapid writing, she listed the main divisions of the model essay:

Neither words nor wide-screen TV can capture

You have to be on the scene to

And, of course

Most thrilling are the

Albuquerque . . . is especially suitable

Besides the

Dates of this year's

4. She decided to try using the structure implied by these transitional words as a generating tool. She tried a quick draft, putting ideas about the Home Ranch into the "slots" she had taken from the model essay.

Read through Kathy's rough draft, noticing how she has used the structure of the model to move her draft along. She has not used any of the words from the original, except for the transitional phrase "and then there's the," but in order to keep a similar structure as the model essay, she found that she used similar transitional words. Notice how the transitional words (which we have underscored) work, as you read Kathy's rough draft:

```
            A VISIT TO A DUDE RANCH

Words can't capture the beauty of the entire scene.
The Home Ranch is in the small town of Clark, Colorado,
about 10 miles north of Steamboat Springs. It's about
the greenest, most lush setting I've ever seen in Col-
orado. The ranch house and the guest cabins are set in
aspen groves; a trout-filled stream runs through the
ranch; trails for hiking and horseback riding are
within view of your front door. Most college students
probably wouldn't even consider going to a dude ranch.
But if they did, I think they'd like it, too.
    Only by being there can you experience the excite-
ment. The bell sounds, beckoning you to join the group
for breakfast. Freshly baked bread, eggs cooked to your
taste, fresh fruit, and more can be taken outdoors to
the tables set along the stream. Anyone who would like
to catch a trout to add to the breakfast fare is wel-
come to try. Fishing rods are readily available,
propped up on the ranch-house porch.
    And then there's the rodeo in the evening. Now don't
expect anything too fancy! The cook, the owner, the
desk clerk, and their friends from town are the star
attractions. The guests are the entire audience. Yet I
```

cheered more for Jodi, the cook, than I've ever cheered for professional bronco riders at the national rodeo in Cheyenne, Wyoming.

Most unusual—especially for a novice—are the horseback rides. Guests can arrange to have a wrangler lead them high above the ranch into the velvety-green mountains. Wranglers help you groom and saddle your horse and give you private lessons to prepare you for the several-hour trek. If you want to eat a hearty lunch on the road, they'll help you fix it. You'll appreciate their experience and help, too. Climbing up the steep, rocky trails takes special horsemanship skills that a novice rider might not know about. For instance, Sam, the wrangler along on my ride, warned me to move my weight either forward or backward to help ease the horse's load as we ascended and descended steep cliffs. Then, when a wide open meadow appeared, he gave me a quick review of trotting and galloping techniques. What a ride!

Clark, Colorado, is the perfect location for a dude ranch. You feel as if you're hundreds of miles from everywhere. And you are. To get there, you can fly or drive to Denver, take route 80 west until you see a sign for Steamboat. Then it's about a three-hour drive north to Steamboat Springs. Ten minutes later, you'll be in Clark.

Oh, I almost forgot. The ranch has special winter rates and winter treats. Guests can cross-country ski from their cabin doorsteps across carefully groomed trails. Horse-drawn sleighs take guests over the river and through the woods. Then it's back to the ranch-house for food around the fireplace instead of a summertime cookout. My summer visit was definitely a treat, so I hope someday to have a chance to vacation there in winter, too.

Using Prewriting Techniques

When you have found a topic that feels good to you, or when you have personalized an assignment or found a model you want to use to guide you, you still may need to spend some time generating ideas. We'd like to suggest a few *prewriting* strategies you can use to develop your ideas. These strategies might more appropriately be called *pre-drafting* techniques, because they do involve some writing. But since some of you may already know the term *prewriting* from other English courses, we'll use the term, too. These prewriting strategies can help you concentrate your attention on developing material. They should help you locate and record for future use an abundance of ideas and details that will help you write an effective paper.

■ Strategy 7—Use Prewriting Techniques to Generate Material and Find a Focus

Technique 1—Answer "Who-What-When-Where-Why" Questions

Any time you are writing about an event, you can generate a lot of material and discover several different "slants" by asking—and answering—five questions:

1. *Who* was there during the event? Who is there? Who should have been there but wasn't—and why? Who might have been there if conditions were different? Were you there as a first-hand observer?

2. *What* took place during the event? What did people do to each other, and how did people react? What did people say, and what did conversations sound like?

3. *Where* did the event take place? What were the geographical surroundings? What were the social, political, and economic environments of the event?

4. *When* did the event take place—in time and in relationship to you? How "close to" the event are you in time or emotional distance? How accurate are your impressions of what went on, or are you coloring things with your mind?

5. *Why* did the event take place? Why did people do the things they did? Why did people say the things they said? Are there clear-cut causes, or do you have to speculate about causes and human motives? If you are speculating, why have you formed the judgments you have?

Since personal writing often focuses on times of interaction—conflict, cooperation, shared joy or sadness—with other people, the who-what-when-where-why questions are often an excellent strategy for starting a personal writing project. You can search your memory for an experience that, on later reflection, strikes you as "significant" for some reason. Then you can start to explore the experience by writing brief but detailed answers to these questions.

Sample Student Response. Here is a sample response to Technique 1; it was written by Eric, a student preparing to write about a trip to Hong Kong.

Jottings About Hong Kong

1. *Who* was there?

   a. Steve was carrying his camera? (Or was it attached permanently, so that he never forgets it like I do?)

   b. Craig and Kirby, who shared a room with us.

   c. Me, of course.

   d. Old cleaning woman in the hotel who spoke no English. She just smiled no matter what we said.

   e. Crowds downtown. Everybody seemed to have an umbrella and that made it seem all the more crowded on the street.

2. *What* did we do?

   a. We rode across the harbor, somehow getting through the mass of little boats.

   b. Steve took a picture of our reflection in the mirrored glass of a building.

   c. Moved into the White House Hotel.

   d. Got lost once when the wrong elevator opened at the third floor game room instead of the third floor of the guest rooms.

   e. Steve and I ordered two suits each from a tailor because prices were so cheap.

   f. He gave us beer every time we came for a fitting.

   g. Rode the ferry over to the mainland—Kowloon City.

   h. Told Steve about the Staten Island Ferry ride.

   i. Followed the two old Americans to the Sheraton.

   j. Stopped at the Sheraton for a drink at the "Giraffe" bar. Silly name for Hong Kong. Flirted with a waitress who spoke English. Steve spilled a drink. Steve wanted to do all the "touristy" stuff—ride the bus to Victoria Peak in the center of the city, take pictures. But I didn't feel like exploring so much. Wanted to stay closer to the hotel. Compromise: looked for the highest building. I led us up to the roof. The view was great but I sort of panicked up there.

3. *Where* were we?

   a. Hong Kong area, built-up city, boathouses.

   b. Looked like New York in some ways, freighters in harbor areas.

   c. Ferry ride across harbor.

   d. Crowds in the market; contrasts between business districts and slummy areas.

Source: Sample student responses and essay on Hong Kong by Eric Reed.

e. All the land right in the middle of the city.

f. The White House Hotel, strange set-up, with one elevator to the hotel rooms and another to the game rooms, one on each of six floors.

g. Sheraton Kowloon Hotel, "Pink Giraffe Nightclub."

h. Bank of America Building: thirty-six floors tall and a good view of the city if you could get to the top; roof top, great view standing on the narrow wall; rusting equipment for lowering window cleaners kept cosmetically out of view of the roof-top restaurant.

4. *Why* did I react as I did?

a. Why did I react so oddly on the roof? I never thought I was afraid of heights but I sure felt afraid that day. Had we been in the "Giraffe" too long? I don't think that it was that so much as feeling so vulnerable out there, out in the air in the middle of that strange city. I'd not wanted to ride the bus all through the town.

b. Was I afraid of being too close to too much strangeness? On the ferry, almost immersed in Oriental life—what I thought of was the ride to Staten Island. I'd acted brave bluffing my way up to the roof. But something struck me there on the roof. And its stuck with me ever since. Sort of changed me. I don't have it all straight in my mind yet.

Notice how details from the preceding student response show up in Eric's essay, "Hong Kong Skyscrapers."

HONG KONG SKYSCRAPERS

Skyscrapers don't stand as tall in Hong Kong as in Manhattan. But then, the people are smaller, too. The skyscrapers congregate in the flatlands of downtown Hong Kong. Behind these rise the mountains which occupy the interior portion of the island, like a swollen Central Park. Victoria Peak, the highest of the mountains, gives a view of the island; green and mountainous in the middle and ringed by the various districts that constitute Hong Kong.

The harbor surrounding Hong Kong is glutted with boats and ships of every type and size. These travel around the harbor in a complex pattern. The residents of Hong Kong, in the way they navigate their boats, in the way they drive their cars, and in the way they walk around their streets, seem to follow patterns derived from some of the more complex video games. Perhaps it's some lingering form of Zen directing them on a random course around the universe.

Across the harbor is Kowloon, on the mainland. It's where you go if you want to ride the ferry, like Staten Island in New York. Even if you have no business or even any interest in Staten Island, you have to go there, because there is where the ferry takes you.

And somewhere in the middle of all this is the Wan Chai district and the White House Hotel. If you stand on Victoria Peak and look down, it's about ten degrees to the right of downtown. I suppose. I never went to Victoria Peak. It's where the bus takes you.

You have to walk or take a bus to the White House Hotel. And an elevator takes you to the third floor. Make sure that you take the right elevator, though. That's the one on the right. The one on the left takes you to six consecutive floors of identical game rooms. It's eerie, like the Twilight Zone. If you get on the left elevator, the wrong elevator, and push the button for the floor where your room is supposed to be, you end up in a game room. Then you try to get back to the first floor and every floor looks the same. We took the stairs down to the lobby. Then we got on the right elevator, the one on the right, and got to our rooms.

It had been a long day. Steve was taking pictures and I was tagging along. I often tag along with people taking pictures because I often forget my camera. Steve had taken pictures from the ferry. Then, of course, he had to take pictures in Kowloon. We stopped at the Sheraton Hotel in Kowloon to have a drink. They have a nightclub there called the Pink Giraffe. I wanted to ask someone where the name came from, because I'm always interested in such things. But there was no one to ask. The cocktail waitress looked like she wouldn't know. She spoke English well and she looked fairly bright. She was also very attractive. But she didn't look like the type who would ever think to ask where the name Pink Giraffe came from.

The ferry takes you away from Kowloon, too. Steve and I returned to Hong Kong after our drinks. Hoping to get a picture of the whole city, Steve suggested that we catch a bus to Victoria Peak. Since I wasn't interested in tagging along, I suggested that we go to the top of a skyscraper instead. The Bank of America building seemed a good place to start: it rises 36 stories above the center of the business district. So we walked to the Bank of America building and entered the lobby from the east side.

The lobby had several shops in it. We stopped at a newsstand to look at the latest issue of <u>Playboy</u>. It had come out that day.

The elevator took us to the thirty-sixth floor. On

this floor is a restaurant with a greenhouse and terrace. I suppose Steve could have taken his pictures from this terrace, but I wanted to go up to the roof.

Somehow, we had switched roles. I was no longer tagging along. Now I was leading. And I'm the type of leader who feels invulnerable as long as the troops have confidence in me. There is safety in numbers, they say. Or maybe courage is enhanced by a need to show off. A hero is just a man who can visualize his likeness in marble.

So the courage that comes with leadership led me to look for a door marked "Employees Only." I knew this would take us to the roof. A man dressed as a busboy passed us as we found the door. We asked him where the restroom was. He pointed to a door we had just passed.

After he had left us, I opened the "Employees Only" door and found a staircase leading up to the roof. This, I guessed, is used to lower a scaffold for men who clean windows.

Steve and I climbed from the roof to the landing where the idle winch rested. From there, we balanced on the rail and carefully made our way to the top of the wall.

I'm not an acrophobe. Heights seldom bother me. I can look down from thirty-six floors and feel no unnatural fear. But standing on a two-foot-wide wall with a six-foot fall behind him and a 400-foot drop in front of him would make even the bravest of men nervous. As I stepped onto the wall, I had a vision of my likeness carved in marble. After a 400-foot fall!

I knelt and grabbed the rail.

From this vantage point, crawling on my knees and grasping a winch track, I saw Hong Kong. It is this image which lingers. In the moment of panic my eyes became cameras to record what they instinctively thought would be their last sight.

My eyes, of course, lived to see other sights. They would burn in the harsh sun reflected from the Pacific as they travelled to other countries and finally home. But not before they adjusted themselves to the view from the top of the Bank of America building in Hong Kong.

Skyscrapers don't stand as tall in Hong Kong as in Manhattan. But then, the people are smaller, too, especially when viewed from a wall atop the Bank of America building. Beyond the office buildings and hotels of the business district lies a harbor littered with boats and ships. One of those ships brought me to Hong Kong. And one of those boats is a ferry. It takes you to Kowloon.

> And high above the city, two young men were looking
> down. One held a camera. The other held a monorail.

Technique 2—Create and Shuffle Lists

There are three parts to this technique: (1) listing details, (2) adding
to your list, and (3) looking for helpful organizational patterns in the
list of details.

1. *Create a list of details on your paper topic.* Do not worry about the order
   of items in your list. Instead, concentrate on the number of items
   and the amount of detail in each item. Use some of the
   "brainstorming" techniques discussed earlier (p. 163) to help you
   develop your list.

2. *Add to your list in light of later thinking and research.*

3. *Look for possible patterns within your list of details.* It's impossible to say
   just how long a list you should try to develop in the first part of this
   list-shuffling strategy. But after you have accumulated a good number of details and feel that you are developing a point of view on
   your topic, you should try to figure out the possible patterns of
   thinking that are buried in your list. As you work, new ideas may
   occur to you. And, of course, you may add things to your list at any
   time. But to begin, study the list, looking for underlying patterns
   that suggest the focus or "point of view" you are developing on
   your topic. You might consider these four questions:

   a. Are there items in the list that deal with a similar idea—ideas
      that seem to cluster together around a key point?

   b. How can the point of each cluster be stated in a clear sentence?

   c. How do the different clusters relate to each other? Are some clus-
      ters similar or supportive? Do some contradict each other? Do
      some clusters seem to support a single, overall theme?

   d. Can you write a single sentence that suggests the kinds of rela-
      tionships that exist among the clusters of details and the points
      they support?

Sample Student Response.   Here is an example of how one student applied Technique 2, creating a list and analyzing it for possible
patterns or clusters of ideas.

Topic: "Responsible and Practical Education"

Topic Statement: To be "practical," an education has to reach
beyond the demands of job-preparation for the years immediately following graduation, and reach into the less-certain future.

List of Details

1. Liberal education is flexible, a broad exposure to many things.

2. Education of "the whole person."

3. Pragmatic, utilitarian education is needed to find a first job.

4. "You can't eat a diploma. It's skills that count." (From a TV ad for a technical school.)

5. Almost any well-known figure in politics, government, or top-level corporate management has a liberal arts education.

6. Vocational education provides specific training in a narrow field.

7. "Practical" education in our changing world is not a narrow, technical education.

8. I've heard that people are going to have three or more *different* vocations in their lives.

9. Who is successful in business—the person with a broad education or with narrow training?

10. Must there be differences between liberal and vocational education?

11. Vocational training leaves out too much—like hobbies, leisure time, general skills to learn a new job, the ability to make informed aesthetic judgments on films and books, standards to use in analyzing political events and vote intelligently.

Clusters of Ideas: In the list of details on "Responsible and Practical Education," for example, there seem to be three clusters of ideas:

Cluster A: (Items 1, 2, 3, 4, and 6.) Vocational and liberal education have different aims and provide different kinds of preparation.

Cluster B: (Items 2, 5, 7, 8, 9, and 10.) Liberal education contributes to a person's success in life.

Cluster C: (Items 8, 10, and 11.) Rather than fragment education into "vocational" and "liberal," it makes sense to speak of "career education," which includes both, but is not limited to, the concerns of either.

A number of common threads seem to run through the three clusters:

1. The fact that broad flexibility must augment technical skills to make job-changing possible.

2. The way that promotion to managerial positions may depend on broad education.

3. The fact that one overall concept of career education can embody the ideas of vocational and liberal education.

For example, this sentence brings out relationships among the clusters of details on the education topic, and so points toward a "focus" for a paper on this topic:

> "Since both liberal and vocational education are important to a person's success, professionally (getting a first job, winning promotions, changing careers) as well as personally (making friends, leisure reading), a responsible college education must include the ideals of liberal and career education."

IDEA FILE: COMPUTER WRITING

Computer Shuffling

1. List all the details you can think of about your topic. List one item per line.

2. Review your list, using the MOVE command of your word processor to group similar items on your list.

3. Press RETURN a few times after you form a cluster of similar items so that you'll be able to see each cluster as a separate unit.

4. Review each cluster and write a topic idea. (Be sure INSERT is turned on. Your word processor will allow space on the screen for you to add your ideas.) Use capital letters to make your topic idea stand out.

5. Write down a focusing statement. Then, if you feel ready, begin drafting. If you want, you can continue adding ideas if you think of some as you draft.

6. Save your file at any time. When you are ready to begin drafting, you can load the file and draft, keeping your ideas at the top of your screen for as long as you need them. (Note: If your word processor has windows—or a split screen function— then you can load your prewriting ideas in the top window and open a separate file for your draft in the bottom window.)

Technique 3—Question Your Topic

The point of the preceding technique, creating and shuffling lists, was to capture ideas and then organize them, in order to clarify your view of a topic. This next technique continues that process of clarification, and also helps you generate more information about it through the natural, human process of asking and answering questions.

You can *question* your topic at just about any time in a writing project. You could do it as a follow-up technique after you have created and shuffled lists or otherwise worked your way to a fairly precise topic and focus for a paper. Or you could use questions about a very general topic as an alternative way to build up a good long list of details. You could also turn to questions when you feel yourself running dry in a drafting session.

If you are working with a general topic ("Education," "Vocations," "Personal Health Care," "Building My Financial Future," etc.), just make that topic the target of your questions. If you have already developed a more precise thesis statement, and want to explore it further, highlight the key phrases in the statement so that you can use each of them as targets of questions. Working with the thesis statement for a paper on "education," for example, you might underscore three words or phrases: "A responsible education must <u>combine</u> the ideals of <u>liberal education</u> and <u>career education</u>." Then, you might focus some who-what-when-where-why questions on each of these words or phrases.

Questions for Probing Your Topic

In exploring your topic, answer the following questions as fully or as minimally as you like:

1. *What* is a full, accurate description of it?

2. *What* are its most characteristic features or functions?

3. *What* are its most unusual or surprising features or functions?

4. *What* are the most important things to understand about it?

5. *What* does it mean? Does this judgment vary from person to person? Why?

6. Under *what* conditions does it happen?

7. *Where* is it most likely to happen?

8. *What* people are most likely to be involved with it?

9. *How* do most people react to it personally? Politically? Morally?

10. *How* do I react to it?

11. *What* consequences does it have for people or society? How significant are they?

12. *How* good (or effective, or understandable, or well-made, or entertaining, etc.) is it? Using what criteria?

13. *How* does a person do it?

14. *What* other things can it be compared to? What are the points of similarity or difference?

15. *How* does it compare with other things in effectiveness (understandability, quality of construction, entertainment value, etc.)?

16. *What* arguments can be made to support it?

17. *What* arguments can be made to attack it?

IDEA FILE: COMPUTER WRITING

Questioning Your Topic

Generate your own who-what-when-where-why questions at the computer. If you are using a word processor, you might consider keeping a special file that you call up whenever you want to question your topic along these lines. Here's how to proceed:

1. Open a file called "Questions." In that file, type who, what, when, where, and why as categories for you to use as you think of questions. Then save your file.

   > Questioning the Topic
   > TOPIC:
   >   who
   >   what
   >   when
   >   where
   >   why

2. Now, with your current writing assignment in mind, type in questions appropriate to each category. Don't try to think of all the "who" questions that you possibly can before you go on to "what" or "why" questions. Use your word processor flexibly, moving back and forth as much as you like, adding a "who" question, then a "where" question, then another "who" question, and so on. When you finish, save your file with a new name. Thus you won't have erased your original "template" file. (Remember, if you save the file with a new name every time you use it, then you will always have a "clean" file with your 5 w's listed, but without questions underneath them.)

3. Answer the questions you've created, then use the file with the answers to your questions as the file in which you draft your essay. Just move the cursor to a space below the questions and answers, and start drafting. You can review your responses anytime you want. If you want to move any of your words or phrases from the top of your file to the draft you are creating at the bottom of the file, you can do so quickly. When you finish, save your file.

4. As you move toward a completed rough draft, erase the questions and answers from the top of the file and save the file

with a new name. In this way, you'll still have a copy of your rough draft file *including* the prewriting responses. But you'll now have a separate file to use as you move toward final revising and editing.

Summary

When you are enrolled in five or six college courses, you may face a lot of writing, especially if a college writing course is part of your schedule. In this chapter we have suggested some approaches that will be useful in your writing course or in other college courses. We have suggested ways that you can respond to assignments based on personal experiences, and outlined specialized strategies for exploring and discovering ideas that may save you time.

We have stressed that, as with other writing assignments, you need to find out what you know about your topic and what you would like to say about your topic before you begin drafting a personal experience essay. We hope that you'll practice some of the strategies we have introduced here. Only by trying them out will you discover which ones seem most useful for *you* and for *your* writing needs.

TEAMWORK WRITING

"Creating and shuffling lists" can work quite well with several students collaborating to help each other. Each person can bring a brainstormed list to class. Each group member can look over the list, looking for patterns that suggest the writer's point of view. (Refer to the four questions on p. 182 to guide you.) The final part of Strategy 7, writing a sentence that states a focus on the topic, probably will work best if each writer phrases a sentence for his or her own topic before the group responds. In discussion, the group can point out ideas the writer may have missed from the list, as well as places where topic sentences seem to misinterpret the meaning buried in the clusters.

One important thing to remember about collaborative work is that each person in the group helps the others because he or she wants help in return. This means that you make comments that are candid but tactful. If you sense problems in the way a person is working with details to make clusters, or phrasing the meanings of clusters, or creating a focus sentence on the topic, by all means bring this out. But do it in the spirit of helpfulness. After all, your time will come to be "talked about" in a group, and then you will want the other people to be polite to you.

Writing Exercises

1. Explore additional topics that you could write about. Do some rapid writing in your notebook, guided by these "working" titles:

My Public and Private Selves

A Place from My Past

A Person Who Influenced Me Strongly

One of My Secrets

One way to guide your rapid writing is to divide an hour of drafting time among several different topics. Write on one topic for at least twenty minutes, then take a break. Repeat the cycle on two additional topics. Keep each of the rapid writings for later use, either on separate sheets of paper or saved in a computer file. When you have completed three different rapid writings, read through all of them, looking for hints about which might be the best place to start drafting:

a. Which draft is the longest?

b. Which draft has the most specific details?

c. Which draft is the most humorous?

d. Which draft seems to be the most original?

e. Which draft would you like to spend more time with?

Another way to use guided rapid writing is to concentrate an hour of drafting time on one topic. Pick one of the four working titles, and write about it for at least fifteen minutes. Read over your material and try to sense the direction your writing is taking you. Put the first version aside and out of sight (or save it and clear your screen, if you are doing computer writing). Without looking at the first version, start over at the beginning, and write rapidly for at least twenty minutes. Read your second version, before putting it aside and taking a break. Later, without looking at either of the earlier versions, start at the beginning and write rapidly for at least twenty-five minutes.

2. Do some rapid writing on a personal topic. At the top of a sheet of paper, write a statement about the topic on which you plan to focus your writing project. Just start writing—your fingers moving, even if your brain is not ready to write yet. If you don't have anything to say, just write the topic sentence a few times. Or, close your eyes and write quickly "in the dark" for a few minutes so that your ideas can flow with no chance that you will be distracted by errors or "dumb" ideas. (If you are using a word processor, turn the monitor off or adjust the contrast so that you can't see your words as you type them.)

After ten minutes of rapid writing, read over what you wrote. Mark phrases or words that seem as if they *might* be useful or interesting. Circle one of the things you just underscored. Write this as a new topic sentence at the top of a clean sheet of paper. Start the rapid-writing game over again to see where ten more minutes of spontaneous drafting may take you.

Review both rapid-writings. Make a *list* of ideas, facts, questions, problems, etc., that you generated during the past half hour. Save the list for possible future use.

3. Put a "target" word or phrase at the top of a sheet of paper (or the top of your computer screen). Sometimes you can use words from your general topic, or one of the underscored phrases from a detailed statement, so that your target is simply "Personal Health Care" or "Career Education." Sometimes, you may need to add a few more words to clarify exactly what you are using as your target.

Apply the "Questions for Probing Your Topic" (p. 185–186) to the target word, substituting your target word for the word *it* as you answer the questions. Few, if any, topics could serve as "it" for all of these questions. Work with the questions that seem most applicable or relevant.

4. Go to the library and find several nonfiction books based on an author's personal experience. Skim each of these books, trying to determine how the author has organized and developed his or her experiences. Does the organization seem to be suggested by the topic? Explain. Record your conclusions in your notebook.

5. One of our goals in this book is to encourage you to grow as a writer. To that end, it is important that you monitor your changing writing processes. Take a few minutes to look through your writing notebook. In particular, note which writing strategies seem to be working well for you. Reassess your writing at this point in the semester. When you write, what additional strategies are you using that you did not use earlier in the semester? Have you changed or refined any of the strategies you used in the past? Are you finding it any easier to shift intentions for your writing sessions? Evaluate the strategies that you have used from previous chapters in this text. Which ones do you think you'll continue to use? Which strategies have not been useful for you? Explain.

Suggestions for Writing

1. Write an essay about some current political or social crisis that people are talking about. Develop your personal opinion about the topic. Explain why you believe what you believe. Some topics of continuing interest are: the stock market crash of 1987, the surro-

gate motherhood controversy, nuclear disarmament, politics and privacy, illiteracy, and the plight of the homeless.

2. Write an essay (between 1000 and 1500 words) of personal insight that uses the same basic structure and approach as Annie Dillard's short essay "On a Hill Far Away" [in *Teaching a Stone To Talk* (New York: Harper and Row, 1982) p. 77]. As you begin this project, you could review the first prewriting technique (see p. 177) and use it to develop details about a point in your life when you discovered some insight into yourself or into life. Notice how the "flashback" structure of "On a Hill Far Away" lets Dillard concentrate on one brief event, but put it in the context of earlier events in her life.

3. Write an essay in which you discuss your public and private selves. What do you appear to be to others, and what are you really? How similar or different are the "real" you and the person you try to be, or would like to be, or pretend to be?

4. Write about an experience or a person that was significant to you. Try to recall, as vividly as possible, the "place" of this event or person. (Country? Inside or outdoors? Season and weather? Surrounding sounds, sights, smells?) Also, try to recall the person. What was he or she like? Physical traits? Mental traits? Habits? Peculiarities?

Writing Projects Based on Reading

7

Overview of Writing Strategies

In this chapter, we will focus on the relationship between reading and writing. In the process, we will explore these writing strategies:

1. Critical reading

2. Summary writing

3. Responding to what you read: the "sumaction" paper

4. Compare and contrast

5. Keep an idea file

6. Study an overview article

Reading and Writing Connections

It probably is no great surprise that this book contains a chapter like this, for college writing projects—in all kinds of courses—frequently depend on reading assignments. If your English teacher asked you to write a paper about your own hopes and goals for the future after you read *Megatrends*, John Naisbitt's best-seller that predicts the kinds of changes Americans can expect in the next decade, the assignment would ask for your personal experiences and opinions. But your teacher would expect you to develop your personal observations within the framework of the ten "megatrends" of the future that John Naisbitt predicts. To write your paper you would have to:

1. Read *Megatrends* closely enough to understand what Naisbitt means by the shifts from industrial society to information society, from national economy to world economy, from institutional help to self-help, from hierarchies to networks—and a half dozen other trends as well.

2. Remember the ten trends and use them to "sort through" your hopes and goals for the future—contrasting them with other peoples' goals—so that you can decide which of the ten megatrends are likely to have the greatest impact on you.

3. Extract enough detail on the megatrends you select so that readers will realize that you are organizing your personal writing within John Naisbitt's framework.

Many writing assignments in college classes require that students read and understand written materials before they can really start the writing project. Assignments often require that they examine their reading and then go beyond it as they write about complex issues. For instance:

1. An economics professor might use *Megatrends* as the starting point for a fairly objective research assignment.

   "Select one chapter in *Megatrends* that you see as relating to important economic principles we have explored since midterm. Beginning with the sources Naisbitt cites in his notes to the chapter, develop a 2000-word paper clarifying the economic principles at work in John Naisbitt's chapter."

2. A professor of computer science or communications theory might use the book as the starting point for a research assignment with an argumentative edge.

   "In his chapter on the information society, Naisbitt says that, as computers become more and more important in American life, everyone will need to be computer literate. As you know, though, there are people who disagree with this view; in fact, Naisbitt himself offers contrary evidence in that chapter and other parts of his book. In about 1500 words, develop an argument on one side or the other of this controversy. Support your points with material from Naisbitt's book, from your textbook in this course, and from at least two other sources published in the last year."

3. A professor with futuristic interests might use the book to assign a compare-contrast essay.

   "Alvin Toffler's *Future Shock* and John Naisbitt's *Megatrends* were both best-selling, much-quoted works of futurism—one in the 1970s, the other in the 1980s. Write a five-page review essay that conveys the essential nature and "flavor" of each book, and that compares the two books to each other. (Here are some things you might think about as you read: What are the major similarities of the futures the two books predict and what are the major differences? Does the later book contradict parts of the earlier one, or modify the earlier predictions in some way?)"

Reading—critically and with understanding—is as important to writing assignments like the preceding, as it is to many other types of writing projects that college professors assign to help you learn within their courses. Such reading, of course, can be as time-consuming as it is important to the success of writing projects. So it makes sense to use some special strategies to increase your efficiency and effectiveness as a reader and as a writer. In this chapter we will suggest several strategies that will help you with the kinds of assignments most common in college—writing projects based on reading.

The most important thing you can do to get started on a college writing project involving written materials is to read actively and intelligently—so that you fully understand the material you are going to write about. You should read with pen or pencil in hand, marking key points on the page—*if* the book or journal is yours—or taking notes on a separate piece of paper. As you read, continually challenge the ideas in the book. React, respond, argue with the author. Critical reading requires critical thinking.

Always read for more than "content." As you work, look for the structure of the information, the key points that organize content, the emphasis the writer gives to different sections. Make your own predictions about where the material is heading. Form your judgments about the relative importance of different points and how well the author is making the points.

Relatively few college writing assignments ask you simply to communicate objectively the contents of one specific essay or book. More typically, college assignments ask you to make "connections" of some kind with the material you are reading—either connections to other readings and academic information, connections to your own opinions and life, or connections to other students' opinions. As you work with college writing projects, you will be able to use a variety of reading strategies.

Frequently, college professors arrange writing projects so that you can respond to a reading assignment or apply ideas in the reading to what you have observed in life. For example:

1. In the second chapter of *Megatrends*, John Naisbitt describes a demand for human contact and human values that grows along with technological and social changes that seem to reduce such factors. Based on your own personal experiences (and those of family mem-

bers and other personal acquaintances of yours), would you say that there is a drive for "high touch" to counterbalance the "high tech" in life?

2. As you read *Megatrends,* what are the three or four predictions of Naisbitt's that strike you as having the greatest possible impact on life in the United States? Write an article that emphasizes these predictions and explains why you think they would have so much impact.

3. How do you react to the shift (in economic power, prestige, growth, etc.) of the United States from Northeast to Southwest that Naisbitt describes in Chapter Nine? The thesis of your four-page paper should emphasize your reactions to specific details in the chapter, and the reasons behind them. Be sure that your paper makes it clear what part of the country you are from.

There are a number of reasons why teachers try to make connections between your writing assignments and your life, opinions, and personal values. Writing assignments that make these connections

1. help you to organize the author's views and information according to your way of thinking and feeling so that you realize that academic assignments apply to "real life."

2. test your intellectual ability to do more than read and memorize—since *application* of material is a higher-level thinking ability than *recalling* information.

3. help you to develop your ability to apply material, and to acquire the intellectual habit of letting information from one context "carry over" so that it can apply to other situations.

4. contribute to the learning process—since one is much more likely to learn more working with material of personal significance than material of only abstract or "academic" interest.

So as you read, it makes sense to mark passages (or take separate notes) as you feel strong responses to what you're reading. Keep track of places where you disagree strongly with opinions, or where you agree strongly; places where you know of an example (in your life, town, campus, etc.) that proves or disproves an important point the writer is making; places where you find an important point morally or ethically objectionable; places where you think the writer is contradicting something you have read, learned in college courses, or seen on television news; or places where you find yourself "changing your mind" about something you have known or believed in the past. Here is an example of the type of notes you might make as you read:

Unless banks reconceptualize what business they are in, they will be out of business.

Note: the Indus-
trial Banks in
Colorado have
failed this
year.

In the next few years we will witness many bank mergers and bank failures. When I was a young person growing up with the memories of the Depression all around me, bank failures meant *the end of the world.* Today bank failures only mean that, like the railroaders, some bankers are just waiting around for their virtue to be rewarded. There will still be abundant banking services available from many kinds of institutions.

With the death of the thirty-year fixed-rate loan, companies in the life-insurance industry must reconceptualize what business they are in, or many of them will be out of business.

In discussing the shift from short-term to long-term and the need for almost universal reconceptualization, I have used business examples because the relatively swift and harsh judgments of the marketplace allow us to see what is occurring more clearly. Business knows about change sooner than the rest of us.

But this need for reexamination and reconceptualization applies throughout the society. Here are some examples from other areas:

- Labor unions are now entirely preoccupied with survival. All of their actions are short-term and defensive in nature. Unless labor unions reconceptualize their role in the society, they will continue on their dramatic downhill slide.

Note: a lot of
people have had
to reconceptual-
ize their ca-
reers too.

They still
haven't rede-
fined themselves

- The two national political parties will continue in name only unless they reconceptualize their role in the light of all the changes that have occurred in the last three decades. Because Ronald Reagan is in the White House, what is left of the Republican party has little incentive to examine its status. What's left of the Democratic party is at this writing just waiting for it all to come down on President Reagan, and then they believe they'll just pick up the pieces; that is the road to disaster and continued decline. And the spectacle, beginning in 1981, of the AFL-CIO giving money directly to the Democratic party (under George Meany contributions were made only to favored candidates) and becoming its key source of financing appears to be another case of dinosaurs mating.

Yes. True at
Colorado State
University.

- Universities—with substantial cutbacks in federal funding, changes in their student populations, and the heavy blows of inflation—are hooking up right and left with companies for joint ventures in bioengineering and telecommunication: a new era of university-industry cooperation and a new concept of what a university is.

- Short-term solutions in dealing with the dumping of toxic wastes are catching up with us in all parts of the country.

- And the long-term implications of short-term decisions involving many of our nonrenewable natural resources have been the subject of national debate for a decade. The reconceptualization here is moving from conquerors of nature to a partnership with nature.

I wonder if this is true for all socioeconomic groups.

- Beginning with the granola ethic in California a dozen years ago, and moving through new concerns about nutrition and physical well-being, there has been evolving a reconceptualization of health care from a sickness orientation to a wellness orientation, and from short-term to long-term.

But what happened to all the interest in solar homes?

- In energy during the last two decades, we have moved from "nuclear is the answer" to an emphasis on a diversity of fuel sources, with the mix of fuels varying geographically—all of this, of course, instructed by longer-term considerations.

Source: John Naisbitt, *Megatrends: Ten New Directions Transforming Our Lives* (New York: Warner Books, 1984) pp. 96–97.

■ Strategy 1—Critical Reading

One of the best ways to make sure you are reading critically and intelligently is to try to find—and write down—responses to a number of critical-reading questions. When you are ready to read an article or book that you will write about later, skim over this strategy a few times; then leave this text open to the questions. As you read, look for material that relates to these questions. Highlight important points on the page, or take separate notes. Stop periodically to write down your response to the questions.

Critical-Reading Questions

1. Begin with personal connections to whatever you are reading. What experiences have you had that relate to some of the ideas in the book (or article)? Do you have any personal questions that you are hoping the book (or article) will answer? (Take time to write your questions and experiences in your notebook. You'll enjoy your reading a lot more if you can find some personal connections to the topic.)

2. What are the main parts or sections of the piece? (Note the key sentences—those that make assertions that form the skeleton of the piece.)

3. Does the writer back assertions with specifics? (Note which key

sentences [question 2] have lots of supporting material, and which are backed with fewer details, examples, statistics, quotations, etc.)

4. Are there any places where the writer may not be making literally true statements? (Note places where you see sarcasm; ironic statements, the opposite of what the writer really means; exaggeration for humor; figures of speech; etc.)

5. Which are the more important and less important parts or sections of the piece? (In making this judgment, consider what you observed in answering questions 1, 2, and 3. Note where the central emphasis of the piece is located. How do you know this is the central emphasis? Could you explain your judgment to the teacher you will be writing for?)

6. Outline the main skeleton of the piece. (Create an outline to show the central emphasis, and how the various key sentences relate to the central emphasis and to each other.)

7. Summarize the piece for a person who has not read it. (Write a 100–200-word summary that makes the central emphasis clear and shows how other points relate to the central emphasis.)

An Example of Strategy 1 in Action. As an example of how you might use the intelligent reading of *Strategy 1*, we will look at how one person worked with a brief presentation of the rather complex issue of consumer finance. First, here is one of the regular "Managing Your Money" columns from *U. S. News & World Report* marked up and annotated in response to questions 1, 2, and 4.

Playing the "Float" for Legal Profits

Two kinds of "float": illegal and legal.

Definition and then examples of legal float that consumers use.

The big brokerage firm of E. F. Hutton has pleaded guilty to fraud stemming from illegal use of "float" in handling checking accounts. If individuals are careful, they can make use of float profitably and legally.

Float is money in transit. For example, a taxpayer enjoyed a two-week float, during which he drew interest on the funds, when his check, mailed to the Internal Revenue Service on April 15, was not charged to his account until April 29. Similarly, an American charged a meal on a credit card in Ghent, Belgium, in September, 1984, and was billed in April, 1985. In a more common case, a husband deposits a paycheck in the bank and his wife immediately mails a check against it to pay a charge-account bill, counting on the paycheck to clear before her check for the charge account reaches the bank for payment.

Since 40 billion checks are written each year, the float is enormous. It is widely used in the form of interest-free "loans" by companies.

Example of
illegal float
(like the Hutton
scheme?)

As an example of illegal use, a large firm has accounts with hundreds of banks, many in remote areas with no access to the automated check-clearing system. The company might deposit in a Virginia bank a check for $300,000 drawn on a small bank in Nebraska. The firm does not have $300,000 in this bank but knows that its check will take five business days to clear. So, in three or four days, it deposits by courier or wire $500,000 in the Nebraska bank, drawing on a remote Oregon bank in which the firm does not have $500,000 but in which, just before five business days are up, it will deposit $800,000 drawn on another remote bank and so on.

Banks use float
when they "hold"
checks—not pay
interest even
though they have
"cleared" and
banks can use
the money.

Banks and individuals also use float. A sore point with individuals is that many banks create float by putting an automatic "hold" on deposited checks. As an example, when a customer of First American Bank in Washington, D.C., deposits a check drawn on an Illinois bank, the money will not be credited to his or her account for eight business days. The bank, however, usually will receive the funds in one or two days, the time it takes 90 percent of checks to clear.

First American's hold or "delayed availability" schedule lists 80 areas, showing hold days for each. Many banks list only three types of holds: For local checks, for other in-state checks and for out-of-state checks.

The banks' explanation for holds is that a deposited check might bounce, although the Federal Reserve Board says that only 1 percent do.

Background in-
formation about
length of time
checks may be
held.

The U.S. Public Interest Research Group surveyed 669 banks and savings associations and found that 52 percent put holds of three to five days on local checks, 75 percent put holds of over a week on out-of-state checks and 20 percent held out-of-state checks for more than two weeks. A third of the banks even held local cashier's checks for three days.

A U.S. League of Savings Institutions survey found that the median hold time for S&L's was three days for local, seven for other in-state and 10 for out-of-state checks.

However, many community banks that know their customers do have favorable policies such as next-day credit on most deposits. As an example, the Burke & Herbert Bank in Alexandria, Va., has no automatic "hold until collected" policy. But a hold may be imposed on a new depositor not well-known to the bank, on a depositor who carries a small balance but deposits a large check or on a depositor frequently overdrawn.

It should be noted that most institutions will start interest payments in an interest-bearing checking account or an individual retirement account on the day after deposit, whether or not a hold is imposed.

To use float
safely you need
to know your
bank's hold
policy.

To use the float safely and avoid overdraft charges, you need to know your bank's hold policy and how long it usually takes for a check to go through the clearing system.

Today, businesses try to deposit checks immediately. You can make a table showing the average clearing time

How to find this
out.

for checks you frequently write. By examining the back of a canceled check you will see a stamp that shows the date that the check reached your nearest Federal Reserve clearing facility or local clearinghouse. On that date, the check received "provisional clearance" and was charged to your account.

Source: John W. Hazard, "Playing the 'Float' for Legal Profits," *U. S. News & World Report,* May 27, 1985, p. 75.

Here is a brief outline and a few comments about the "Playing the 'Float'" article:

1. "Float" ("money in transit") can be used legally or illegally by consumers.
   a. Legal examples: earn money while check clears; delay between charging on a credit card and having to pay the bill.
   b. Illegal examples: writing a check on an account with insufficient funds; covering it with a check on a different account with insufficient funds.
2. Banks use float in a way that irritates many consumers.
   a. Banks may hold deposited checks (before starting to pay interest on the money) for much longer than it takes checks to clear.
   b. Example of First American Bank: holds checks 8 days, but for 90% of all checks, the bank actually has the money in 2 days.
   c. Banks claim the delay is to guard against bouncing checks, but the Federal Reserve Board says only 1% of checks bounce.
3. There is a lot of variation in the hold policies and check clearance time of banks.
   a. Same-state checks usually will be held longer than local checks, out-of-state checks even longer.
   b. Established customers with substantial balances in accounts may not have their checks held, while new customers and people with records of bouncing checks may.
4. To use float without risk of overdraft charges, you must know your bank's hold policy and check-clearance time. You can look into this by checking the backs of canceled checks for the dates they cleared a Federal Reserve Bank; that's the date interest was credited to your account.

Some Comments:
   a. The central emphasis of "Playing the 'Float'" is that there is money to be made in the time it takes money to move with checks. The writer seems to want to inform readers about how float works; in the process of doing that, he also informs them of problematic practices banks use to make money from float.

b. There are specific examples in all the points, though many more in the areas dealing with legal float and with banking practices.

c. There is a little information—maybe for background—about how corporations could use float illegally. But this does not seem to be the center of the article.

The suggestions for critical reading discussed in this section do not exhaust the questions you might ask in analyzing nonfiction sources. But following these guidelines—and responding to them in writing as you read—can help you become very familiar with a written source.

■ Strategy 2—Summary Writing

Rick Gebhardt's sixth-grade teacher loved to tell his students, "If you can't write it out in your own words, you really don't know it." There is a lot of truth in that statement. In order to "translate" into your own language the ideas in a book or article you have read, you must understand the writer's ideas. The process of writing about the author's ideas—the coordination of brain, hand, and eyes during writing—helps you learn the material you are writing about. As you write, you think about what you are writing, and see your words with your eyes—something especially important for those of you who are "visual" learners. For this reason, writing summaries is a useful strategy to use when you begin to work with a writing project based on reading.

As you can see from the critical-reading questions in *Strategy 1,* you should think of a summary as growing naturally out of intelligent, critical reading. In a sense, the reason you should try to answer questions 1–4 and outline the skeleton of an article is to help you write a summary of the article, for a summary should communicate the central emphasis and the overall "skeleton" of points compactly. Consider the following summary:

> John Naisbitt's *Megatrends* (Warner Books, 1984) describes, to use the words of its subtitle, "ten new directions transforming our lives." Naisbitt describes these trends in American life—changes of direction in society or human attitudes or both—as a series of shifts: from an industrial to information society; from forced technology to a world of "high-tech/high touch"; from a national to a world economy; from short- to long-term approaches; from centralization to decentralization; from institutional to self-help; from representative to participatory democracy; from hierarchies to networking; from the north to the south; and from simple either/or options to multiple options. Because these trends are now underway and likely to continue for some time, Naisbitt says that we are "living in the time of the parenthesis," in a time between eras that is both unsettling and filled with possibility. And Naisbitt's goal for his book seems to be to help us get a clear enough look at "the road ahead" that we can exploit the possibilities the new era may bring.

This very brief summary (less than 200 words about a 330-page book) captures the central emphasis of the book: ongoing trends that are transforming America. And it sketches the topics of the book in the order the book presents them, and so gives a feel for the structure (or "skeleton") of the book. A person completely unfamiliar with Naisbitt's book would know, from this capsule treatment, that the book is about present changes and their possible future impact. But because of its brevity, the summary does not communicate as much as it would if it treated each of the ten megatrends in a sentence. In fact, to summarize a ten-chapter book, it might make sense to use about a dozen paragraphs: an introduction highlighting the central emphasis of the book; a paragraph on each chapter—each relating to the central emphasis and including illustrative material to help an unfamiliar reader understand the main points; and a conclusion.

The key issue in writing a summary, then, is not length, but whether it communicates to a reader the main points and overall argument of the original. With that criterion in mind, how effective would you say this piece of writing is in summarizing the preceding *U.S. News & World Report* article (pp. 197–199)?

> In "Playing the 'Float' for Legal Profits," John W. Hazard provides information about financial "float" (that is, "money in transit" from the time a check is written to the time it is credited to an account) so that general consumers can understand and use this financial principle. While he mentions that float can be manipulated illegally, Hazard concentrates on legal applications, such as when a consumer's checking account pays interest during the two weeks it takes a check to move through the mail to a business, and then through the banking system into the business's account.
>
> Float works for banks as well as consumers, and Hazard goes into a good bit of detail on banking practices, because consumers need to understand them in order to use float themselves. When a person deposits a check in his or her account, the bank "holds" the check from three days to two weeks to guard against checks that bounce, though, as Hazard notes, the Federal Reserve Board says that only 1% of checks bounce. How long banks hold a check, Hazard points out, depends on a lot of different things: whether a check is written against a local bank, an in-state bank, or an out-of-state bank; as well as whether its depositor is an established customer, a new depositor, or a customer with a record of bouncing checks.
>
> A person who wants to profit from float without risking overdraft charges, Hazard concludes, needs to learn his or her bank's hold policy and how long its checks take to clear the regional Federal Reserve Bank. To find this out, he suggests that you look at the dates on the backs of canceled checks to see when they cleared the Federal Reserve clearing center—and so started drawing interest.

There are some other things to keep in mind as you try to work from the critical-reading questions to a summary. As you read the following list of criteria for evaluating a summary, glance back at the summaries of *Megatrends* and "Playing the 'Float.'" Later, evaluate your summaries using these criteria:

1. Make sure that your summary conveys the article's central emphasis, and indicates how the various points in the article "work together" to give that emphasis.

2. Use connectors (like "then," "next," "second point") and contrasters (like "on the other hand," "but then," "even though") to help readers see how the author's points relate to each other.

3. Use a few specific details or very brief quotes (a few words only, woven into your sentences) to help your readers understand the author's points. But do not try to summarize all the evidence the author uses.

4. Mention the author's name and the title toward the beginning of the summary.

5. Later, periodically use the author's name (or a pronoun that refers to the author) or the title (perhaps shortened, or a pronoun that refers to the title) to "remind" the reader that you are passing on ideas and information from another person. The point, here, is be sure your readers remember they are reading your account of another person's ideas and information. The habit of dropping "credits" into your summary, by the way, will help you avoid unconscious plagiarism when you work with research papers and other papers using material from written sources.

6. Keep your work as "objective" or "neutral" as you can. Don't present your opinions or argue with the author.

IDEA FILE: COMPUTER WRITING

Writing a Summary

Sometimes writer's block can be cured by writing. When you have a summary to write, first remind yourself of the kinds of information you need to include. Begin by typing out the key ingredients of a summary:

> Author's Name:
> Title:
> Main Points:

Add as much information as possible to your "summary file." After you accumulate enough material to get started, you can go back to the start of your file and write out your first few sentences, based on the information you gathered. The following is an example of how a writer might create a summary of *Megatrends* on the computer.

1. Type out the key ingredients of the summary:

> Author's Name:
> Title:
> Main Points:

2. Fill in the blanks:

> Author's Name: John Naisbitt
> Title: *Megatrends* (Warner Books, 1984)
> Main Points: describes trends that are transforming our lives. Says we are "living in the time of the parenthesis."

3. Begin turning the material into a summary, transforming the phrases into sentences.

■ Strategy 3—Responding to What You Read: The "Sumaction" Paper

The critical-reading guidelines of Strategy 1 and the summary skills of Strategy 2 can help you understand individual articles or other materials. But many papers require that you develop a more extensive personal response to what you read. Knowing why you have responded as you did to a text will help you prepare to write about your response. Words on the page may trigger your response, but only if they connect with ideas, attitudes, beliefs, or values within you. To record those responses, try to write rapidly about these questions:

1. What on the page triggered a response? What was my response?

2. What in me contributed to the response?

3. What do I respond most strongly to in the reading—and why?

4. What experience(s) have I had that are similar to the experiences related by the author?

Papers that require a personal response are often some form of what we call the *sumaction* paper. When you get your next assignment based on reading, try writing a several-paragraph *sumaction*—summary plus reaction. Begin with a paragraph that compactly and objectively summarizes the article. Then shift to your responses: what did you respond to most strongly in the article and why? What experiences of your own confirmed or contradicted the author's ideas?

The idea of connecting or blending summary and reaction is important in at least two kinds of academic writing: "literary" papers, and "critical" reports on journal articles.

Application of the "Sumaction"—The Response Paper.
Courses in literature, drama, film, music, or art deal with esthetic
forms that communicate largely through the human responses they
trigger. So professors in these fields often give writing assignments
that encourage students to use their responses to demonstrate their
understanding of a work. Here, for example, a student explores her responses to the way relationships between men and women are treated
in Henrik Ibsen's 1879 play, *A Doll's House,* in a draft of a paper on "A
Central Issue in Ibsen and in American Society."

> I react quite strongly to the sort of man/woman re-
> lationship portrayed in <u>A Doll's House</u>. A definite
> double standard is evident. It seems that a wife's ded-
> ication to her husband is a social requirement, while
> any show of love or consideration on the husband's part
> is due to his kind and generous nature. As Torvald says,
> "You have loved me as a wife ought to love her husband"
> (p. 192). For the majority of the play, Nora accepts
> this viewpoint. She herself tells Torvald, "I would not
> think of going against your wishes" (p. 125). In other
> words, she is living for someone else. Even the world-
> wise Mrs. Linde feels life is meaningless for a woman
> unless she has someone else to live for (p. 125).
> Fortunately, for myself and those around me, I cannot
> accept this viewpoint. Dedicating oneself to another
> is not impossible, nor is it wrong. But before you can
> live for someone else, you must first live for your-
> self. Then if you want to make the sacrifice, at least
> you will realize the cost. Poor Nora had given herself
> up totally without knowing what she was really losing.
> And I know of some other people who are doing much that
> same thing.
> Unfortunately, the problem lies not in what these
> women do, but why they do it. Ibsen shows the preju-
> diced classification of women near the turn of the cen-
> tury. Torvald consistently generalizes that Nora is
> "just like a woman" and even goes so far as to exclaim
> that Nora is incapable of understanding how to act on
> her own responsibility (p. 192). And women believed it
> because society (and husbands!) arranged their lives
> that way.
> In all fairness, Torvald's chauvinism and that of his
> compatriots is undoubtedly ingrained. Many men don't
> realize what they are doing. They are simply following
> social standards. For this reason, I cannot accept
> Nora's solution of escape. The fault lies not with
> women or with men, but with the relationship between
> the two. Thus solutions and changes need to be made in
> conjunction with one another. We all need to grow to-
> gether. It's better than growing apart.
>
> Source: Rosalyn Smith

Application of the "Sumaction"—The Critical Report. Professors in almost any field may assign journal articles that explore in detail specialized features of a course. Often, they structure these assignments so that students report on their readings in a common format, and they may arrange for students to pool their research by making reports to the class. Here, a student follows an education professor's "critical abstract" format—a sort of formalized sumaction.

<u>Publishing information</u> : Myra Sadker and David Sadker, "Sexual Discrimination in the Elementary School." The National Elementary Principal, pp. 41–45.

<u>Purpose</u> : The purpose of this study is to show that young children learn their sex roles through a hidden curriculum, a curriculum provided, not by books and classes, but by living in and experiencing the process of schooling.

<u>Points of discussion</u> : Because boys mature more slowly than girls, they may have more conflicts in school and receive more of the teachers' active attention than girls do. They begin to learn that they are naughtier than girls and therefore more deserving of reprimands. Boys are usually less successful than girls in the race for grades (two–thirds of all grade repeaters are boys).

Girls are praised for being quiet and neat and polite. This can hamper their learning process by leading them to avoid intellectual challenge.

For boys, the elementary school staffed largely by females may conflict with their active lifestyle; but girls experience their own difficulties with staffing patterns. The elementary school tends to be a female world, but its leader is a man. So girls may learn that when a woman functions professionally, she takes orders from a man.

<u>Conclusions</u> : The authors conclude that schools pose more problems for girls than for boys, because they teach inferiority, docility, and submissiveness. They feel it should be the challenge of elementary schools to eliminate sexist practices and make equality of opportunity a daily reality.

<u>My evaluation</u> : I was impressed with this article because it seemed to say the opposite of what I always found myself believing. I always thought that the immaturity of boys and the "dominant mother images" in the schools would mean that boys would be damaged by the schools more than girls.

If I had more time, I would like to read more recent articles on this topic, possibly a recent article by the same authors. It seems to me as if the sex–role situation in elementary schools probably has changed

in the past few years. And yet, I know that there still
are quite a few sharp differences in "acceptable" behavior by men and women in America.

IDEA FILE: COMPUTER WRITING

Report Formats

If you have to write a report, find out early what format your
teacher wants it to be in. Then create a template file for the report
format. For example, to prepare to write the critical report described in this chapter, you could begin by typing the following
categories into your word processor:

Publishing Information
Purpose
Points of Discussion
Conclusions
My Evaluation

Save your file—before filling in the categories—calling it something like creport.fmt (for critical report format). Then, when
you begin writing another report that requires the critical report
format, just load your master file and start writing. You'll have
to save each file with a new name, though, so that you won't
wipe out your template file.

By typing in the categories first and writing later, you can easily move from one section to another as you generate ideas or
draft your paper. For instance, if you feel that it would be helpful
to write down the purpose of your paper first, you can move your
cursor to a blank line below **PURPOSE** and start writing. After
you've run out of ideas, you can move your cursor to another part
of your paper and draft some ideas there. Let your paper grow as
you write, moving from one section to another as often as necessary and returning to previous sections when you think of new
ideas for those sections.

■ Strategy 4—Compare and Contrast

Frequently, college professors assign writing projects in which you
need to explain the connections you see between two or more written
pieces. These assignments may occur as brief essay test questions:

Explain the chief points of similarity and difference between the argument Henry Kissinger made in his essay on mid-East tensions and our
text's treatment of the subject in Chapter 13.

Or the assignment can be complex, such as the comparison of *Megatrends* and *Future Shock* earlier in this chapter (pp. 192–193). As in both

of those examples, writing assignments can be sharply focused and require a fairly explicit "comparison" and "contrast" of similarities and
differences between two written pieces. Or, you may be asked to work
more loosely with sources in order to develop an essay based on the
general background and common subject of your sources:

> Treasure hunting is an unusual sport. Read a chapter from *Treasure of the
> Atocha* by R. Duncan Mathewson and an essay called "Treasure Hunt,"
> from the *Wall Street Journal,* to get an overview of this topic. Use ideas
> and material from these readings in an essay based on your response to
> the material. (Pay special attention to areas where the two authors seem
> to be in greatest agreement and to areas where they seem to disagree.)

Whether sharply focused or fairly loose, comparison-contrast assignments are valuable intellectual exercises, since they force you to

1. develop a good understanding of two or more sources.

2. sort out key ideas from minor points or supporting details.

3. judge whether ideas from different sources are similar, different, or
   unrelated.

4. create statements that pull your judgments together and express
   them to other people.

The intellectual challenge of these activities makes it helpful to use
the following guidelines when you begin to work on a writing project
involving the comparison of written sources:

1. Read each source critically and study it separately so that you can
   outline or summarize its important points and not be thrown off its
   main argument by minor points or interesting pieces of supporting
   evidence.

2. Decide which key points from the different sources relate to each
   other—which are similar or different, and how. Decide what points
   in the sources are unrelated, and therefore incomparable.

3. Specify, in your words, the relationships between specific points.

4. Develop (out of the work you did for items 2 and 3) a general
   "thesis" statement about overall similarities or differences between
   the sources.

The first guideline—studying written sources separately so that
you understand them well—implies that you should make use of the
critical-reading questions discussed earlier in this chapter (see pp.
196–197). After you understand the two articles (or other written
sources) you are going to compare, you can use a *Comparison Chart* to
help you explore how the sources are similar or different.

To create a Comparison Chart about two sources (articles or books), use a large sheet of paper. Divide your paper into three columns. Then follow these directions:

1. Decide which of your two sources will serve as the "master source" in your comparison. This should be the longer or more detailed piece, the one that you find easier to follow, the one with the most up-to-date information, or simply the one you "like" better.

2. In the first column, state each point from the master source, compactly, in a complete sentence. Use your words, but include brief quotes of words or phrases where useful. Give page numbers of points in parentheses.

3. In the second column, state a parallel point on the same issue or subject from the second source. Be sure that each point stated in this column is on the same issue or subject or idea as the point stated in column 1. Line these points up with the points that they match in column 1.

4. In a third column, for each "hit," write a few words or phrases to show how the statements that line up relate. State the points compactly, as in the directions for column 1. Note "shadings of" as well as "absolute" differences or similarities.

When you've completed your chart, use it to write three detailed, specific sentences, each of which summarizes a different relationship between the way the two sources treat their common subject. Think of these sentences as potential thesis statements for a paper comparing the sources. Table 7.1 is an example of a comparison chart.

As you compare the sources in order to come up with summary sentences or thesis ideas, use the master source as a frame of reference for your thinking.

An Example of Strategy 4 in Action

1. First, the student writer set up a Comparison Chart using the headings suggested in Table 7.1.

2. Then, he filled in each of the spaces in his chart. (See Table 7.2 for an example of a completed chart.)

TABLE 7.1 *Comparison Chart*

Key Points (Master Source)	Key Points (Source Two)	Comparative Points
A.	1.	a.
B.	2.	b.
C.	3.	c.
D.	4.	d.
E.	5.	e.

(Continue in this fashion, adding as many points as necessary.)

TABLE 7.2 *Completed Comparison Chart*

Key Points (Master Source)	Key Points (Source 2)	Comparative Points
"Treasure Hunt" by D'Arcy O'Connor	*Treasure of the Atocha* by R. Duncan Matthewson III	
A. They haven't yet found the "money pit" and one woman—whose husband and son died as a result of the project—thinks that there isn't any treasure. They hope that a new shaft that they are about to sink will finally get to the pit.	1. Treasure Salvors, a salvage company, located a sunken treasure ship off the coast of Florida near the Marquesas Keys on July 20, 1985. They found the wreckage of a Spanish galleon.	a. search for treasure
B. Daniel Blankenship, a Miami contractor, has been searching for 22 years.	2. They have been searching for 16 years.	b. length of search
C. He is quoted as saying, "We're almost there."	3. Fisher often told his workers, "Today's the day."	c. unbelievable optimism
D. He put $97,000 of his own money into the search. A Montreal consortium of wealthy individuals is financing this, the "world's longest running and most expensive treasure hunt." They have put about $3 million into the venture.	4. The project cost $8 million. "They adapted every useful instrument of modern technology" in order to locate and retrieve the treasure.	d. expense involved
E. He almost died eleven years ago. A shaft dug to get close to the	5. Mel Fisher's son died ten years earlier.	e. risked lives

(continued)

TABLE 7.2 *Completed Comparison Chart*

Key Points (Master Source)	Key Points (Source 2)	Comparative Points
"money pit" caved in around him. A total of six people have died as a result of the search. But he kept going because he's got an "obsession to be part of the team that brings this crazy search to its conclusion."		
F. The company's president, David Tobias, feels that "in all probability "this will be the deepest and most expensive archeological dig ever made in North America."	6. They had to be quite resourceful in order to find the treasure. (according to the introduction)	f. archeological interest justified expense and difficulty
G. Samples from some test digs at the pit have turned up pieces of wood, charcoal, and china, among other items.	7. The treasure consisted of, among other things, over 1,000 silver ingots.	g. items found
H. Carbon-14 analyses shows that the wood dates to about 1575. Some farm boys found the site of the money pit in 1795 when they came upon some "rotted, moss-covered stumps." They dug a hole as deep as they could, but they hit a slab of rock with hieroglyphics on it.	8. He died shortly after finding an important clue—a bronze cannon.	h. clues

(continued)

TABLE 7.2 *Completed Comparison Chart*

Key Points (Master Source)	Key Points (Source 2)	Comparative Points
Then, mysteriously, the pit filled up with water.		
I. Different people have different theories about where the treasure came from. Blankenship thinks that the Spanish hid the money there. Tobias thinks that Francis Drake hid his loot there.	9. The project revealed much information about what life was like in the New World in the 17th century.	i. historical interest
J. Tobias has had to go to court to try to claim some lots that another man claims.	10. Fisher had to go to court to gain ownership of the booty from the ship.	j. court cases

Source: The pieces discussed are from the following sources:
D'Arcy O'Connor, "Treasure Hunt: Adventurers Still Try to Get to the Bottom of Fabled Money Pit," *Wall Street Journal,* July 20, 1987.
R. Duncan Matthewson III, *Treasure of the Atocha,* (New York: Pisces Books, 1986), pp. 12–15.

3. Finally, he summarized the relationships between the passages by writing several possible thesis statements:

Summary sentences:
I. A reader of R. Duncan Matthewson's *Treasure of the Atocha* would not expect to find another treasure hunt to match the one described between those pages. But "Treasure Hunt," an article in the *Wall Street Journal* proves otherwise. The similarities between the two searches are uncanny.
II. It's hard to believe that people put treasure above human life. But in the case of the Atocha treasure hunt and the search for the "Money Pit," the treasure hunters never gave up, even after close relatives died during their searches.
III. Why do grown men and women risk their lives and their fortunes to search for treasure? Two recent treasure hunts—one still in progress— indicate that it is not just the treasure that keeps hunters searching. Instead, the key ingredient in these searches, Mel Fisher's search for the Atocha and Daniel Blankenship's search for "The Money Pit," seems to be the quest in and of itself. Along with the quest, the search parties in each case seem to share a deep interest in archeology.

When the writer was ready, he moved from reading strategies to drafting. Completing the comparison chart left him with several parallel ideas and summary (or possible thesis) statements. He used some of the ideas as he drafted a short essay. As you can sense in the following example (a second draft on the project), the writer began to draft by staying very close to his first summary sentence, and he kept coming back to other summary sentences for ideas. The draft combines ideas in different ways—and moves its way toward "sumaction" with the last paragraph—and so turns out to be something quite different from a direct "translation" of the summary sentences.

DRAFT

Why do grown men and women risk their lives and their fortunes to search for treasure? Two recent treasure hunts--one still in progress--indicate that it is not just the treasure that keeps hunters searching. Instead, the key ingredient in these searches, Mel Fisher's search for the Atocha and Daniel Blankenship's search for "The Money Pit," seems to be the quest in and of itself. Along with the quest, the search parties in each case seem to share a deep interest in archeology.

Mel Fisher has already succeeded in his quest. On July, 20, 1985, his Treasure Salvors company found what it had been searching sixteen years for--the wreckage of the Spanish galleon Atocha. One wonders how many times Mel Fisher told his crew, "Today's the day." The reader of Treasure of the Atocha is amazed by most of what the book reveals. Fisher's search took sixteen years and cost over $8 million. The search also led to his son's death. But Fisher kept searching for the Atocha after his son, his son's wife, and their crewman died--ten years before the day his crew screamed, "We found it."

Daniel Blankenship, a former contractor from Miami, hasn't been so fortunate, though he has had similar misfortunes. And his perseverance rivals that of Fisher. For twenty-two years, Blankenship has been involved in trying to find a treasure called "The Money Pit," believed to be located under an old oak tree on an uninhabited island off the coast of Nova Scotia. Blankenship almost died himself one time, when a shaft that was dug to get close to the "pit" caved in around him. All told, a total of six people have died as a result of the search, yet Blankenship's commitment to the search is unrelenting. In July, 1987, Blankenship had not yet found his treasure, but his words to the reporter who wrote the Wall Street Journal article were, "We're almost there."

        In both cases, the treasure doesn't seem as important
    to the people involved as the search itself. Blanken-
    ship admits that he has an "obsession to be part of the
    team that brings this crazy search to its conclusion."
    Fisher kept going for ten more years after a clue kept
    him interested in the quest: his son found a pile of
    bronze cannons near the site shortly before his death.
        Both treasure hunting parties were also inspired by
    the possibility of making monumental archeological
    findings. As a result of Fisher's expedition, we have
    learned much about the way people lived in the New
    World during the 17th century. David Tobias, presi-
    dent of the company that is financing the "money pit"
    search feels that, "in all probability, this will be
    the deepest and most expensive archeological dig ever
    made in North America."

According to the student who wrote the preceding essay, setting up
a Comparison Chart was helpful:

        This strategy seemed quite useful. When I have to
    write about topics that I don't really know anything
    about, I get very nervous. This technique helped get
    me started even before I had an idea of what I wanted
    to say. I'm not crazy about starting to write this way
    (it seems too mechanical) but I needed to get this
    assignment done and I'm glad we had to try this stra-
    tegy.
        I didn't use as many of the matched details as I
    thought I would. After I wrote the third trial thesis
    statement, I had a good idea of what to say and how to
    organize it, so I started drafting. I thought I'd use
    the details, but when they didn't fit, I didn't force
    them in.

As our student has observed in his log, strategies can seem mechanical to a writer who enjoys plunging into a discovery draft. But when
you have several papers due at the same time, you'll probably appreciate using a time-saving strategy just as our student did.

■ Strategy 5—Keep an Idea File

Most of the strategies suggested in this chapter can be used when
your professors assign specific written sources for you to write about.
Such reading-based projects are quite common in many kinds of college courses. But so are research papers and other assignments for
which you need to use written sources, even though your teacher does

not assign specific articles and books. You will find that keeping an *idea file* will help you begin this sort of writing project.

When, early in a course, you know that you will later need to write a paper on a topic of your choice, you can use a simple but effective method practiced by professional writers. Here is how two experienced authors and editors describe the strategy:

> Writing well for publication demands, first, that you pick a subject that excites you and will attract others, and, second, that you flesh it out with examples, images, anecdotes, facts, and characters. Among the writers we've canvassed, most meet these requirements with the help of the pack-rat process, which involves hoarding printed materials that interest them, along with scribbled notes about ideas, snatches of conversation, and nuggets of information they find provocative.
>
> In the beginning, these bits and pieces may not mean much but as they accumulate they'll start to form patterns, and eventually a number of items may cluster around a subject. . . . At that point, the next step is easy: label a folder with that article or book, notes on background reading, research materials, people to interview, associations to contact, relevant data from the *Congressional Record,* preliminary reflections, and angles of approach.
>
> *Source:* Nancy Evans and Judith Appelbaum, *How to Get Happily Published* (Harper and Row, 1978), p. 12.

Evans and Appelbaum are writing for people who want to write and sell magazine articles and other sorts of professional prose. But their ideas can help you find leads for a research project that "excites you and will attract others"—especially the professor who will grade your work. You can keep your eyes and ears open in the course (as you do assignments, listen to lectures, participate in discussions) and as you watch the news, read papers and magazines, attend other classes, and talk with friends at lunch. You never know when a project-idea may come to you. So if, throughout the semester, you actively look for ideas—and keep a file of clippings, photocopies, jotted names, book titles, and stray nuggets of information—you probably will have less trouble when it comes time to decide on a research project.

This strategy does not take the place of systematic library research techniques, a thorough description of which would take far more space than this whole chapter. In fact, this strategy will work better if you are familiar with your college's library and its reference staff, and if you know how to use *Reader's Guide* and other "periodical indexes" to locate articles. In turn, this strategy can help you to utilize recent articles in exploring an assigned subject, so that you know what topics to look for in the library.

IDEA FILE: COMPUTER WRITING

A Computer Idea File

1. If you happen to have a simple data base program such as PFS: File or Appleworks, you can use your data base to sort your ideas by topics, by bibliographic data, and whatever other categories you set up.

2. With a word processor, a good way to set up an idea file is to dedicate an entire disk to idea collecting. (Or, if you are using a computer with a hard disk, you can devote an entire subdirectory to your ideas.) Establish some general categories. Then as you find a reference that fits into that category, open the appropriate file and insert the reference. For example, suppose you are writing a paper about the criticism of public school education. Begin by dividing your topic into subtopics: problems, criticism, solutions. When you have an idea about the problems, just open the file and insert your idea. Or, if you have come upon a quote that you might be able to use to develop one part of your paper, you can insert the quote in the file.

■ Strategy 6—Study an Overview Article

One of the most effective ways to find research leads or to explore a subject you know little about is to read an article that gives an overview of the subject. From the reading, you may learn that a topic you expected to be technical and boring really has a lot of promise. Or, you might discover that a topic you had wanted to write about really is not for you. You might discover from an overview article that the subject you had wanted to research is too broad, but that there are several subtopics you can look into by doing some library research. Or you might find, in your reading, the names of some of the "experts" in the field or the title of a recent book you could turn to for more information.

Finding a good overview article is often, at least partly, a matter of luck. That's one reason to get in the habit of keeping an idea file of useful material—you may just "find" a useful overview article. But here are some things you can do to help with your search:

1. Browse the current periodicals collection in the university library. If you get in the habit of looking through new magazines in the library (part of the "pack rat" approach of the previous strategy), you will have a general sense of the sort of places to look for overviews on different topics. For instance:

a. *Newsweek, Time,* and *U.S. News & World Report* can be excellent sources of overview articles on subjects currently in the news. They have regular columns to which you can turn for material on politics, science, business, finance, medicine, etc. And their cover stories typically are dozen-page clusters of articles filled with background information, charts, statistics, and interviews on a single subject.

b. *The Atlantic Monthly, Harpers Review, Saturday Review,* and Sunday issues of the *New York Times* and other large newspapers are places where you may find overview articles on art, music, architecture, theater, and other cultural and intellectual trends.

c. *Smithsonian* offers overview articles, for general readers, on a wide range of topics in science and natural history. But, for scientific topics, you would find more focused treatments in *Science* and even more detailed articles in *Scientific American.*

d. *Money* would be a place to look for nontechnical information on all sorts of subjects related to personal finance, but *Forbes* would be much more likely to provide insights into corporate financial matters and *Barron's* provides more specialized information on investing.

e. In the field of computer science, you might find general treatments of computer developments and their social impact in popular magazines like *PC World* or *Creative Computing,* more technical concerns in *BYTE,* and special-focus concerns in periodicals, like *Computers and the Humanities,* that deal with specific areas.

f. For general subjects dealing with education, you might look for articles in *Educational Leadership,* but for current issues at universities in the U.S., you would want to look at *The Chronicle of Higher Education.* For ideas about teaching in a specific field you would want to check journals related to that field (*Mathematics Teacher, History Teacher, English Journal,* etc.)

Summary

In this chapter, we've suggested a variety of strategies you can use as you read college materials—strategies that should be useful if you have to write a paper based on your reading or if you simply need to read your sources closely in order to prepare for an exam. As you learn to read more closely and more critically, you will be able to modify the techniques we have suggested and develop your own strategies. Remember, in order to grow as reader and as writer, you have to take charge of your own development. We can only point you in what we think are useful directions.

TEAMWORK WRITING

Teamwork Agenda A

It can be very helpful to work with other students on most of the strate-gies in this chapter. The underlying reason for all the strategies, after all, is to help you better understand the written materials about which you are going to write. And you'll develop confidence in your own under-standing when you begin to realize that your reaction to something you have read is acceptable even though it is different from other students' reactions. Here are two suggestions for working in a group:

1. Choose one member of your group to locate a brief, opinionated piece of writing—perhaps an editorial in your local or campus newspaper. Xerox the piece, and distribute it within the group.
   a. (Complete this step individually.) Skim the article quickly. Then, reread the piece and mark things to which you respond. Also, reread the piece using the critical-reading questions of Strategy 1. Finally, write down your reactions.
   b. (Complete this step as a group.) Compare your reactions with the reactions of other students in your group. What is similar? Differ-ent? Can you account for your differing responses?

2. Write *sumactions* of something you have all read. Then answer the following questions.
   a. Is there a clear difference—objective vs. personal—in the two parts of the sumaction (the summary part and the reaction part)?
   b. Is it clear what the writer responded to in the article, and what the response is?
   c. Are the background influences or other personal causes of the re-sponse clear?

Teamwork Agenda B

If your instructor will permit, try writing group reaction papers. Here's one way you might proceed. Read an opinion essay and share your indi-vidual responses. Account for differences in your individual perspectives, but try to achieve consensus. Next, each student should write what he or she *thinks* is the group's reaction. When you finish writing, share your papers to determine how accurately each person has described the "group's attitude" toward the essay.

Teamwork Agenda C

You can develop your summarizing and reaction skills by responding to one another's writing. Trade rough drafts. First, summarize one another's assignments; then write a reaction to what your partner has written.

Writing Exercises

1. Develop your summarizing and reacting skills by writing about the books, essays, or chapters that you need to read for other courses. Before you begin, determine the *writing situation* for each book, essay, or chapter that you read. Keep your summaries and your reactions in your writing notebook.

2. Good readers are usually reflective thinkers. To reflect is to muse, ponder, contemplate, meditate. Practice reflective thinking by keeping *double entries* in your notebook. Draw a line down the center of several pages in your notebook. Use the left-hand side of each page to summarize your reading. On the right-hand side, reflect on your summary: What does it make you think of? What is your reaction? Why do you think you are reacting as you are? Contemplate the similarities and differences between your responses and those of other students in your class. Reflect on reasons for your different perspectives.

3. Earlier, we asked you to write about your writing processes. Now, try to write about your reading processes. After you finish reading an essay or a story, immediately begin writing about what you did as you read. Did you read straight through from beginning to end? Did you go part way through the essay and then double back? Did you daydream for awhile about your own personal experiences? Share your observations about the way you read with your classmates.

Suggestions for Writing

1. Prominent American poet William Stafford discusses the naturalness of writing in an essay included in *Writing the Australian Crawl: Views on the Writer's Vocation* (University of Michigan Press, 1978, pp. 21–28). If you are interested in creative writing, read William Stafford's essay, "Writing the Australian Crawl," as you begin to write on the topic, "How 'Natural' Should Writing Be?" Write a "sumaction" paper in which you summarize Stafford's main ideas in the first paragraph and then respond to those ideas in the balance of the paper.

2. Instead of writing a *sumaction* paper based on one source, write a *synthesis* paper based on three sources; that is, after reading, summarizing, and reacting to three separate essays, write a paper in

which you synthesize or "pull together" your overall view of the topic. Use this format to guide you as you prepare to write:

Summary of Source A:
Summary of Source B:
Summary of Source C:

Response to Source A:
Response to Source B:
Response to Source C:

Statement of Synthesis:

3. After reading *Megatrends* (or another book), write a paper based on one of the sample assignments on *Megatrends* mentioned in this chapter, or on a similar assignment designed to match your book. Be sure that you use strategies from this chapter to help you understand the author's ideas, and that you provide enough summary so that readers unfamiliar with the book will be able to understand your writing.

4. Write a 1000–2000-word paper in which you incorporate several published sources, either to support your opinion or to note contrasting views. Take as your starting point for this project one of the following overview articles. Or, work with another article assigned or approved by your teacher.

"The American Male: 'New and Improved.'" *U.S. News & World Report* 3 (June 1985): pp. 44–55. (A cover-story cluster of material.)

Connel, Christopher. "Drinking on Campus." *Change: The Magazine of Higher Learning* (January–February 1985): pp. 46–51.

Jolly, Allison. "Can Animals Think?" *Smithsonian* (March 1985): pp. 66–75; reading list, p. 203.

"Weekend Athletics." *Consumers Digest* (June 1984): pp. 54–61. (Safety and sports injuries.)

Note: this assignment points you toward a broad topic area for a writing project but does not specify your purpose for writing. As you explore the overview article, look for additional material, and draft toward your finished version, you will need to clarify whether you are writing an objective report, an "opinion piece," an argument to convince others, an article intended for campus readers, or for a more general audience. Regardless of how you clarify these issues, one fact is clear: your finished article will need to use sources honestly and clearly, so that readers can give you credit for your ideas and know when your sources are supporting your points.

5. Write an essay on a subject featured on the "Opinion" page of *USA Today* during the past three weeks. Use Strategy 6 ("Study an Overview Article") as you begin to work on this project, as well as other strategies in this chapter.

   Draft your way toward an article that explains your point of view and convinces readers that this is the "right" perspective on the topic. Within your article, you should highlight the strongest arguments on both sides of the issue, and work to "disprove" the argument against your view. Besides referring to editorials from *USA Today* you should use at least three other recent sources.

Writing Projects Based on Reasoning

8

Overview of Writing Strategies

In this chapter, we will explore the importance of clear reasoning and the thoughtful use of evidence in effective writing. We have outlined several writing strategies that will help you develop thoughtful and logical papers with strong supporting evidence.

1. Discover what you think

2. Evaluate the evidence in source materials

3. Evaluate the evidence in your own writing

4. Evaluate the logic in source materials

5. Evaluate the logic in your own writing

6. Determine whether a solution "solves" a problem

7. Use formulas when you need them

In a way it could be said that all writing projects are based on reasoning. After all, you're always expected to write clearly and convincingly in college and on the job. But some kinds of assignments require particularly clear and careful thinking:

- essay-test questions that require you to take a side

- letters-to-the-editor

- letters to politicians

- critical reviews

- position papers

Producing clear and logical answers to essay-test questions, arguing intelligently and rationally in letters-to-the-editor, or taking a stand in a position paper is not an easy matter. Yet the ability to think and reason clearly is the one outcome that most students expect from their college careers.

In the book *Higher Learning* (Cambridge: Harvard University Press, 1986), Derek Bok stresses the importance of reasoning and thinking skills for college students. He writes:

> It is time . . . to think seriously about multiplying the opportunities for students to reason carefully about challenging problems under careful supervision. Such an effort will presumably call for greater emphasis on promoting active discussion in class, stronger programs to prepare instructors to teach Socratically, and increased efforts to create more thought-provoking written assignments and exams.

This chapter will help you prepare for the kinds of assignments that Bok encourages and that, increasingly, teachers are including in their courses. We will suggest strategies to help you tackle a wide range of thought-provoking assignments. You can work with these strategies to enhance the clarity of the logic and the strength of the evidence in your written responses to these kinds of assignments.

Thinking and Evidence

A blend of rational thinking and supporting evidence is important to success in most college writing assignments, as well as in most writing you will be called on to do in your future career. On the one hand, writing requires sound ideas and thesis statements, close analysis of issues, and the discovery of the underlying relationships between ideas or events. But sound ideas alone do not produce good writing. Most academic and professional writing requires that generalizations and assertions be clarified and supported by examples, statistics, quotations from experts, and other sorts of evidence.

How does this differ from what you've been doing in previous chapters as you worked on writing assignments based on personal experience or on writing assignments based on reading? In all honesty, there is no real difference, just a difference in emphasis. To give you practice with a variety of writing assignments, we began with personal experience writing. Then we moved to writing based on reading. We suggested strategies for summarizing source material, for responding to what you read, and for answering essay questions.

You can't concern yourself with everything at once, so we didn't ask you to consider your reasoning or your evidence in your earlier papers. But logic and evidence are at work, nevertheless, in personal writing and in writing based on reading. In some descriptive writing, specific details work as a kind of evidence that you have an accurate understanding of what you are describing—a person's personality, the physical environment of a place, the series of stages in a process, and the like. Without evidence and carefully reasoned examples to support them, even your best ideas are simply assertions that readers may or may not understand or agree with. This is why the author of the essay "Carnival," in Chapter 5, created a greater effect using carefully selected details about the carnival than she would have if she had just asserted her personal opinion that carnivals are terrible, dangerous places.

Some college assignments are more demanding. They almost require you to think consciously about reasoning and evidence. They expect you to be convincing—to move an audience to your position, to encourage a reader to agree with your thesis. At times, you need to convince critical or even hostile readers, readers who would love to find overly general statements that they could counter with their own generalizations. By writing carefully reasoned answers to essay tests (supported by appropriate references to textbooks, library assignments, and lectures) you can convince the grader that you understand course materials and how specific facts, theories, and statistics relate to the assigned question. With enough evidence that is accurate and up-to-date, and with carefully reasoned arguments, you can convince readers that you know what you are writing about, and maybe even that they should view your subject the way you do.

Applying Reasoning Skills in Daily Life

No matter what we do in life—no matter what job we get—we want to feel in control of our thought processes. We react strongly to the kind of society George Orwell writes about in *1984*, a society in which the government attempts to control thinking. If leaders attempt to control people's thoughts, then people gradually lose the ability to think on their own.

To think for yourself implies conscious choice, though, not just knee-jerk response. If you don't cultivate the habit of thinking for yourself, you will lose the ability to think independently, not because of government-sponsored mind control as it existed in Oceana, the fictitious society Orwell wrote about, but because it is often easier not to think. If someone asks you what you think of some recent political controversy, do you ever respond quickly with an opinion? But how did you form your opinion? Why do you think what you think? Because your parents think that way? Because most people in your home community would respond that way? Or because *you* have reasoned through issues like that before and have arrived at an independent position?

Some stock issues almost ask for an automatic response instead of clear reasoning. Many of you are probably tired of hearing people discuss such standard topics as capital punishment, abortion, gun control, or the drinking age. You have heard standard arguments on both sides of these issues. But standard responses are easy to come up with. Original thinking—based on direct evidence—is not so easy.

What would you say if someone walked up to you and asked you to give your opinion about raising the drinking age? Many young students quickly respond by saying something like, "If you're old enough to fight for your country, you should be old enough to drink." Or, they might say, "We can vote at 18 so we should be allowed to drink at 18." But prefabricated answers like these are not expressions of what *they* think. Nor are these responses based on evidence and careful reasoning. Quick responses like these are similar to clichés, time-worn phrases such as "tried and true" or "the American way" that people use without thinking about what they mean. They are prefabricated sets of words that substitute for honest thought.

Consider the difference in the following responses to the issue of raising the drinking age:

Student 1

Last summer, Colorado legislators passed a law that raised the drinking age from eighteen to twenty-one. I don't like that law personally, but I can understand its necessity. The federal government is making an attempt to curb the number of traffic-related fatalities. If Colorado legislators had not raised the drinking age, the state would have lost hundreds of thousands of dollars for highway repair.

Personally, I wish the drinking age had not changed. My friends who turned eighteen before the new law went into effect can go to dances at such local night spots as "Boomers" and "Comedy-Works," places that have nighttime entertainment, but I can't. Yet I can understand the necessity for the law. A lot of young people don't know how to drink responsibly. And they aren't always mature enough to admit when they've had too much. More specifically, though, the legislators almost had to change the drinking age. If they had not passed a new drinking law, not only would they have had to raise highway money from other sources, but they might have felt personally guilty whenever a drunken teenage motorist was at fault in a traffic accident.

The new drinking age law has helped control some problems already. Last year, many students attended

football games primarily to drink. Now, there are
fewer students at the games, but most of those who are
there want to watch football, not drink. And the sta-
dium is not cluttered with as many broken beer bottles.
Furthermore, the law has led to a greater sensitivity,
among university officials, of the student drinking
problem. In other years, many students partied in the
parking lots throughout the entire football game. This
year, the university has ruled that pre-game tailgate
parties can last no longer than fifteen minutes after
the game begins.

Of course, laws won't eliminate all problems related
to illegal drinking. Teenagers who want to get drunk
will find a way to do it. And some of them will drive
while intoxicated. A few weeks ago, a woman was killed
after a tailgate party at the football game. The
driver was an eighteen-year-old who had been drinking
illegally. The law didn't save the woman's life. But
it does absolve the legislators of personal responsibility for her death.

Alcohol is a problem for adults and teenagers alike.
Passing a law that limits drinking by these people is
not an easy matter—as the Prohibition Era has docu-
mented. By curbing teenage drinking, however, the new
law may limit alcohol intake among teenagers. Further,
by curbing their drinking until they can drink legally,
the new law may help some teenagers. It may give them
time to develop a more mature outlook on drinking. It
may give them time to reflect on the problems excessive
drinking can cause and as a result, the law may encourage teenagers to be more responsible drinkers when they
do reach legal age.

Student 2

The drinking-age law is unfair. When people are 18,
they are old enough to fight for their country and they
are considered an adult, yet they cannot buy beer. I
always thought that when I was 18 I was considered an
adult, but now I feel I am still a child because I have
no privileges. I was hoping that on my 18th birthday I
would be able to go to bars and to nightclubs.

I believe the state was blackmailed into raising the
drinking age by getting pressure by the federal government by withholding Colorado's highway funds. I believe that the highways do not need that much work in
Colorado. They should at least use the money they're
giving Colorado for their highways on things they
really need to improve, like improving the cities in
Colorado.

Even if people are not 18, it's not that hard to get

```
beer. There are always friends who barely made the
drinking age who can buy you beer for awhile. I be-
lieve that Colorado should have waited until January
1988 to change the law.
    I don't think the drinking age is a good law because
once you're 18, by most laws, you're considered an
adult and can be treated as an adult.
```

The second student is parroting ideas she's heard others speak. Phrases like "they are old enough to fight for their country" or "once you're 18 you're . . . an adult" do not convince the reader that the author has thought through the idea herself. On the other hand, the first student does appear to be searching for her own ideas. When she says "I don't like that law personally, but I can understand its necessity," a reader immediately senses that this is an honest piece of writing. The author is taking her time. Instead of responding to the question hastily, she is trying to think through her reasons for an opinion. She is taking a second look at the evidence. Then she is reformulating her opinion. With practice, you'll get used to using more careful reasoning processes. As a result, your answers will be *your* answers instead of repackaged versions of responses you've heard many times before.

We would urge you to write like the first student. It's difficult, of course, to think a topic through carefully and logically. In this chapter we'll encourage you to clarify your thoughts for yourself in early writing sessions so that you can rework them later for your audience. British novelist E.M. Forster was fond of saying, "How do I know what I think until I see what I say?" We'll suggest a variety of writing strategies that will help you determine what you think. The process of forming opinions about everyday issues is the same process you should use as you prepare for writing assignments based on reasoning.

A note of caution. As you clarify your own opinions on different issues, you will no doubt find that no matter how logically you arrive at your evidence, not everyone will agree with you. Why is that? Why do people have widely divergent opinions on the same ideas? Each person is the product of a lifetime's experiences. He or she understands new experiences in the context of old experiences. All learning is that way. If you want to teach someone how to play a new sport, you can do it more easily if the person has played similar sports before. You can build on the person's previous knowledge. If you've never been to a city, you will have difficulty imagining what a big city will be like. But once you've been to a large city, you are in a better position to learn more about cities by reading books about city life. You can relate what you read to your experiences. Thus, you can use more of what you read as evidence for your own opinions.

Because your friends' experiences are different from yours, the evidence they have to draw on as they formulate their own opinions is different, too. If you belong to a conservative religious group or organization, it may be almost impossible for you to understand some of your classmates' responses to issues like abortion and AIDS. Don't think that everybody has to be the same, though. Just learn how to respect one another's differences. And learn how to choose who you want to be. Most important, critically evaluate your beliefs. Know why you believe what you believe.

Developing Thoughtful and Logical Papers

Some people try to avoid issues that confuse them. But if they'd think about more things, they'd make their life more interesting. They'd notice more connections. They'd feel part of a larger world. When Dawn Rodrigues first asked her students in New Mexico to read *Newsweek* as one of their assignments in freshman English, her students said that they weren't interested in what happened in the world. They were only interested in what happened in their town. "Isn't your town in the world?" she asked. Finally, a local issue that was also a national issue emerged: Should cab drivers in El Paso, Texas (fifty miles away from Las Cruces, New Mexico), be required to speak English? "Of course. Everybody should be required to speak English," said several students. But not everyone in the class agreed. Some students whose relatives had lived on and farmed the land—long before Texas was a state—disagreed. They argued that their parents didn't speak English, and that seemed legitimate. So why should cab drivers speak English? And if Spanish-speaking cab drivers should be required to speak English, then why shouldn't English-speaking cab drivers learn Spanish? Her students were finally thinking through an issue. Dawn volunteered to make a chart on the blackboard to list the "pros" and "cons" of the situation. Students kept talking—and they were thinking as they talked. The papers they produced were the best they had written all semester. Read through the following sample of student writing from that course, noticing how the student has managed to subdue his emotional reaction to the issue as he attempts to reason logically:

EL PASO CAB DRIVERS

Recently, pressure has been mounting in El Paso, Texas, to require cab drivers to pass a test in spoken English. The proponents of the test have noted that many cab drivers cannot speak English, and the result, they maintain, is that visitors to El Paso are discouraged, frustrated, and angry. They fear that tourists will not come to El Paso and that the economy will suffer.

The second major argument that the advocates for testing in English give is that English is the official language of the United States, and therefore anyone in a public position, such as a cab driver, must be able to speak English. That argument is fairly easy to rebut, since the United States—Texas included—does not have an official language. Granted, most people do speak English in the United States, and it would probably help the cab drivers if they could speak English, but to require that they be proficient in English is to impose something on them that simply is not necessary.

The more compelling of the two arguments for requiring cab drivers to have their English ability tested is the impact upon tourists and others who must use cabs to get from one section of El Paso to another. But if we examine the context in which these cab drivers work, then we realize that the ability to speak English fluently or even fairly proficiently is simply not necessary.

First, the name of a street in El Paso is the same whether the cab driver speaks English or not. Alameda or El Paseo or Wilson Boulevard are the same to a cab driver regardless of what language he speaks. The cab drivers know English numbers equally well, and they all know the major hotels and motels in town. So they can communicate with a monolingual English speaker.

Second, El Paso is a bilingual city. Many people who live here are primarily Spanish speakers. They have little trouble communicating with a monolingual Spanish-speaking cab driver. Furthermore, they can even tell a monolingual English-speaking cab driver where they want to go. People who have grown up in a bilingual environment are accustomed to dealing with someone who does not speak their language proficiently. Spanish speakers are not demanding that monolingual English speakers pass a test in spoken Spanish, so why should cab drivers have to pass a test in English?

Third, if tourists are the primary people who suffer because cab drivers only speak Spanish, what do those tourists do when they go to Juarez? In fact, the primary reason why tourists come to El Paso in the first place is to go to Juarez, Mexico, where they do not complain when everyone speaks Spanish. If they take an American cab to Juarez, they probably are extremely grateful that their cab driver can speak Spanish.

So, where does that leave the proponents of the English proficiency test? The argument is one of values, not one of whether monolingual cab drivers can take their passengers to the correct destination. Those who

argue for English testing are probably unwilling to
learn a little Spanish themselves. To them, Spanish
speakers are foreigners, even if they have lived in
El Paso for their entire lives. In a city that depends
upon Mexican citizens for many public services, and a
city whose economy is closely tied to that of Juarez,
we cannot afford to turn our backs upon Spanish speakers, for to do so might hurt the economy much more than
would the loss of a few tourists who refuse to tolerate
Spanish-speaking cab drivers.

Good thinking makes for good discussions. And good discussions
lead to good writing. Personal interest in a topic, coupled with convincing evidence, leads to the kind of compelling writing that is rewarded anytime. And more fundamental than any techniques for research, topic exploration, drafting, or revision is the awareness that
writers usually write for men and women who do not share their own
knowledge, attitudes, and personal experiences. Understanding your
readers' assumptions and their biases can help you develop a more
reasoned, logical response to an assignment.

■ Strategy 1—Discover What You Think

You won't convince anybody about anything unless you care about
your point yourself. What is your opinion about your topic? What
really intrigues you? What is worth arguing about? Answering these
questions will help you clarify your attitude toward your topic early.
Remember, though, that you may change your opinion somewhat as
you read. In fact, you should expect to change. But by having some
sense of how you feel about your topic, you can read with an argumentative edge. Maybe one of the sources you read will convince you
to change your thesis. If so, then you will be aware of how powerful
effective evidence and effective logic can be.

1. State your opinion (state the case—as is done in legal arguments).

2. Consider the arguments against your opinion. (What is the opposition's position?)

3. In rapid writing, rebut the opposition's position.

4. List the best arguments you can think of to support your own position. Use your best argument last.

5. Read several essays, chapters of books, or editorials. Take careful

notes. Then return to items 1–4. Reread your responses and revise your original opinions wherever necessary! Record your response to this exercise in your notebook.

An Example of Strategy 1 in Action

Topic: Surrogate motherhood

1. State your opinion (state the case—as is done in legal arguments).

    Surrogate mothering is fraught with too many problems to make it practical.

2. Consider the arguments against your opinion. (What is the opposition's position?)

    Some—especially those who can't have their own children—would like to think that it's okay.

3. In rapid writing, rebut the opposition's position.

    These people are only thinking of themselves. They want a child so badly that they block their minds and don't think about the effect of their decision on their child's life. Nor do they think of how the woman who agrees to be a surrogate mother really feels. Maybe she hates what she is doing, and is only doing it for the money. But her emotions may overwhelm her. She may become psychologically ill as a result of the ordeal. The people who are wealthy enough to "buy her body" ought to be smart enough to consider her mind.

4. List the best arguments you can think of to support your own position. Use your best argument last.

    a. The unborn child needs to be considered, too.

    b. Just because someone is willing to be a surrogate mother doesn't mean she should be allowed to be one.

    c. Not everyone needs to have a child.

    d. Surrogate parenting is unfair to everyone involved: the wealthy people who pay others to bear their children, the woman who agrees to have someone else's child, the unborn child, and the couple who hires the surrogate.

5. Read several essays, chapters of books, or editorials. Take careful notes. Then return to items 1–4. Reread your responses and revise your original opinions wherever necessary! Record your response to this exercise in your notebook.

    After doing this exercise, I feel good. I had read a lot about the topic before I began, and that may be why I still feel okay about the ideas I've generated. Some of the additional news stories I have read do support my opinion. I wonder if others in class will write on the same topic. If they do, I wonder if they'll come up with different opinions.

IDEA FILE: COMPUTER WRITING

Computer Rebuttal

1. List all the points you want to make about your topic. You can use phrases rather than complete sentences if you want.

2. Trade computers (or disks) with a classmate. Move your cursor to the line after each of your partner's points. Typing in "all caps," rebut as many of your partner's points as you can.

3. Return to your own computer (or disk). Reread your list of ideas and your partner's rebuttals. Revise your list, adding points that you think of as a result of your partner's comments.

Use Convincing Evidence

The quality of your thinking counts for a lot. But you've got to have convincing evidence to support what you say. Students sometimes question the grades they receive on tests without examining the evidence they have used to support their answers. The student who wrote this essay for an economics test was not happy with his grade:

```
                    PRODUCTIVITY

    Productivity in the private economy, as measured by
output per man-hour, fell 2.6 last year. What caused
this decline in productivity? Some economists feel this
decline was caused by the economic downturn. I feel the
economic downturn was caused by a constant decline in
productivity over the past several years. This constant
decline in productivity is the result of labor agree-
ments and government regulation.
    When was the last time you read or heard of a local
union or the AFL-CIO going out on strike and demanding
increased productivity? You probably never have. What
unions usually demand is higher wages, longer paid cof-
fee breaks, more hospitalization insurance, time-and-
a-half for over forty-hours worked, and double-time for
holiday work. I have not yet heard of any union promis-
ing to increase productivity in return for these in-
creases in wages and benefits.
    One gets the distinct impression that labor wants to
be paid more for producing the same or in some cases
even less. John Doe, an assembly line worker, is a good
example. John has worked at an auto-assembly plant for
three years. His job is to fasten the lug nuts on the
```

left front and rear wheels as cars come down the assembly line. There are ten lug nuts on his side of the
car.
   John's starting wage was $8.50 per hour. After 90
days he got an automatic $2.00 raise. Each year for
three years John got a $1.00 an hour raise. Now, after
three years of service, John is earning $13.50 an hour.
A new contract is being negotiated and the union is
asking for a $4.00 raise over the three years and free
dental care.
   John is still fastening lug nuts on the assembly
line. But since the company is now producing a smaller
car, the two wheels have only eight lug nuts. It is
plain to see that John wants to be paid more when he
is producing less.

You probably noticed several problems with the quality and effectiveness of evidence in that example. Effective college writing is quite
different from the writing in the essay, "Productivity," with its limited
research, its logical gaps, and its unsupported assertions. Where the
essay, "Productivity," gives the impression that its writer is struggling
to make some kind of point in spite of the evidence, effective academic writing shows a writer's active intelligence

- exploring a subject thoroughly enough to arrive at plausible generalizations and conclusions about it.

- shaping generalizations about the subject into a thesis that holds
  the writing project together.

- locating key ideas and subpoints, and determining an effective order for them to be presented to readers.

- evaluating evidence and selecting material that works to clarify
  and support thesis and subpoints.

- weaving assertions and supporting material together so that conclusions seem natural and valid, rather than manipulated or re-
  sulting from persuasive tricks.

- working to help readers understand intended relationships between ideas, between ideas and evidence, and between items of
  evidence.

Often, just looking carefully at a piece of writing lets you find
places where there is little or no evidence, or where facts are erroneous or completely out-of-date. And this suggests a technique you
can use to strengthen the quality of evidence in your own writing.
Late in a writing project, you can look at your own draft as if someone

else had written it in order to find unsupported assertions and weak evidence that could undermine the effectiveness of your writing.

Solid background reading and thorough exploration of your subject during early drafting sessions result in more effective writing. Many college writing assignments ask you not just to use written materials as evidence but to develop your whole thesis within the context of assigned readings or library research. Your writing on such assignments will be more effective if it grows out of background readings that are reliable, and if it uses as evidence the most credible details, quotations, and statistics from those sources. One way to strengthen the evidence you present in your writing projects is to be a demanding and critical reader when you are doing the background research on academic assignments.

Strategy 2—Evaluate the Evidence in Source Materials

Here are questions you can ask to probe the quality of evidence in source materials. It is unlikely that you would want to answer all these questions about any one source. But it can be very helpful to answer the most appropriate questions on this list for any source you think may be important to a project you are working on. If you find yourself giving negative or unflattering answers to very many of the questions, you should take that as a signal that the source probably is not one you want to rely on too much in your writing project.

Evaluating the Quality of Evidence in Source Materials

General Questions About Evidence

1. Does the writing use a variety of evidence—details, examples, opinions, statistics, quotations, etc.?

2. Does the evidence seem reasonable and accurate or does it vary widely from other things you know about the subject? If it varies, who is wrong: you or the writer?

3. Is evidence consistent throughout the writing, or do some items of evidence contradict or throw doubt on other items of evidence?

4. Does evidence seem up-to-date?

Questions About Details Used in Description

5. Do details emphasize central and important points in the subject, or do they focus attention on minor points?

6. Do details help the reader experience the subject—see what it looks

like, hear what it sounds like, understand its sequence of actions, etc.?

Questions About Examples

7. Do events used as examples seem consistent with your general observations about life and human behavior, or do they seem artificial, incredible, or fictionalized?

8. Does the person upon whose observations the example is based seem to be a qualified observer-reporter?

9. Does the person upon whose observations the example is based seem to have any personal biases that might cause him or her to slant the example in a distorting way?

Questions About Opinions Quoted as Evidence

10. Does the opinion seem to be grounded in fact? Does it seem to represent the conclusions that a person has drawn from personal observation or from research?

11. Does the person whose opinions are quoted possess the knowledge, training, and experience from which to formulate reliable conclusions about the subject?

12. Does the person whose opinions are quoted seem to let personal biases get in the way of sound judgment? Are there obvious omissions of points that would contradict the person's view? Are there conclusions that run counter to the evidence given by the person?

Questions About Statistics

13. Are statistics understandable and clearly relevant to the points they are used to support?

14. Does the handling of statistics seem honest, or does reading the piece remind you of the old saying, "Figures can't lie, but liars can figure"?

15. Does the writer identify the sources of statistics and are they reliable sources? Does the writer let you know where and when statistics were collected, as well as who collected material, analyzed data, and arranged the statistical results?

16. Do statistics seem to be based on samples large enough and random enough to give believable results? This is a hard question for a nonspecialist to answer. But do you have the feeling that the researcher may have looked at such a narrow range of data that the conclusions are shaky?

Questions About Charts, Diagrams, Tables, Appendixes

17. Do these materials help the reader understand the subject, or do they seem confusing, distracting, expendable?

18. Does the writer explain the relevance of such materials, or does the writer seem to expect the reader to figure out how they relate to the words and ideas of the paper?

Questions About Quotations, Paraphrases, Documentation

19. Are quotations and paraphrases handled accurately and honestly? Does the writer misquote sources, or attribute to them words they did not use? Does the writer plagiarize?

20. Does the writer use a consistent form of documentation to indicate sources of evidence?

IDEA FILE: COMPUTER WRITING

---

*Keeping Track of Your Sources
and Reading Them Critically*

You need to keep a record of your sources. And you also need to read them critically. Why not combine both tasks in one computer file? Here is a suggestion for how you might proceed.

1. Create a template for a bibliography file, a file that contains all the sources for a specific paper or project. After you have designed the format you want to use, use the "block copy" command of your word processor to copy the categories as many times as you wish; then you'll have a ready-made form to fill in whenever you want to add new items to your bibliography. Save the template file with a new name, something like "bib.tmp." When you use the file to create a bibliography for a specific paper or project, remember to rename it so that your template file can be reused.

   > Author:
   > Title:
   > Publication Data:
   >
   > Author:
   > Title:
   > Publication Data:

2. Create a template that incorporates critical reading comments with bibliographic information. If you have already created a bibliography template, you can revise that template in order to create this template. First, load your bibliography template.

Then insert the categories you will use to help remind you of criteria for reviewing your sources critically. Finally, save your revised "temp.bib" file with a new name, something like "crit.tmp."

> Author: Hirsch, E. D.
> Title: *Cultural Literacy*
> Publication Data:
> > Evidence:
> > Details Used in Description:
> > Examples:
> > Opinions Quoted as Evidence:
> > Statistics:
> > Charts, Diagrams, Tables, Appendixes:
> > Quotations, Paraphrases, Documentation:

3. Load the "crit.tmp" file. Move the cursor to the criteria you want to comment on, and insert information about that point. You don't need to respond to all the items or respond in any specific order. Save your file with a new name so that it won't write over your template.

■ Strategy 3—Evaluate the Evidence in Your Own Writing

The quality of the examples, quotations, statistics, and other evidence you use to make assertions and general statements clear and convincing is important in good writing. But even more important is the reciprocal way that evidence and ideas work together. Whenever you have a fairly complete draft of a writing project based on reasoning, you should begin to read it the way you think your most skeptical or hostile reader might. One way to begin doing this is to apply to your own draft the same questions about the quality of evidence that are listed in Strategy 2.

An alternate approach is to recall the critical, argumentative "clone" you invented to discuss drafts with in Chapter 2. Bring that helpfully obnoxious reader back to look for weak spots in your evidence.

An Example of Strategy 3 in Action

Imagine that you are the author of the earlier essay, "Productivity." Let's look at how your "clone" would be able to help you analyze your own writing.

Analysis of Essay by Your "Clone"

```
Paragraph 1: The paper starts by using statistics and
refers to experts ("some economists") who suggest a
cause of the problem. Then it just drops the expert
```

view and asserts a contradictory personal opinion without any evidence to show why you feel this way. How do you know there has been a constant decline? No evidence. In fact, the salary figures are so low, I wonder just what years you are writing about. I get the feeling that your mind is made up, and that you don't care much about answers other people may have.

Paragraphs 2 and 3: Your assertion in the third paragraph ("labor wants to be paid more for producing . . . less") rests on evidence in the second paragraph. But that evidence is shaky. Saying you haven't heard of any unions promising productivity does not prove that unions haven't done exactly that. Saying I probably haven't heard of it doesn't prove anything either.

Paragraphs 4 and 5: In paragraphs four and five, you use one worker as an example. You talk about what John does, how much he makes, how his salary increased over several years. And say what the union is demanding as a raise. Then you conclude that John wants more pay for less work. Really, there is no evidence at all about John's motives, so the conclusion you reach in paragraph six is not logical.

IDEA FILE: COMPUTER WRITING

Disk Commenting

Here is one way that you can respond to your own text or have others respond to your writing.

1. Make a copy of your entire file. Save it with a different name.

2. Turn on the "caps lock" key on your computer so that you can use capital letters to comment on your writing or to have your classmate comment on your writing.

   Productivity in the private economy, as measured by output per man-hour, fell 2.6 last year. What caused this decline in productivity? Some economists feel this decline was caused by the economic downturn. I feel the economic downturn was caused by a constant decline in productivity over the past several years. This constant decline in productivity is the result of labor agreements and government regulation.

   THIS PARAGRAPH STARTS BY USING STATISTICS AND RE-FERS TO EXPERTS ("SOME ECONOMISTS") WHO SUGGEST A CAUSE OF THE PROBLEM. THEN IT JUST DROPS THE EX-PERT VIEW AND ASSERTS A CONTRADICTORY PERSONAL OPINION WITHOUT ANY EVIDENCE TO SHOW WHY YOU FEEL

THIS WAY. HOW DO YOU KNOW THERE HAS BEEN A CON-
STANT DECLINE? NO EVIDENCE. IN FACT, THE SALARY
FIGURES ARE SO LOW, I WONDER JUST WHAT YEARS YOU
ARE WRITING ABOUT. I GET THE FEELING THAT YOUR
MIND IS MADE UP, AND THAT YOU DON'T CARE MUCH
ABOUT ANSWERS OTHER PEOPLE MAY HAVE.

When was the last time you read or heard of a local union. . . .

Logical Thinking

Writing based on reasoning should include logical arguments. Teachers expect students to support their broad generalizations with specific
details—examples, illustrations, and so on. But where do you get your
broad generalizations? How are generalizations formed?

Making generalizations involves making connections. When you go
to different college classes, and you notice that you have writing to do
in each one (and you remember, perhaps, that not all your previous
instructors valued writing), you can make the generalization that your
college instructors value writing. After making many generalizations
about a topic, you can make broad statements about your generalizations. These statements are your conclusions. You might, for instance,
make the generalization that high schools don't require enough writing. Then, you might generalize that your college requires a lot of
writing. But when you visit a friend, you discover that his college
classes require very little writing. From all of this evidence, you might
draw the conclusion that teachers are not consistent in the way they
incorporate writing into their courses.

The intellectual act of forming conclusions is important because,
without it, you cannot maintain control over the dozens of factors—intended meanings, memories, quotations, statistics, ideas, graphs, and
generalizations based on all of these—that confront you whenever you
write. Generalizations and conclusions allow you to

1. *recognize significant patterns* in the separate items of information you
   uncover during your research.

2. *generalize* about the significance, the possible consequences, or underlying causes of the phenomena you are examining.

3. *form hypothetical answers* that you can examine in light of other information.

4. *create possible thesis statements* around which to organize your writing
   projects.

It is all too possible, of course, to form conclusions that are inaccurate or only partly accurate. Gaps in evidence and lapses in logic can undermine conclusions and reduce the credibility writing has for readers. It's possible that you may assume to be true ideas that really deserve critical thought and reasoned argument, or you simply may not care enough to do the hard work of drawing accurate conclusions. We'd like to recommend several strategies for making your writing logically convincing. But in order to use these strategies, you need to understand that there are two general ways to form conclusions—deduction and induction.

■ Deductive Thinking and Inductive Thinking

In *deductive* thinking, you begin with an assumption (an idea, belief, fact, etc.) that you consider to be true about a subject. You form a conclusion by basing your thinking on this assumption or examining information in light of the assumption. For example:

> *Assumption:* Cooperation is a key element in all team sports.
> *Data:* Basketball is a team sport.
> *Conclusion:* Cooperation is a key element in basketball.

In *inductive* thinking, on the other hand, you begin with specific items of information (observations, statistics, ideas, experiences, etc.) and you examine them in order to discover an underlying pattern or relationship. You form a conclusion by drawing a generalization from specific items of information. You analyze each piece of data separately, moving from one piece of information to the next:

Data
Cooperation is a key element in football, soccer, hockey, basketball, polo, baseball, volleyball, and water polo.
Inductive Thinking

↓

Data
These sports are very different. Some encourage body contact, while others penalize it; some use elaborate equipment and some use little equipment; some are played indoors, outdoors, on ice, in water, on horses; some are more popular in the United States and some are more popular in Europe.
Inductive Thinking

↓

Data
One thing that these very different sports have in common is that they are team sports rather than individual sports.

Inductive Thinking

↓

Conclusion
Cooperation is a key element in team sports.

If the deductive process begins with an erroneous or only partly accurate assumption, conclusions usually turn out to be invalid or at least questionable. If inductive generalizations are based on too little information, conclusions are likely to be invalid or only partly valid.

The professors who assign and grade college writing projects usually look for "logical" conclusions and connections in quoted sources and in the writer's overall argument. So you increase the likelihood of success in academic writing if you try to determine the validity of important conclusions and generalizations when you are selecting source materials for writing projects, and when you are working to improve your own drafts.

You need to cultivate the habit of thinking logically. One way to help you get accustomed to using logical thinking in your writing is to practice probing commonly held assumptions. Only by questioning your assumptions can you be sure that they indeed have any validity or support.

A lot of people have misguided assumptions about the world around them. Think about college students, for example. What kinds of assumptions do people have about college students? Read the following statements, mentally completing them.

> Most people think college students are . . . Most people think that students are in school to . . .

One commonly held notion is that all college students are more interested in partying than in studying. But it is unfair to label an entire group of people based on experience with only a few members of that group. It is also illogical.

People have many misconceptions about lots of other things, too. For instance, some people have misconceptions about male and female roles in life. As a result, many people have stereotypes of men and women. What kinds of assumptions do some people have about these topics?

> Men are usually . . .
> Women are usually . . .

Think about other commonly held assumptions. Explore how misconceptions and stereotypes have developed and why they persist. By examining everyday assumptions, you have an opportunity to practice becoming a more critical and rational thinker.

The Reciprocal Relationship Between Logical Thinking and Information

In effective writing, thought and evidence work together. Readers sense that the writer is working out of a broad and solid background with his or her subject, and they can easily locate the writer's own ideas and assertions. Items of evidence clearly and obviously fit the assertions they are used to support, so readers do not need to guess at the intended relationship between generalization and example. At the same time, assertions seem to be natural extensions or logical conclusions of the information and evidence used for support, so readers never feel that a thesis or other assertion is being forcibly imposed in spite of the evidence.

The way ideas and evidence work together is important in all writing. Frequently, questionable conclusions are formed due to a lack of reasoning in the relationship between thought and information.

When you need to prepare for an assignment that involves logical thinking, try using the Critical-Reading Questions in Chapter 7 to help locate key conclusions and generalizations in an article or book that you are planning to use as a source. Pay close attention to how accurate and valid these conclusions seem to be. Use the suggestions given earlier in this chapter (*Strategy 2*) to evaluate the evidence your source uses to support its conclusions. Then, apply the questions and suggestions from the following section (*Strategy 4*) to evaluate the logic used in forming those conclusions.

■ Strategy 4—Evaluate the Logic in Source Materials

In addition to evaluating the evidence in your sources, analyze the logic. Be sure that you base your conclusions on adequate information and that your argument is logical.

1. Is a deductive conclusion based on inaccurate or only partly accurate assumptions?

    Faulty conclusion: Since Linda Monroe stayed in that cult, she must be a spiritual weakling without a real commitment to God.

    Faulty assumptions: Nobody with strong faith joins a cult. Cults never grow out of feelings of religious commitment. There are no sociological or psychological forces that push people toward cults. Cults never apply psychological or physical force to attract and retain members.

2. Is a deductive conclusion based on inaccurate or only partly accurate information?

    Faulty conclusion: The FDIC and FSLIC provide U.S. government insurance on accounts in banks and savings and loan associations. So it really is pretty foolhardy to keep your money any place except a bank or S&L.

Inaccurate information: FDIC and FSLIC do not cover *all* banks and savings and loans, only the federally-chartered ones. There are limits on how much FDIC and FSLIC insurance will pay on any one account, and there is no assurance that the payments will come quickly and conveniently. Money in federally-chartered credit unions is insured for just as much by the government-backed NCUA. Stock market investors who leave their securities with their brokers for safekeeping are protected by SIPC insurance. People who want to put their money in certain kinds of bonds and money-market instruments can look for investments that carry private insurance.

3. Is an inductive conclusion based on too little information?

Faulty conclusion: The Wyoming fish and game authorities are really behaving oddly. They are poisoning a stretch of river to kill brook trout just because the fish is not native to the area.

Information that is not reflected in the writer's conclusion: The brook trout, released by a fisherman to stock his favorite stream, have a record of outcompeting and taking over from the native cutthroat trout. Since brook trout spawn at a different time of the year and have a different protein quality than the cutthroat, displacement of the native trout means that eagles and grizzly bears—both endangered species—will have a major source of spring food interrupted.

4. Is a conclusion questionable because a writer confuses sequence with cause (implying that because B follows A, therefore A caused B)?

Faulty conclusion: Each spring, the grizzly bears wade into the river at that same point, grabbing cutthroat trout in their jaws or tossing them onto the bank with their paws. And each spring, there are fewer trout able to get past the bears to their spawning ground. If we don't do something about those bears, in another couple of years there won't be any trout left.

Overly simple statement of cause: In a balanced ecosystem, natural death by predators does not wipe out a species. An unnaturally large number of grizzly bears on one particular river might be a problem; if so, that would be something the writer would need to show.

5. Is a conclusion questionable because a writer fails to realize that a given phenomenon may have more than one cause?

Look again at the grizzly bear problem in question four. The writer sees hungry bears and the dwindling number of trout and assumes that one causes the other. But there could be other causes of the problem—for instance, the brook trout takeover referred to in the example for question three.

6. Is a conclusion questionable because a writer oversimplifies a complex issue so that it seems to have only two or three possible dimensions (causes, solutions, explanations, etc.)?

Faulty Conclusion: That criminal's behavior is inexplicable. He is neither insane nor poor.

Overlooked dimensions of the issue: Prejudice and discrimination, uncaring or brutal parents, America's love of violent heroes and violence in sports, psychological conditions less severe than insanity, drug dependence.

7. Is a conclusion questionable because it rests on a false analogy? Does the writer use principles from one area to prove or explain a point about a fundamentally dissimilar thing?

Faulty conclusion: A balloon can expand only so far without exploding. Similarly, there are limits on how much population growth Central America can accommodate without rupturing its agricultural and economic resources.

False analogy: The flexible expansiveness of a balloon is not similar or comparable to the physical, political, and religious realities of population growth in developing countries.

"Logical" problems such as these usually indicate that something has gone wrong in the relationship between a writer's thought and information. For example:

• The conclusion that it is foolhardy to keep money any place but a bank or savings and loan (item two) begins with correct assumptions: that most people consider security desirable, and that FDIC and FSLIC insurance increases the security of the saver. The problem comes from limited information about FDIC and FSLIC insurance, and from missing information about several other savings and investment arrangements.

• The conclusion that something has to be done about the grizzly bears in order to save the cutthroat trout (items four and five) rests on the accurate assumption that it is desirable to prevent the extinction of a species, and it reflects a mind drawing conclusions from observed information. The conclusion may be invalid because the assumptions and conclusion-drawing are focused on insufficient and inaccurate information about trout, bears, and ecosystems; because of the intellectual disposition to oversimplify complex issues; or because of a combination of the two.

■ Strategy 5—Evaluate the Logic in Your Own Writing

At different times during your writing, read over either your predraft or your draft with the seven questions from the preceding strategy in mind. Try to detach yourself from your writing, and look for thinking problems the same way you would if you were trying to find weak spots in writing you disagreed with. *Revise your thesis if it no longer appears to be a logical conclusion of the ideas and evidence you have included in your draft or in your rapid writing. Revise your thesis, too, if it no longer appears to be a logical conclusion of the ideas you discovered in your reading.*

Inexperienced writers are frequently reluctant to reexamine their original ideas in light of what they have learned while exploring their topic. They may feel that this revision of their original thesis will necessitate doing all of their work over again. It is important to realize that this is not the case. If all of your evidence leads you to a conclusion different from the one that you originally stated, it is easier to formulate a new thesis based on your evidence than to deny (or ignore) the evidence and force yourself to write a paper based on a thesis you cannot support.

Another way to evaluate the logic in your own writing is to work with a group of writers so that each person helps the others find the thinking problems that would confuse readers or reduce the credibility and effectiveness of your projects.

Assignments Based on Reasoning: The Problem-Solution Paper

When college teachers use writing to help students learn and to test their learning, they usually assign projects that require more than the presentation of facts. Indeed, most college writing assignments ask you to use materials from the course or from your research in some way and apply your knowledge toward analyzing a subject or issue, weighing alternatives, or persuading readers about the correct course of action. One of the common ways teachers do this is with projects that focus on problems and their solutions. The following examples illustrate this type of assignment.

Sample Assignment for a Biology or Ecology Course

As you know from your reading, the Wyoming case of a declining cutthroat trout population is not unusual in modern America; naturalists and fish and game authorities frequently must analyze and try to keep species from declining or becoming extinct. Select one such ecological disruption (the trout case or one of those summarized in our text) for further research. Write a well-documented report outlining what your study shows to be the best solution to the incident. Work to convince your readers that your analysis is correct.

Sample Assignment for a Sociology or Criminology Course

A recent CNN news story featured a Texas program in which selected prisoners are given plastic surgery to correct facial deformities (broken noses, scarring, twisted mouths, etc.). According to the report, there is some evidence that this treatment reduces the number of repeat-offenders. Basing your paper on material you have read throughout the course, analyze this approach to the problem of repeat-offenders and explain whether facilities and resources should be committed to plastic-surgery therapy for career criminals.

Writing successfully on such problem-solution assignments requires clear thinking and solid evidence. For example, the preceding biology/ecology assignment requires that a writer outline all the major causes of one specific ecological situation (such as whether the numbers of cutthroat trout declined because of overfeeding by bears, being chased away by brook trout, having their food eaten by the growing brook trout population, being poisoned by pollution, etc.), and select the most likely or important cause. Then it requires the examination of how different approaches might work to alleviate the central cause. The assigned paper itself would need to reflect all this thinking and this sorting of information, as prelude to the task of proposing a solution and demonstrating that the solution would be likely to work.

The assignment proposed for a sociology or criminology course does not just ask for a response to the plastic surgery treatment. It requires a writer to sort through various causes of criminal behavior (such as socioeconomic pressures, drug addiction, early home life and parental treatment, psychosis, feelings of inferiority and poor self-image, etc.), looking for those that would seem to be addressed by improved physical appearance. It also requires weighing the importance of the various causes; for instance, does feeling that "nobody would hire a person who looks like me" lead to as much serious crime as drug dependence? All this background would need to be reflected in the paper. But the assignment also calls for an evaluation, based on that background, of whether there would be enough reduction in repeat-crime to justify spending money on this program rather than on solutions to other problems.

Since problem-and-solution writing requires a lot of coordination between your own thinking and the information you locate through reading and research, you may find the following strategy a useful take-off point for some of your college papers.

■ Strategy 6—Determine Whether a Solution "Solves" a Problem

After you have done some general research so that you understand the issues and facts involved in your assignment, write out detailed answers to the following questions. If you are working with a computer, it will be easy to go back later to add information and new ideas; if you are working with pen and paper, use a separate sheet for each question so you will have room to add details later.

1. What is the "problem" for which you need to find a "solution"?

2. What are the "causes" of this problem? List specific facts and issues

and possible causes. For each one, add some notes about the sources you have found that deal with the cause.

3. What are the major causes of the problem, and what solutions might help with each of those major causes? From the longer list in question #2, decide on the most significant underlying cause of the problem you are writing about. State this cause in a sentence. Then list as many responses or corrections as you can for that one cause, and add some notes about the sources you have found that deal with each solution.

4. What is the problem and how might it be "solved"? Draft an overview paragraph that sketches the problem and outlines its solution the way you might in the introduction to a paper.

5. Why will the solution solve the problem? Explain—using evidence from your research—why the solution you outline in question #4 will solve the problem. Be sure to include any evidence you have that your solution (or a similar one) has worked with a similar problem.

6. Does the solution overlook any significant causes of the problem? Assume the role of your critical clone as you review questions 2, 3, 4, and 5. Argue against your solution by pointing out the causes it does not address.

   As a variation to questions 6 and 7, use teamwork strategies to let other people point out objections to the course of action you are recommending. Or, share your work with a roommate or friend, and ask them to look for "loopholes" in your thinking.

7. Will the solution cause other problems? Assume the role of your critical clone as you review questions 4 and 5 and the notes you have kept on your research. Work out the complications that might be caused by putting your solution into practice.

8. Can you overcome reasonable objections to your solution? Review questions 4, 5, 6, and 7, as well as your research notes; do additional research if necessary. Draft several paragraphs explaining why the skeptical readers are wrong and arguing that the course of action you are proposing can solve the problem without itself creating worse problems.

Assignments Based on Reasoning: The Critical Review

A common college assignment requiring logical thinking and evidence is an essay often called the *critical review,* a carefully reasoned response to a book, film, play, or something similar. Critics look with a trained eye. They observe their material carefully and logically. Based on the evidence, they report their generalizations and conclusions.

If your teacher assigns a critical paper, take some time to observe how critics review books, movies, and television shows. You'll note that in any given magazine—*The Atlantic Monthly* or *The New Yorker*, for example—the reviews will follow some general formats, but each author creates his or her own internal organization to fit the subject of the review. You'll also note that the same movie or book often will receive different reviews from different critics. We'd like you to read the following reviews of the same movie, each organized differently, and each with different conclusions based on the same evidence. Which of the reviews is more convincing? Why?

Sample Critical Review 1

NICHOLSON, STREEP AREN'T BELIEVABLE
AS BUMS IN *IRONWEED*

Jack Nicholson and Meryl Streep play two alcoholic bums in the movie adaptation of William Kennedy's *Ironweed*, but no matter how talented these actors are, they can't do it. They're too famous and glamorous to bring off the deep sadness of insignificant people, leaving *Ironweed* with some big gaps where its soul and loneliness ought to be.

It's 1938 in Albany, N.Y. Signs of the Depression are all over the debris-strewn streets, where bums linger on corners and in front of small fires on vacant lots. Francis Phelan (Jack Nicholson), a 58-year-old former major-league baseball player, hangs around with his friend Rudy (Tom Waits), takes a day's work burying coffins in the cemetery, and carries the guilts of his lifetime.

Francis pays for his violent past with memories of the infant son he killed when he accidentally dropped him on the floor, and of the scab busman whose brains he purposely splattered during a strike, with a rock thrown like a baseball.

As he wanders the streets of Albany, his many dead friends and enemies appear to him, often in brightly lit, posed groups, wearing white suits and dresses, until it all becomes one floating landscape where Francis merely endures the course his life has taken.

Francis has been on the bum ever since the infant Gerald died, but for years he's maintained a relationship with Helen (Meryl Streep), a fellow drinker and bum, who also has a sad past. She was a singer and now she has a family that refuses to acknowledge her.

Helen and Francis meet in bars and, when they have some money, they share a cheap hotel room. When they don't, Francis helps her find a space among some other bums in an abandoned car while he sleeps in the weeds.

The combination of Streep, Nicholson, and Brazilian director Hector Babenco's (*Pixote, Kiss of the Spider Women*) great eye for poverty and desperation ought to work. Nicholson has always had the soul of a bum anyway, and here, in baggy, filthy clothes with plenty of gray stubble on his face he looks the part.

Streep does fine accents, and her whiney, pathetic voice yanks at Francis as well as the audience.

But we always know it's *them*, those great and famous actors, who live glorious lives and pick up lots of awards. Streep is like a national treasure; it's impossible to disregard who she is—and she's not a bum.

You can see that Babenco knows he's got a problem because he hides the actors' faces. Francis and Helen pull their hats down over their eyes, the focus goes soft in the close-ups, and they're shot from a distance as much as possible. But when they speak, Francis and Helen still have too much glamour. They're movie stars, not derelicts.

To make things harder, the script (and the book) is squishy the characters have too much give to them. The other current movie about alcoholic bums, *Barfly,* doesn't give an inch—the characters have nowhere to go. But in *Ironweed,* Helen and Francis can escape, into either fantasy or actual refuges (Francis has dinner with the wife and family he deserted more than 20 years before).

Ironweed may be an unfilmable movie. No matter how well the scenes are done, Francis's memories are awkward. In a book, a character thinks in words, but in a movie, the audience has to see those things, and it's too literal. Although it's done with care, the technique looks cheap.

The strength of *Ironweed* may also harm the movie. The story is about a man bringing his past and present together, and refinding the hope of family love. You want it to happen, and the movie has incredibly touching scenes, but it doesn't dig into the material deeply enough and it feels too easy.

We never forget that it's just play-acting.

Source: Howie Movshovitz, "Nicholson, Streep Aren't Believable as Bums in *Ironweed,*" *The Denver Post,* February 12, 1988.

Sample Critical Review 2

IRONWEED

William Kennedy's Pulitzer Prize winning novel *Ironweed* has been recreated on screen with subtlety, intelligence, and heart by director Hector Babenco and actors Jack Nicholson and Meryl Streep.

Though the South American director of *Kiss of the Spider Woman* may seem an unusual choice to direct this American story of Albany, NY, hobos in the 1930s, Babenco is obviously at home with the tale's complex emotional textures.

Since he filmed on location in Albany, and used a script by novelist Kennedy, the American aspects of the story take care of themselves. It is the emotional turf of *Ironweed* that is more important, anyway. Though the film is a little too long and slow, Babenco successfully releases the story's powerful humanity.

Ironweed is a personal odyssey of self-discovery by a Depression Era Ulysses whose life was forever changed when he caused the death of his infant son. *Ironweed* catches the man—Francis Phelan—at the point in his life where he wants to assess what it has all meant thus far. He needs to analyze what he has—and what he has given up. He needs to tie up the loose ends of his life before he can move on.

Francis needs to understand his on-again, off-again relationship with Helen, his companion in the flophouses and soup kitchens; the feelings of his wife, Annie, and his two now-grown children he abandoned years ago; and his feelings toward the ghosts of his past who continue to haunt him with a mercurial, netherworld glow.

Thinking himself undeserving, Francis gave up on a conventional life years before. It's apparent he's not ready to return to that life—but it is important to him that he understand it, and that those he left behind understand him. That's enough for Francis.

As a subtext, *Ironweed* offers the character of Helen, a woman with more basic concerns—she wants to be warm, and she wants peace. Little else concerns her.

Helen had been a singer, and one of the most touching moments in *Ironweed* occurs when she imagines herself successfully singing a song in a tavern. It is a momentary flash of interest, though, from a woman who has basically surrendered to the world. She has no fight left in her.

Francis and Helen are showcase roles for Nicholson and Streep, and both actors have approached the performances with artful intelligence. Streep uses lots of physical touches in her performance—a tight-lipped way of talking; a heavy, cumbersome walk; and a wrap-around hat that nearly envelops her in a cocoon.

Nicholson, on the other hand, employs quiet restraint and low-key movement, relying instead on telling facial expressions and evocative uses of the eyes. It is a remarkable interior performance that suggests the character's depth, hunger, and pain.

In support, Carroll Baker is memorable as the kindly Annie Phelan. Though abandoned by Francis many years ago, she still manages to call upon reserves of love and forgiveness. Diane Venora is also quite good as Phelan's daughter, Peg, who can't as easily forgive her father; and singer Tom Waits has a few choice moments as Rudy, Francis's main buddy in the breadline.

Ironweed is a book of complex emotions that hide beneath subtle, almost nondescript behavior. It is very much an "interior" book in which much that is important happens within the mind of Francis Phelan. It is only because of the skill and awareness of Babenco and Nicholson that the challenges to film this novel have been so successfully met.

Source: Jack Garner, "*Ironweed*," Gannett News Service, *Fort Collins Coloradoan*, February 12, 1988, p. B1.

Assignments Based on Reasoning: When Time Is a Factor

When you have time to work out your own organization based on your ideas, you should use the strategies we have suggested in this book and other strategies of your own as you draft your paper. But frequently with college assignments, you will find yourself in the position of having to draft a coherent answer on the spot. If you have a *formula* in mind, you can apply that formula to the task and thus ease the demands on you as you write.

■ Strategy 7—Use Formulas When You Need Them

One way of answering essay questions that ask for your opinion of a chapter or a book that you have read is to use this formula:

> My opinion
> Summary of first part of the author's opinion
> Rebuttal
> Summary of second part of the author's opinion
> Rebuttal
> Summary of third part of the author's opinion
> Rebuttal
> Conclusion

This strategy gives the writer time. Before he or she begins writing, the writer does have to come up with an overall opinion, but with an organization in mind, the writer can discover ways to rebut the source opinion during the writing process. As the writer works through the answer, he or she need not think about the overall structure of the piece. Having determined his or her opinion, and having decided to use a formulaic structure, the writer can focus on expressing each sentence as he or she writes.

An Example of Strategy 7 in Action

Recently, students at Colorado State University were asked to write an argumentative essay on the topic of animal rights. They were given the following assignment:

> *Instructions:* Read the following passage. In an organized and detailed essay, explain why you agree or disagree with what the article says. Support your agreement/disagreement with specific examples from your experience or from outside reading and/or with an analysis of the essay's argument.

ANIMALS IN AMERICA

In the last few years a new animal ethic has emerged, one which asks, simply, that we treat animals humanely. The new animal ethic, spokesman Peter Singer explains, demands that "we cease to regard the exploitation of other species as natural and inevitable, and that, in—

stead, we see it as a continuing moral outrage. . . . Speciesism is as indefensible as the most blatant racism." To avoid speciesism, we should stop experiments on laboratory animals, quit interfering in the lives of wild animals, and cease our abusive and unnatural treatment of domestic animals and pets.

Although animal research may lead to breakthroughs in heart disease, cancer, or AIDS, most research is really no more defensible than Hitler's "experiments" in purifying the Aryan race. We have no right to inflict suffering on mice or dogs or cats just to prolong the life of a few human beings.

In our well-intentioned efforts to save wild animals from exploitation or extinction, we interfere unnecessarily in their lives. We tag them, collar them, vaccinate them, feed them, or "save" them by bringing them to "rehabilitation" centers or to zoos. Take the example of the California condor. According to the best estimates, there are no condors left in the wild. "The last free condor," reports one naturalist, "was trapped in April, 1987, by a team of biologists hoping to save this species. Condor AC9, as biologists named it, will join the last 27 condors already in captivity at the San Diego and Los Angeles zoos."

And finally, we are guilty of speciesism in our treatment of domesticated animals and pets. Farmers regularly confine thousands of chickens in cramped, disease-ridden, perpetually lighted quarters; they keep calves immobilized in tiny, dark pens in order to produce veal; and they herd cattle in unsanitary feedlots for months prior to slaughter. As far as our pets are concerned, sometimes we abuse and neglect them, but often we pamper them excessively, which is just as abusive.

If we are to give up our brutal and brutalizing dominion over the animals, we need to cease all scientific experimentation on animals, release wild animals from zoos and eliminate human populations from the animals' natural environment, and quit pretending that our treatment of domestic animals and pets is anything better than blatant and racist speciesism. Only then can we look forward to a world where two-footed and four-footed creatures stand together on an equal ethical basis.

Source: Dudley Erskine Devlin, essay prompt for placement exam at Colorado State University, 1987.

Here are two students' responses to this passage. Read through them and then be prepared to discuss why the first student's response is less effective than the response of the second student.

Student 1

I believe this opinion that animals suffer needlessly in experiments and that we experiment cruelly on animals in the name of research is correct. Many things that happen to animals do not benefit humans or the animals in the long run. I also feel we do not need to destroy any more wildlife areas. I do feel that the author's opinion that having house pets is being abusive to the animals could be considered incorrect. People need animals to feel loved and needed. House pets also need that love and food that is provided by the human race. What is wrong with giving someone you love the best things possible? Whether that is a cat you give liver to or your own child who you give a toy to. People need love and some do not receive that love, so they look for other things. Those other things might be money, or a pet. A pet that will love them unconditionally, listen to them without giving judgment, and cuddle with them.

This kind of love cannot be abusive to anyone, whether it be a pet or a person. If animals do not like this treatment why don't they run away from their owners? Some people may claim that pets are chained or kept in the house, which is true, but if something is hurting badly enough it will escape and survive. Animals are not dumb, they understand what is going on, and how these things are affecting their lives.

The author did make good points concerning the lives of animals that are used by science or used for food, but his point about pets did not consider love. Love is the main factor and will always be one.

Student 2

As guardians of our world we are faced with many ethical dilemmas. We can't profess to have all the answers. We are not perfect and we are saddled with the delusion that the world was created to revolve around us. But even through our stumbling selfishness and ignorance we usually make the effort to correct our past mistakes and in the process, I feel that we create a better world.

The author of this opinion piece speaks of an inhuman race of people involved in "speciesism" in his article "Animals in America." He maintains that these inhuman people are interested only in their personal gain as a species at the complete expense of helpless animals. He claims that medical research, involving experiments made on animals, is not only cruel but outrageous. This view slants the purpose of research

irreparably by ignoring the very fact that research--
when completed--often saves many human lives.

Next the author returns to his point that the world
was not created solely for us but for the lower orders
of animals also. We share this world, he maintains, but
we have been given the intelligence to change it and
make it useful and productive as the animals haven't.
To this point I must respond by saying that it is a
well-known fact that we have a thirst for knowledge and
a desire to make things easier and better for all. Medical research on animals allows us to probe possibilities. And while it can be abused, as many other professional tools are, it can also prolong life for those
who, without it, would have no chance.

The author also addresses the cruelty of human interference in wildlife. He claims that we no longer really
have "wildlife." It is all tagged, monitored, artifi-
cially bred, and imprisoned presumably for its own benefit. Through his actions, man has altered the animal's
world--on that point I will agree. But some of the alterations are positive ones. Animals live today and
species survive that probably wouldn't without man's
help. The giant panda, for example, is quickly becoming
extinct not through man's interference but through nature's. At birth, it is a tiny, vulnerable animal, pre-
cariously in danger even of its own mother rolling over
and suffocating it. Zoologists observe and protect it
during its most vulnerable time.

Yes, man has upset the balance through hunting and
exploring new territory. But we have never claimed
perfection. Furthermore, we are faced continually with
confronting past generations' mistakes. To condemn us
totally by looking at only one side of our actions is
unfair. In many instances, we are doing the best we
can, attempting to preserve what is left of the animal
species, and trying to avoid future problems.

Analysis of Student 1. Student 1 had no plan. He began writing
too soon. This was not the kind of situation where he had time to discover an opinion as he wrote. He could have used the back of the paper or the margin to do some quick listing of ideas or even to write a
practice thesis statement. But the groping quality of the first part of his
essay mars its effectiveness. The reader doesn't want a reiteration of
the author's points. The reader wants to see a forceful explanation of
the writer's points.

Analysis of Student 2. Student 2 consciously decided to follow a
formula. Note how each part of his answer develops a different part of
the formula:

Paragraph 1:
The author responds rationally. The author concedes a point. Then, the author gives his own view.

Paragraph 2:
The author summarizes the opinion piece. Then he evaluates the piece.

Paragraph 3:
The author continues with the summary and again responds.

Paragraph 4:
The author continues with the summary and responds

Paragraph 5:
The author ends by stating his own views.

Summary

If you have worked your way through this text with us, you have done a considerable amount of writing. We hope that our strategies, exercises, and assignments have helped you grow as a writer. We have not tried to include every possible assignment you will face in college or in your career, but we have tried to prepare you for the variety of writing that you will do. As you face additional writing assignments, we hope you will have confidence in your own writing processes and intentions, and that you will adapt them flexibly to each new task. Happy writing!

TEAMWORK WRITING

1. Use the questions outlined in Strategy 2 (see pp. 233–235) as the agenda for a writing-group session in which you work to evaluate weaknesses within the evidence used to support a piece of writing, and share ideas about how to find stronger supporting evidence.

   Share drafts with each other and discuss trouble spots in thinking and evidence using the questions from Strategies 2 and 4 (see pp. 241–243 for Strategy 4). Decide at the start of the session which people will evaluate for logic and which will concentrate on evidence. If drafts are more than a few pages long, you could also arrange for some people to concentrate more on the first half of each draft, while others just skim the beginning and focus on the last half.

   Spend ten minutes discussing each paper. When one person brings up a problem regarding logic or evidence, others should suggest ways to improve the paper. And the writer of each paper should try not to talk, but just listen closely and take notes.

2. Write a problem-solution paper about a campus problem. Choose a problem that everyone in your group would like to explore. To gather information, have each member list everything that he or she would like to know about the specific problem. Then divide the tasks so that each group member does research on one part of the problem. During the next class meeting group members should present their findings to one another, sharing evidence they have collected about the problem, including reports and documents, newspaper articles, notes from interviews with professors. Each person might decide to write his own problem-solution paper based on the evidence that the group members have collected.

Writing Exercises

1. Explore the following statements with your classmates and find out how much their opinions vary on each of the generalizations.

   a. English should be made the national language.

   b. Women who stay home with their children are better mothers than career women are.

   c. Children of divorced parents are likely to have problems in life.

   d. College students are only interested in money and practical subjects.

   e. Yuppies are spoiled kids grown up.

   f. Capital punishment deters crime.

   In your notebook, explore the assumptions on which your differing attitudes are based.

2. Evaluate the logic in the following essay by Ed Quillen. Read through the essay, noting the quality of the author's evidence. Discuss your response to the essay with your classmates.

THEY CAN'T WANT AN EDUCATED PUBLIC

Every candidate for president has come out in favor of improving American education, but just why is a mystery. It would be much simpler to be president if Americans continued in their blissful, uneducated ways.

Consider how Ronald Reagan continues to enjoy his presidency, just because Americans have failed to master elementary logic.

Last Tuesday, a federal grand jury indicted four men. Among them was Lt. Col. Oliver North, considered a hero in some right-thinking circles because he once took an oath to preserve and defend the U.S. Constitution and then indulged in some extra-constitutional foreign policy.

Essentially, North and the others were charged with stealing $11 million by overcharging the Iranians for arms that the United States wasn't even supposed to be selling to Iran. The ill-gotten proceeds then went to the contras in Nicaragua.

Oliver North said, "I did not commit any crime." President Reagan has insisted that no laws were broken, that these men are not criminals.

But they have been indicted so they are certainly suspects. In the pre-Reagan days, criminal suspects were entitled to the presumption of innocence.

However, Ed Meese, whom Reagan appointed as attorney general, is now the chief law enforcement officer of the United States. And it was Meese who once declared "If a person is innocent of a crime, then he is not a suspect."

By Meese's reasoning, then, North is guilty, merely because he has been charged. But by Reagan's statements, North is as pure as the driven snow.

Now, if we had all received the solid classical education that conservatives think we should receive, we'd know a great deal about formal logic. Every American would realize that North could not be both innocent, as Reagan insists, and guilty, as Meese presumes.

A rigorous logician would be forced to conclude that either Meese or Reagan doesn't know what he's talking about. The logician might even begin to wonder at the fate of a nation that so enthusiastically re-elected Reagan, who in turn appointed Meese and seems to like his work.

Fortunately, our inferior educations have spared us such worries. But suppose American education really is made rigorous, and our citizenry becomes learned in logic. What might happen then?

Would we continue an expensive and corrosive all-out "war on drugs," whose major function appears to be to raise the price of illegal substances so that their thuggish importers and dealers make even more money?

Would American transportation policy still favor the automobile with ever more freeways, beltways, and highways, even though these cures for traffic jams are at best temporary? Even though the cars consume vast quantities of an irreplaceable resource and convert it into the toxic clouds that blanket many cities?

Would we believe that "defense" spending of $280 billion a year— about $1,160 apiece—really makes us prosperous and secure? As secure and prosperous as say, the Swiss, who spend about $310 apiece each year to defend their borders? Whose per-capita income is $14,408 compared to our $13,451?

Can you imagine how different this presidential campaign would be if American education had truly been improved? What potential president could possibly want an educated populace? A population that couldn't be hoodwinked and conned, but would have to be persuaded by cold logic?

Despite all the talk about upgrading American education, it's a safe bet that no matter who gets elected, we will never see any substantive improvements. Presidents want to be leaders, and sheep are easy to lead.

Source: Ed Quillen, "They Can't Want an Educated Public." *The Denver Post,* March 20, 1988.

3. Practice reviewing one another's drafts to check for problems with evidence or reasoning. Review the following draft according to the suggestions in the Revision-Planning Guide provided in Chapter 4 (see pp. 101–102). Be sure to question the author's evidence. Can you believe the data if no citations are included?

THE NATIONAL LANGUAGE ISSUE

Currently, the United States is 60 percent Hispanic. That means that 60 percent of our citizens consider Spanish their first language. Fearful of the threat to the Anglo-establishment, lawmakers in California have introduced legislation to make English the official language. This sounds logical. After all, for years the United States has assimilated immigrants from all countries and English has remained dominant. Certainly we want to be sure to keep it that way.

I don't think that we should legislate what the language should be, however. I think that the power structure is already controlled by Anglo-Americans and will stay that way. The only reason whites seem to need to legislate English as the official language is that they are afraid of losing control. Hispanics, however, stand to lose their identity. Saying that English is the official language sounds to them as if the United States is saying, "your language is bad." Other ethnic groups have felt the need to learn English without being told they have to accept it officially. Hispanics are just going to see the "English as a National Language movement" as a slap in the face—a real put-down.

Before the English as a National Language movement gained force, Hispanics were able to push for Bilingual Education for their children. They were able to convince state legislators that it made sense to offer their children an opportunity to think in Spanish temporarily as they learned reading, writing, and arithmetic. Simultaneously, they were learning English. But by having a chance to think in Spanish until they made the transfer, children of Hispanics had a chance to hold their own in schools. This may not be possible. The English as a National Language advocates want to get rid of Spanish. If English is our language, they argue, then let's not allow children the opportunity to grow in Spanish. Let's force them to learn English from the outset. But if that happens to these children, our whole country stands to suffer. By the year 2000, 90 percent of our population will be Hispanic. Do we want 90 percent of our population to be intelligent or not? If we do, then we don't want to cut off the opportunities for the children of those people to learn when they enter our schools.

Another reason why we need to continue Bilingual Education is so that the pride of Hispanic children can continue. If you go to school thinking that your first language is second rate—not even good enough to think in—then what does that tell you about yourself? It tells you that something is wrong with you. That simply is unfair to our children.

4. If you have to write a paper about a difficult issue, you might have trouble deciding how you feel about the topic. Try looking at the topic from different perspectives—in particular, from the perspectives of the individuals involved rather than from your own point of view.

The news media present many "problem" stories. The following exercise refers to one you may have read about—the Baby M case. By now, you may know what happened. But take yourself back, for awhile, to the early stages of the Baby M case. Imagine how you would have reacted if you were one of the people involved in the situation. First, to remind you of the case, here is a summary of the early events:

> William Stern's wife, Elizabeth, was advised not to try to have a child of her own for medical reasons and so, along with her husband, signed an agreement to have Mary Beth Whitehead become a surrogate mother so that they could have a child.
>
> Mary Beth Whitehead, twenty-nine, gave birth to Baby M under a surrogate-mother arrangement in which she was artificially inseminated with William Stern's semen. However, following the child's birth, Whitehead decided she could not surrender the child.
>
> The Sterns desperately wanted to keep the child and sued for custody.

Answer the questions below as if you were the person involved.

a. You are Mary Beth Whitehead, the woman who agreed to bear a child for a New Jersey couple. You have decided that you want to keep the child you have given birth to. Write a letter to Elizabeth and William Stern in which you express your change of heart.

b. You are Elizabeth Stern. Write a letter to your attorney telling him or her how you feel about the situation.

c. You are William Stern. Write a letter to Mary Beth Whitehead expressing your current feelings.

d. You are Noel Keane, a Dearborn, Michigan lawyer who has brought the Sterns and the Whiteheads together. Write an abstract stating your position on the case.

e. You are Judge Harvey R. Sorkow. You must decide whether the contract signed by the Sterns and Whitehead was valid. You also must decide who will get custody of the child. What do you write in your diary after hearing the first few days of testimony?

f. You are Baby M—twenty years from now. What has happened to you? Write an opening statement for your autobiography.

Use your answers as the basis for an essay on the surrogate motherhood issue.

5. If you have kept a Processes and Intentions Log, read through all of your entries and reflect on what you have learned and how you have changed as a writer. Write a final entry in which you summarize your attitudes toward your writing, toward the notebook you have kept, and toward this course.

Suggestions for Writing

1. Choose some national issue that interests you. Follow the topic for several weeks, collecting newspaper stories and magazine articles about it. Also, listen to the news and to television talk shows that cover the topic. Take notes as you listen. Then write an essay in which you establish your own view of the topic. Use evidence from your sources and logical thinking strategies to make your point as convincing as possible. Use strategies suggested in this chapter to think through your own opinion and to evaluate the evidence of others.

2. Collect some letters requesting your support of a politician, an environmental issue, or a campus issue. Examine the strategies each writer uses to make his or her case convincing. Choose one of these letters to use as a model for your own to a politician.

3. Write a paper in which you challenge some widely held assumption. For example, blondes are more popular than brunettes; college graduates are more successful than non-college graduates; professional authors have little trouble writing. Establish why you believe as you do, then explore how people who disagree with you feel. Why are the opinions of these people invalid? Wrong? In your paper, try to incorporate your personal opinions and ideas in addition to specific examples and details that can capture, for the reader, the vision you have. Also, try to incorporate several outside sources for your argument: feature stories in newspapers, popular nonfiction books on the topic, essays in magazines, personal interviews. Interview the people on your dorm floor, the workers at the student union, the students in your class. They can add credence to your assertions and illustrate that not just one group of people feels this way.

4. The editorial page of *USA Today,* a nationally distributed newspaper published five days a week, can help you get started when you want to write on current topics about which there is a fair amount of controversy.

   Each "Opinion" page is organized as a "debate" on a single issue stated clearly at the top of the left column. Immediately under the theme-statement for the page is the paper's own editorial on the subject, and across the page from it is a second editorial, presenting an opposing view of the topic. Elsewhere on the page are two or three other articles that line up on one or the other side of the issue. Filling up the page are a political cartoon related to the topic, one-liner quotes from people involved in the controversy, and a half dozen "man in the street" statements by people from around the country.

Glance at a couple of weeks of "Opinion Pages" and find a topic to write about. (You'll find such topics as "Defense Contracts" one day, "Stop and Test Strategies to Combat Drunk Driving" another, and "Acid Rain" on a third.) If the topic printed at the top of a page catches your attention, you can study the page for an overview of the issue. Then, depending on when your assignment is due, you can either take time to generate ideas or you can move right to drafting. You might start by summarizing the two sides of the debate, or you could compare the two most clearly opposing articles, or you could respond personally to a topic.

Appendix A: Computer Writing

In each chapter of this textbook, we have included Idea Files with computer-writing tips. These files demonstrate ways you can use the writing strategies suggested in the textbook with the word processor of your choice. The files are intended as suggestions only. After you try a few of them, you will be able to customize them to suit your own writing processes. You will be able to create your own files, suited to your special writing needs. This appendix provides some additional information about how computers can help you develop writing ability.

Some Terms to Know

If you are not yet a computer writer, you may be confused by computer terms—like the words "save," "disk," and "cursor." And so we'd like to conclude by offering you a tongue-in-cheek glossary:

- **Disk:** a square with mysterious stuff inside it. A disk, that comes with a manual about how to work the computer after you "load" the program into the computer is a *software package*. A disk that is so blank that you have to "initialize" it before the computer even knows it is there is just a disk, and it has room to hold up to a hundred pages of text.

- **Disk drive:** a piece of hardware that costs at least as much as an inexpensive computer. It does things electronically with disks so that the stuff in a software package gets rammed into the computer, so that the stuff you are working on with the computer has a place to go for storage when it is "saved," and so that you can load stored stuff into the computer later.

- **Hardware:** machinery—the computer, keyboard, disk drive, printer, and assorted connections between them. *Software* is invisible, electronic stuff, stored on disks, that makes the hardware work like a word processor and not an "Attack of the Cretins" game.

- **Keyboard:** it looks like a typewriter keyboard, but it uses electricity to activate characters on the *video monitor* and simultaneously in the *memory* of the computer, and it has magic *control keys* that change a simple key like "n" into a powerful command like "delete everything." It also has *cursor control keys* that govern the movement of the *cursor*—a mobile bright spot on the screen that marks the place where the next key stroke will put a character on the screen, and simultaneously in the memory.

- **Printer:** something like a typewriter that prints on paper the words and other symbols you have created with the computer.

- **Word processor:** a software package that can turn a microcomputer into a word processor, a computer that is working as a word processor, and a person sitting at the keyboard of a word processor.

Why Computers Can Help Writers

One of the best things you can do to "free" your writing is to write at a computer. You need to have some keyboarding skills to do this, of course. But if you can touch-type at all and if you have access to a computer with word processing software, then computer writing can be a powerful tool to help you become a more spontaneous writer.

Why is this? It is largely because computer writing lets you sense the dynamic, changing flow of words and ideas. It allows you to write in a way that suits your writing processes. It also encourages you to develop new strategies for generating, drafting, and revising your text.

If you already are a computer writer, you know what we're talking about. If you aren't, you'd probably enjoy reading what computer writer Warren Self has to say:

> When I am working with my composition on the screen, the words are written in light, not ink. Their transiency makes it possible for me to manipulate them without feeling as if I have to labor to alter concrete form. Moreover, I know that whenever I make any of these changes, I am merely experimenting. . . . What has been added can be deleted;

what has been moved can be returned to its old position; what has been deleted can be restored.

Source: "Computers: Changing Writers' Relationships with Their Composing Process," *FOCUS,* 9 (Spring, 1983), 19–20.

Computer writing, then, lets you experiment with a moving flow of words, which is less restrictive than committing the words to paper with ink. Computer writing allows you to be a more spontaneous writer. Working on paper, you cannot easily go back to previous parts of your text to add ideas that may occur to you as you write. You have to crowd words between the lines or draw arrows from a balloon of words in the margin to the proper point on the page—a time-consuming task that generally stops the spontaneous flow of language. But with a word processor, you can add productive new thoughts effortlessly, without losing your train of thought.

Also, when you write with a word processor, you do not need to worry about errors or try to censor "dumb" ideas—two things that often prevent the pen-and-ink writer from writing freely. It is so very easy to make changes in computer writing that it really doesn't matter whether there are typographical errors, misspellings, silly ideas, unsupported generalizations, and the like. Knowing that such things can be cleared up easily later, the computer writer does not have to worry about them during early drafting sessions.

For such reasons, we would suggest that you try at least some of the computer-writing ideas in this textbook. If you touch-type badly, don't worry. Keyboarding with a computer is a lot easier than working a mechanical typewriter, and knowing that it is easy to correct errors later also seems to help people "type better" on a computer. (If you want, you can use a typing tutor software program to let the computer help you brush up your keyboarding skills.)

Word Processing Software

Don't worry too much about what word processing software you use. As long as your word processor has a few standard features, you will begin to notice a difference between writing with pencil and paper and writing with the computer. Some essential features of a good word processing package are:

1. *Automatic Re-formatting.* Most word processing programs now come with this capability, which means that you can add additional text anywhere in your file and the program will automatically readjust your right margins for you. With older software, writers often had to remember to use a special "adjust" or "fill" key whenever they reworked a passage of their text.

2. *Full-Screen Cursor Movement.* This means that the writer can freely enter text anywhere on the screen. In some early word processing software, writers had to escape to an edit menu just to delete a word in a preceding line.

3. *Wordwrap.* With "wordwrap," you don't have to press the carriage return at the end of a line. The word processing software automatically moves a word to the next line if it doesn't fit on the current line.

4. *WYSIWYG Display.* WYSIWYG stands for "What-You-See-Is-What-You-Get." If your software has this feature, then your text on the screen matches printed versions of your text. Thus, when you read your hard copy, words appear in the same places as they do on the screen, simplifying revising and editing.

If you are new to word processing, you should start by getting comfortable with the basic features of your program. Begin by learning just what you need to know—how to enter, delete, save, and print a file. Don't get bogged down with too many computer commands. And, *for the most part, steer clear of tutorials.* They frequently present word processing commands in isolation.

You will learn how to use a word processor best if you plunge in, using it from the outset for your own writing. In that way, you can focus on drafting, not on learning computer commands. Gradually, you should add to your repertoire of computer-writing skills, learning new commands when you *need* them. By not rushing yourself, you'll learn how to delete, move, and copy text effortlessly. You'll begin to use a word processor as intuitively as you used the eraser on a pencil. Thus, as you learn advanced commands, you'll be able to customize the word processor so that it suits your writing requirements.

Adapting Word Processing to Your Writing Needs

You can remain in control of your writing just as easily when you draft with a computer as you can with pencil and paper. Just be sure to adapt word processing to your own needs. Develop computer drafting strategies that suit your writing processes. Some writers like to "rough out" a draft, writing a key sentence here, an idea there, and maybe even a conclusion before going through and writing complete sentences, paragraphs, and sections. This kind of drafting is less inhibiting for some computer writers. Other computer writers draft at the monitor in ways very similar to the way they draft on paper: they move from paragraph to paragraph, following an organization that they have already mapped out in their notes or in an outline. When writers draft with the word processor, they can change their minds as they go, all with the satisfaction of knowing that even if major sections of their text need to be reworked, they will not have to retype their entire manuscript.

Some writers' drafting strategies include so much revising that many people would have trouble determining whether they are drafting or whether they are revising: they may draft a few paragraphs in one file one day, move to another file and finish a paper and then not return to the first file for weeks. When they do return to that earlier paper, are they drafting or are they revising? The question is moot. One person's drafting is another person's revising.

Writers also need to develop their own word processing strategies for revising and editing. Here are some suggestions:

1. When you want to add or substitute text, *add first and delete later.* You may like your original version better than your revised version.

2. Save each draft with a new name. That way an idea that you cut out in an early draft can be restored in a later draft if you change your mind and decide to use it.

3. Write yourself notes in the body of your text. Use all capital letters or other markers to identify your comments easily. Then when you revise, you won't forget to deal with your note to yourself.

4. Use the cursor to guide you from the end to the beginning of your text as you do final editing and proofreading.

Some writers have a great deal of difficulty revising on screen. Most computer monitors do not display more than twenty-five lines of text at a time, and writers sometimes get lost as they attempt to "scroll" or move forward and backward in their text. Other writers are comfortable revising at the monitor. They quickly develop an ability to retain the gist of their text in their minds. You need to do what is most comfortable for *you.*

Almost all writers, however, need to do at least one round of editing on paper. Errors that slip past them when they edit on-line leap out at them when they read their text on the printed page. As you read your printed draft, mark places where you need to make a correction. When you re-load your file at the computer, you can use the "search" function of the word processor (most word processors will allow you to "search" for a word or phrase) to find the particular point in your text where the error occurs.

As we stress repeatedly in this text, all writers are different. Those writers who remain in charge of their own writing tend to be the best writers. So don't let other students' computer-writing processes affect the way you use the computer. You need to find strategies that work well for your own writing needs and idiosyncrasies.

If you've been using a word processor for awhile, some of our suggestions may seem obvious to you. But remember, what is obvious to one person may be totally new to the next. And even experienced computer writers may continue to discover new ways of adapting the computer to their writing needs.

Supplemental Software

With a good word processing program, you don't need other software. You can tap the features of your word processor and adapt it in the ways we suggest in this textbook. Of course, other software is available. Writers can choose from a wide array of prewriting, revising, and data base aids. This section will provide you with a brief description of the kinds of writing aids you may want to consider using.

■ Outline Generators

Stand-alone outlining programs such as *Think Tank* and *More* help some writers brainstorm ideas and organize them at the same time. When the writer is ready to draft, the outline can be "ported" (moved) to the word processor. After that, you can finish drafting with your word processor. Unfortunately, most outline generators do not allow you to move between word processor and outline generator.

Microsoft Word, a popular word processing program, is unique in that the word processor comes with a built-in outliner. This feature allows writers easy movement between outline and text.

■ Prewriting Software

You may want to purchase some "prewriting" software—special software that comes with sets of questions to help you generate ideas and find a focus for your writing. Just as loading different software will turn the same computer into an accounting tool, a filing system, a word processor, or a game machine, this software can help you get started on a writing project. In general, these programs ask you questions and respond to the answers you type in. They prompt you to subdivide your general subject so that you can find a more precise paper topic. They help you to develop specific points you could build into a paper on that topic, and to organize the points in different ways.

Clearly, such exploratory software is no replacement for the active coordination of you brain, hands, and eyes as you work at spontaneous drafting, brainstorming lists, and the like. But this sort of computer aid is a tool you can use to help you write more effective college papers. If you are seriously looking for prewriting software, you should try it before you buy it. Some older prewriting software does not allow a writer to move back and forth between one question and the next. Newer programs such as *Writer's Helper,* 2nd edition, and *Seen* have been revised to allow writer to review early responses.

Style Analyzers

Some computer software checks your writing for lapses in diction (word choice), and style scanning for such problems as excessive use of "to be" verbs, and for overuse of the passive verb form. These programs are called "style checkers" or "style analyzers." (*Grammatik, Right Writer,* and *The Writer's Workbench* are three such programs.) If you buy this kind of software for your own use (note that *The Writer's Workbench* is not available for personal computers) or if your school has a style checker in its computer lab, be sure that you use the program judiciously. Remember: computers do not read your writing. They check to see if the kinds of "errors" in your writing match the errors that have been pre-programmed into the computer.

When you get the results of a computer style analysis of your writing, do not take the "advice" too seriously. Only make the changes that *you* want to make. Do not let yourself be intimidated by the authority of the computer.

Spelling Checkers

Most college computer labs have spell-checking software. In fact, many word processing packages come with fully integrated spelling checkers. That means that you can access the spelling checker directly from your word processor, without leaving your file. If you have access to a spelling checker, by all means consider using it. Even though spelling checkers are not foolproof (they cannot tell you whether you have confused "it's" for "its"), they can help you proofread and catch typos.

Data Base Software

Data base programs allow writers to enter, arrange, rearrange, and retrieve their text. If writers enter bibliographic information (such as name of book, date, place of publication, page number, etc.), then they can retrieve their notes easily when they are ready to prepare a bibliography for their research papers.

If you plan to purchase your own data base software, be sure that you select a package that handles text well. Some data base programs are designed primarily for mathematical computation, not for storing and retrieving text.

Appendix B: Teamwork Writing

Throughout this text, we have stressed the value of teamwork writing. You can consult each chapter to review specific ways teamwork strategies can be useful to you at different times in your writing.

This appendix provides you with an overview of teamwork writing—or collaborative writing, as it is often called. Also, it offers some general guidelines that you may want to read before you participate in teamwork-writing activities in your own classroom. Finally, we include two additional teamwork exercises for you to try.

The Importance of Collaboration

How do you know whether your writing is clear, your arguments convincing, your evidence sound, your language appropriate to your intended emphasis? Ultimately, the only way to determine whether your writing succeeds or fails is by noticing the reaction of your readers. Similarly, the playwright listens for the laughter of an opening-night crowd to test the effectiveness of a new comedy; the architect awaits the clients' response to a model of their home; the carpenter or masterbuilder anticipates praise from the homeowner.

In your courses, you can write a paper, turn it in, and notice the grade on it when it is returned. Or you can build a collaborative system for trading audience response with other students so that you know something about the effectiveness of your writing before you turn it in for a grade.

You may have been surprised by the term *teamwork* being applied to something as individual as writing. How, you might have wondered, could other people help you decide what you want to write? And even if they could, how could a group of students help you write more effectively?

If you had such reactions, you are not alone. Most people think that writing has to be a lonely activity in which a writer confronts appallingly blank sheets of paper and tries to fill them with words that will convey his or her ideas to other people. In schools and colleges, most people assume that writing should be an individual effort—something mainly between students and teachers. This emphasis on individual, rather than collaborative, efforts extends throughout American society.

While individual effort may be encouraged more than collaborative effort in the United States and its educational institutions, cooperative teamwork is a potent force—often a more effective force than individual achievement in motivating action. Thus in science, where the popular myth of the eccentric scientist still lives, major activities such as cancer research or space exploration are group efforts, combining the talents of thousands of men and women. In writing, too, cooperative teamwork is an important fact of life, as the number of multiple-author texts (including this one) in your college's bookstore shows. The different perspectives, the moral support, and the editorial assistance that a writer can receive from other writers often work to increase the overall effectiveness of writing.

The support of other writers is also important to the student writer. Students can help each other write better papers, and by editing other people's work, students can improve their ability to write and edit their own papers. By talking about ideas in small groups, students have an opportunity to engage in extended conversations with one another, giving and receiving feedback on their ideas about a topic, and helping one another learn how to develop their ideas through lively conversation.

The Value of Feedback

Once on a plane trip, Rick Gebhardt overheard two salesmen talking about one salesman's writing. This salesman had written a speech on the merits of some little plastic part used in industrial cooling equipment, and he was reading sections of it to the man next to him. Together, they discussed the intended meaning of an important section, the selection of illustrative details, and the appropriateness of an opening joke in another section. The writer did not want to wait for the do-or-die moment of the presentation to test the effectiveness of his speech against an audience. He was using a cooperative colleague to get some early feedback.

That term, *feedback,* is a second key idea that you should understand. It is an important concept that refers to the signals that inform you whether you have performed an action well, or whether you should modify the way you perform it the next time.

For writers, response to writing can be destructive (in the form of a poor grade), too late (in teacher comments on a paper you have submitted but do not have time to revise), and informal (in the puzzled looks of a roommate who reads your paper for spelling errors and finds that she cannot follow your central argument at all). Or, such feedback can come in the more constructive, timely, and systematic way suggested in this textbook.

What to Expect in a Teamwork-Writing Session

If you are expected to take part in group exercises, you should do the best you can to make the experience a success. Collaborative writing strategies are used in English classes across the country in a wide range of high schools, colleges, and universities—with varying degrees of success. When groups work, they give you some of the most valuable college learning experiences you can get.

By learning how to talk with and write for your peers, you will be involved in the kinds of experiences and activities that you will face throughout life. For instance, after you graduate, you'll need to get along with people on the job. You'll need to plan projects and move them to completion just as you are asked to do in teamwork-writing sessions.

We feel that college classes should not be isolated communities—unrelated to the rest of society. So even if you are a loner, or a shy student, and resist working with your peers, please understand that writing is never an individual act. When you write, you are trying to communicate with someone else—and unless you test your ideas on them and receive their criticism, you'll never know the effect your words have on your readers.

Making Teamwork Sessions Work Effectively

Just because you're put into a writing group doesn't mean that you'll know what to do. Giving your classmates feedback on their writing isn't easy. So much depends on how the criticism is given. Some people have learned how to tell others what they are doing well and what they need to improve on, but other people are just not as naturally sensitive.

Consider people who say things like, "You really don't know how to organize your life." "What you should do is . . . ." Sometimes you just tune out people who make such comments.

Now, you don't want your peers to tune you out. And you don't want to tune them out. So what can you do to learn how to give and receive criticism? Here are some ways to ready yourself for criticism:

Giving Criticism

- *Give negative criticism tactfully.* Start with a positive phrase and then add a conditional comment: "I liked *X*, but . . . ." or "Even though you do *X*, you don't really do *Y*."

- *Phrase advice in the form of questions:* "Do you think that you might be able to . . . " (add a more precise word, delete this long phrase, move this sentence, combine these sentences, etc.); "What would happen if you moved this paragraph from this position to another position?"

- *Tune in to the writer's purpose* as you read his or her draft. Remember, it is not your paper. So, always say, "Given that the writer wants to do *X*, I think that he or she needs to do *Y*."

- *Be honest.* If you don't understand something that you feel you should be able to understand, let the writer know.

- *Give advice kindly.* If all your art teacher did was put a big "X" all over your drawing of a flower, you'd be unhappy. You drew the flower the way you wanted it. You don't know how to make it better unless he or she tells you what didn't work well in your drawing. Similarly, if someone reads your paper and does nothing but tell you how bad it is, you won't feel like reworking it.

Receiving Criticism

- *Realize that your own paper is probably not finished.* If you think you are finished before you ask for help, then you'll be upset when you hear your reader suggesting that you make changes.

- *Ask questions.* Don't just sit and listen, interact with your reviewer. Here are some questions that you might want to ask your reviewer:

  a. What do you think is the strongest feature of my draft?

  b. What is the biggest problem?

  c. Where do I lose you?

  d. Should I add another example here?

  e. How do you think I might go about revising my draft?

- *Accept criticism* without being defensive. If your reader tells you that he or she doesn't understand a given sentence or passage, work together to determine where the problem lies. Avoid saying things like, "But I said that down there." If your reader can't follow you or hasn't understood a given point, chances are that you haven't stated the point clearly or you haven't explained a concept early enough in the paper.

- *Respect your reviewer's opinions.* Realize that your partner's comments are intended to help you do a better job on your paper, not to evaluate your ability as a writer. If your partner tells you that you may need to rework your entire paper, pay attention to your critic's reasons for feeling this way.

- *Remain in control of your own writing project.* Teamwork activities help you learn whether your writing is communicating to your reader. But what if you don't like what your reader has to say? What if your reader wants you to revise your writing in a way that seems inappropriate? Ultimately, only the writer knows whether feedback is useful. Writers should never follow their reviewers' advice if it isn't helpful and accurate, or if the reviewer suggests that the writer move in a direction other than what he or she intended. If advice is useless or unhelpful, disregard it.

No matter how easy you think it will be to give or receive advice, you may not be prepared for the emotional responses some people have to criticism. You may have difficulty giving and receiving criticism. You can, however, prepare yourself by following the advice in this section.

TEAMWORK WRITING

Teamwork Agenda A

ROLE-PLAYING ASSIGNMENT

Directions for the Group: Spend ten minutes discussing each paper in one of the following ways. Be candid, detailed, animated, imaginative. If you get ideas about how a paper could be made more effective, explain them to the writer later. But do not interrupt the role-playing situation to do this.

1. *Honest Reactions Group.* Members should discuss how much or how little they know about the subject of the paper, what their attitudes and assumptions about the subject are, and how they react intellectually and emotionally to the draft.

   It is likely that any group of four or five people will have quite a range of knowledge, attitudes, and assumptions about any given subject. A short, candid discussion can give the writer a sample of this diversity and help build an intuitive sense of how readers may respond to a writing project.

2. *Devil's Advocates.* Instead of giving honest reactions to the paper, group members should express critical views that somebody, somewhere might hold. Each group member should have fun pretending to be a petty, critical sniper so that the writer can see how the paper might need to be modified for hostile readers.

3. *Improvisational Scene.* Group members should discuss what the most likely audience is for the project. They should try to make up some plausible situation in which several members of this audience could discuss the paper. Then they should act out this situation for five minutes—being as imaginative and animated as possible.

   For example, to explore audience reaction to a paper that is going to be graded by a writing teacher, each member of the group could play the role of a specific writing teacher he or she has known. Then the group could act out a scene in which one teacher shares a paper with several other teachers during a coffee break.

Teamwork Agenda B

EVALUATION ACTIVITY

On occasion, take time to evaluate your group's performance. The following questionnaire should be filled out by each group member individually before the results are discussed by everyone.

Evaluation of Group Member

Name _____

1. Does this person come to group sessions with his or her work completed?

2. Does this person take the group projects seriously? That is, when your group is given a task, does this person focus on what needs to be done? If not, what does the person do?

3. How would you describe this person's contributions to the group discussion? For example, does this person add ideas? Does the person only react to other people's ideas? Does this person keep the discussion moving along?

4. What advice would you like to give this person to help him or her be a more productive group member?

Index

Robert
444-2516